Judaism and Story

Chicago Studies in the History of Judaism

EDITED BY

William Scott Green and Calvin Goldscheider

Judaism and Story
The Evidence of The Fathers According to Rabbi Nathan

Jacob Neusner

The University of Chicago Press

Chicago and London

The University of Chicago Press, Chicago 60637
The University of Chicago Press, Ltd., London

01 00 99 98 97 96 95 94 93 92   5 4 3 2 1

ISBN (cloth) 0-226-57630-2

Library of Congress Cataloging-in-Publication Data

Neusner, Jacob, 1932–
    Judaism and story : the evidence of The Fathers according to Rabbi
Nathan / Jacob Neusner.

        p.   cm.—(Chicago studies in the history of Judaism)
    Includes bibliographical references and index.
    1. Talmud. Minor tractates. Avot de-Rabbi Nathan—Biography.
    2. Talmud. Minor tractates. Avot de-Rabbi Nathan—Legends.
    3. Rabbis—Biography—History and criticism.   4. Legends, Jewish—
    History and criticism.   I. Title.   II. Series.
    BM506.4.A943N48   1992
    296.1'2—dc20   91-37130
                                                                                CIP

⊚ The paper used in this publication meets the minimum
requirements of the American National Standard for Information Sciences—Permanence of Paper for Printed Library
Materials, ANSI Z39.48-1984.

JACOB NEUSNER is Distinguished Research
Professor of Religious Studies at the University
of South Florida.

For

GERD and ELKA LÜDEMANN
Göttingen

A token of
esteem and affection

Contents

Part Two
Logic and Proposition: Narratives in
The Fathers According to Rabbi Nathan
41

Part Three
Comparisons and Contrasts: The Story in The Fathers According to Rabbi Nathan in Canonical Context
113

Appendices

Preface

The Judaism of the Dual Torah, written and oral, makes its statement in three media: exegesis of the Mishnah, exegesis of Scripture, and stories about biblical heroes and rabbinic sages. Here I ask whether a particular sort of statement found its voice in storytelling in preference to the rereading and rewriting of Scripture and the restatement of the teachings of the Mishnah. Where in a particular sequence of a literary tradition do we find the movement from one mode of discourse to another—for example, from the aphoristic, as in the Mishnah and its exegesis, to the narrative? In earlier books I have traced what happens when authorships within the Judaism of the Dual Torah write with Scripture, and I have also shown what happens when authorships within that same Judaism respond to the Mishnah, making a statement that is continuous with the statements of prior authorships and yet also distinctive. In this book I show precisely the same pattern in the movement from an aphoristic document to a continuous yet distinctive narrative document. In the details, I have tried to show a phenomenon that may prove illuminating for historians of religion in the West. For here before us is one example of a broad phenomenon in which people find narrative in general, and the story in particular, a distinctively appropriate way of saying what they wish to say about their encounter with God on earth.

I spell out in the introduction what is at stake in the use of stories to convey a religious message and experience. An explanation of why I have addressed the appearance of storytelling in a literary tradition that began in indifference to the appeal of stories appears in *Judaism: The Classical Statement. The Evidence of the Bavli*, in which I showed that, by the conclusion of the Bavli (ca. A.D. 600), the editorial processes of the canon of the Judaism of the Dual Torah had found ample place for (1) exegesis and amplification of the Mishnah and (2) exegesis and amplification of Scripture.[1] But the authorship of the Bavli, like that of the Yerushalmi, had not resolved the problem of what to do

1. Further studies of mine on the Talmud of Babylonia and its literary situation are in the following monographs: *The Bavli and Its Sources: The Question of Tradition in the Case of Tractate Sukkah* (Atlanta: Scholars Press for Brown Judaic Studies, 1987); *The Talmud: Close En-*

with the sizable corpus of sustained and important stories about sages that both editorships received from an indeterminate past. Their dilemma drew me to make a more systematic inquiry into how people made use of stories about sages and why such stories were deemed to serve important purposes within the Torah.

While at stake are considerable questions in the history of religion, I closely analyze a given text, as is my way, in an inductive search for some larger rules and descriptive laws of religion, taking Judaism as an example. I ask, specifically, whether and how the authorship of The Fathers According to Rabbi Nathan experimented with the solution to the problem of dealing with the sizable production of stories about sages. I demonstrate that, among the five species of narrative, stories about sages are used in a far higher proportion by the authorship of The Fathers According to Rabbi Nathan than by the authorship of any other canonical document sampled here. I show furthermore that the role assigned to the sage-story proves central to the purpose of our authorship in composing the document before us. We will see here sustained experimentation with a genre of writing formerly used less frequently and, on the whole, for a more limited purpose than to bear a document's fresh messages. Since my

counters (Minneapolis: Fortress Press, 1991); *Tradition as Selectivity: Scripture, Mishnah, Tosefta, and Midrash in the Talmud of Babylonia. The Case of Tractate Arakhin* (Atlanta: Scholars Press for South Florida Studies in the History of Judaism, 1990); *Language as Taxonomy. The Rules for Using Hebrew and Aramaic in the Babylonian Talmud* (Atlanta: Scholars Press for South Florida Studies in the History of Judaism, 1990); *The Bavli That Might Have Been: The Tosefta's Theory of Mishnah-Commentary Compared with That of the Babylonian Talmud* (Atlanta: Scholars Press for South Florida Studies in the History of Judaism, 1990); *The Rules of Composition of the Talmud of Babylonia. The Cogency of the Bavli's Composite* (Atlanta: Scholars Press for South Florida Studies in the History of Judaism, 1991); *The Bavli's One Voice: Types and Forms of Analytical Discourse and Their Fixed Order of Appearance* (Atlanta: Scholars Press for South Florida Studies in the History of Judaism, 1991); *The Bavli's One Statement. The Metapropositional Program of Babylonian Talmud Tractate Zebahim, Chapters 1 and 5* (Atlanta: Scholars Press for South Florida Studies in the History of Judaism, 1991); *How the Bavli Shaped Rabbinic Discourse* (Atlanta: Scholars Press for South Florida Studies in the History of Judaism, 1991); *The Bavli's Massive Miscellanies. The Problem of Agglutinative Discourse in the Talmud of Babylonia* (Atlanta: Scholars Press for South Florida Studies in the History of Judaism, 1992); *Sources and Traditions. Types of Composition in the Talmud of Babylonia* (Atlanta: Scholars Press for South Florida Studies in the History of Judaism, 1992); *The Law Behind the Laws. The Bavli's Essential Discourse* (Atlanta: Scholars Press for South Florida Studies in the History of Judaism, 1992); *The Bavli's Primary Discourse. Mishnah Commentary, Its Rhetorical Paradigms and Their Theological Implications in the Talmud of Babylonia Tractate Moed Qatan* (Atlanta: Scholars Press for South Florida Studies in the History of Judaism, 1992); *The Discourse of the Bavli: Language, Literature, and Symbolism. Five Recent Findings* (Atlanta: Scholars Press for South Florida Studies in the History of Judaism, 1991); and *How to Study the Bavli: The Languages, Literatures, and Lessons of the Talmud of Babylonia* (Atlanta: Scholars Press for South Florida Studies in the History of Judaism, 1992). In addition, certain problems ancillary to those dealt with in the present book are amplified in a repertoire of charts set forth in the companion work, *Form-Analytical Comparison in Rabbinic Judaism. Structure and Form in The Fathers and The Fathers According to Rabbi Nathan* (Atlanta: Scholars Press for South Florida Studies in the History of Judaism, 1992).

argument unfolds systematically in six stages and is explained in context stage by stage, there is no need for more extended reprise of what is to follow.

It remains, however, to specify the limitations of this study, so that readers will not expect to find what is not here. Specifically, while I have asked a question important in the history of religion, with special reference to the history of a particular system of Judaism, I have not addressed issues of narrative as framed by literary critics. I am the first to express admiration for the acumen and acuity of literary criticism. When it reads biblical narrative and poetry, literary criticism (exemplified, to take three paramount names by Robert Alter's *The Art of Biblical Narrative,* Meir Sternberg's *The Poetics of Biblical Narrative,* and David Jobling's *The Sense of Biblical Narrative*) allows us to understand biblical texts as though we had never seen them before, just as the great social anthropologists, such as Edmund Leach and Mary Douglas, teach us to read these same texts as though they were discovered this morning. But issues of literary criticism are not the issues of this book, which attends to questions that derive from the history of religion. Literary critics and narratologists will therefore find little of interest in what I have to say about materials on which they might have a great deal else to say. Secular literary studies engage with biblical studies in striking ways, but I do not promise to contribute to that engagement. My interest is in the advent of narrative of a very particular sort, viewed as a datum in the unfolding history of a religion. My interest is not, then, in narrative itself, except as an exegetical device. That is why I propose to divide narrative into sage-story, story of the biblical hero, parable, and the like. These categories point to differences in narrative technique, but they do not derive from a taxonomy of narratology. In placing this caveat at the beginning of my discussion, I hope that I may gain a hearing for what I propose to contribute, rather than out-of-hand rejection for not speaking to issues that, to begin with, lie beyond my horizons.

My translation of *The Fathers According to Rabbi Nathan* (Atlanta: Scholars Press for Brown Judaic Studies, 1986), based on Solomon Schechter, *Aboth de Rabbi Nathan, Edited from Manuscripts with an Introduction, Notes, and Appendices* (repr., New York: Philipp Feldheim, 1945), forms the foundation of the present work. I therefore call attention to my use, in my translation, of the prior translation of the same text, that of Judah Goldin, *The Fathers According to Rabbi Nathan* (New Haven: Yale University Press, 1955). I made ample use of Goldin's translation in three ways. First, where I had difficulty with an unusual word or phrase, I consulted his version, and when I found his rendering suitable, copied it. In such cases I have preceded his rendering of the word or phrase with [Goldin:]. Points in this book at which his rendering is used are listed under his name in the index. Second, I treated his translation and notes as a commentary, and from time to time have inserted into my translation his reasoning or his explanation of a passage. This too is indicated by the use of square brackets in the translation. Third, I often consulted his (that is, usually the Jewish Publication Society's) English rendering of verses of Scripture, although I have usually tended to a freehand rendition of my own.

In addition, I consulted Anthony J. Saldarini, *The Fathers According to Rabbi Nathan (Abot de Rabbi Nathan) Version B: A Translation and Commentary,* Studies in Judaism in Late Antiquity, vol. 11 (Leiden: E. J. Brill, 1975). Ample bibliographies for The Fathers According to Rabbi Nathan as well as for The Fathers are in Saldarini's *Scholastic Rabbinism: A Literary Study of The Fathers According to Rabbi Nathan* (Chico, Calif.: Scholars Press for Brown Judaic Studies, 1982), 155–61. Saldarini's treatment of the present text in that excellent study pursues its questions and analyses just as I have done here. Approaching the same text through diverse methods, he and I have reached points in common as well as points of difference. I believe that the program of inquiry I follow here is sufficiently distinctive to justify my not engaging in argument with Saldarini point by point. His basic question seems to me historical; mine is religious and literary. My respect and esteem for him and his work need hardly be emphasized, even as I pursue my own interests in my own way. My thanks go to Professor Saldarini for his counsel in this project.

While various aspects of storytelling in the religious writings of Judaism have received ample attention, for example, storytelling in Scripture and in rabbinic writings, I have not found any books that pursue the questions studied here. However, I did commission a systematic bibliography of the use of stories and other narratives in Judaism. Published in *New Perspectives on Ancient Judaism* (Lanham, Md.: University Press of America Studies in Judaism, 1987), 3: 185–218, the "Bibliography on the Story in Judaism" by Joseph M. Davis lists more than five hundred items relevant in a general way to the theme of narrative. If anyone else has asked why a Judaic document without a narrative substrate was supplied with one and where and how that process took place, I do not know where that work has reached the light of print.

It remains to express thanks to my friend and co-worker, Professor William Scott Green, whose knowledge of the theoretical literature relevant to this study guided me in substantial measure.

Jacob Neusner

The work was completed on the day before Erev Rosh Hashshanah, 5748
September 23, 1987

Marking fourteen years since the death of my
father-in-law and friend, Max Richter

Department of Religious Studies
University of South Florida
Tampa

Introduction:
From Aphorism to Story and from Epistle to Gospel in Judaism and Christianity

From Aphorism to Story

In 250 C.E., the Mishnah tractate Avot, The Fathers, delivered its message through aphorisms assigned to named sages. A few centuries later—we do not know how many—a vast secondary expansion of that same tractate gave flesh and blood form to those sages, recasting the tractate by adding a sizable number of narratives. In this book I show how aphoristic form and syllogistic discourse were joined by narrative form in general and stories about sages in particular. In seeing how this happened, we follow a process of transformation in the way people make their religious statements, and we gain an understanding of the appeal, in transmitting truth, to the story in preference to the syllogism and the saying. A moment's thought will show how the movement from Paul's letters to the Gospels of Mark, Matthew, Luke, and John (as well as the numerous apocryphal gospels) finds a striking analogy to the process I shall trace in these pages. Within the limited setting of the Synoptics, what I am showing is analogous to the movement from Q to Mark and Matthew.

The authorship of The Fathers presented its teachings in the form of aphorisms, rarely finding it necessary to supply those aphorisms with a narrative setting and never resorting to narrative to present its propositions. At an indeterminate time, possibly ca. 500, the testamentary authorship of The Fathers According to Rabbi Nathan provided a vast amplification and supplement to The Fathers, introducing into its treatment of the received tractate a vast and varied corpus of narratives. In this way the later authorship indicated that it valued narrative in general, and stories about sages in particular, as modes of discourse for presenting its message that the earlier authorship did not utilize. The choice of the medium bore implicit meanings, also, for the message that would emerge in the later restatement of the received tractate.

A document that spoke in aphorisms was transformed into a set of propositions delivered, in part, through narratives. This case represents in a small way a much larger tendency of religions to receive religious truths as propositions in the form of syllogisms, and to restate them as propositions in the form of narratives, particularly stories about holy men. That movement, in the unfolding of a complex religious tradition, is already familiar to us, though the details of how the movement took place are not in hand. We realize what is at stake in tracing the movement from aphorism to story when we reflect on the simple fact that the first Christian writings took the form of syllogisms, argued as philosophers argue, while the next layer of Christian writings took the form of stories and sayings spun out as sustained narratives, for example, the words and actions of Jesus Christ presented as cogent gospels. The evolution of the earliest Christian writings is analogous to the movement traced in this book and indicates how much is to be learned.

From Epistle to Gospel

When the apostle Paul sought a medium through which to convey his encounter with Christ, he chose to state propositions in the form of abstract arguments, syllogisms conveyed through letters as well as sustained essays, such as the remarkable letter that he wrote to Christians in Rome. He did not tell stories about the life of Jesus, and he did not regard as critical to (what we should now call) his Christianity the framing of aphorisms in the name of Jesus. He had not known Jesus when the Master lived and taught, and he did not seek stories about things Jesus had done and said during His lifetime. Since we know such stories and collected aphorisms enjoyed the loving attention of other Christians, who collected and memorized them even in the same years in which Paul was representing Christ, we must regard Paul's medium and method as distinctively congruent with the message of Christ and the meaning of faith in Him that Paul sought to compose and communicate.

Within a decade or so of Paul's statement of Christianity in the medium of letters and the form of aphorisms, a quite different approach to expressing in words the encounter with Christ led other writers to different medium and form. To them, the very things that Paul had thought trivial—stories about what Jesus had done, records of what He had said—formed the center of discourse. These other Christians chose to tell stories, and not only to tell them as episodes but to write them down in connected compositions, Gospels. They filled out those stories, moreover, with collections of aphorisms that recorded things Christians remembered Jesus had said. From Mark, writing in the sixties, through Matthew and Luke and finally to John, writing four decades or so later (not to mention the authorships of important extracanonical Gospels), Christians resorted to storytelling in the statement of Christian truth.

Both modes of religious writing—the composition of letters and essays in syllogistic form and the telling of stories in connected narratives of the life and teachings of Jesus—attracted continuators and imitators. Consequently, the diverse Christian communities received both apocryphal Gospels and also letters pseudonymously assigned to Paul's authorship. These two initial modes of putting down in words what it meant to encounter Jesus Christ and to become part of His body, to die and live again in Him, competed with many others, for the stunning word of the death and resurrection of Jesus Christ provoked, in the imaginative life of Christians, both experimentation with and also renewal of the possibilities of language. Indeed, as we review the diverse types of writings through which the Christian message gained literary form, we may find astonishing both the renewal of received and the invention of unprecedented modes of recording in words what God had done.

In this book we can see one kind of literary program available to Christians but not explored by them—one that took as a principal task the demonstration of continuity, coherence, and essential uniformity among writings produced over a long span of time. This program, in its stress on the traditional process of transmitting truth and the traditionality of the truth transmitted, lay emphasis upon demonstrating the continuities. In terms of literary form, the program required the form of commentary, not autonomous and original writing. It required glossing, not pronouncing, amplifying in unanticipated ways, not forthrightly allowing the new to look new; the new was inserted within the framework of the old. This process of imposing the emblems of traditionality characterizes the larger part of the received writings of the Judaism of the Dual Torah, there being only two important compositions within that canon which in no way attach themselves to prior writings: Scripture and the Mishnah. But no Christian writings proposing to formulate and transmit the pattern of Christian truth thought it important to make statements through a process of agglutination and conglomeration, exegesis of a received text and systematic citation of prior writings. And that brings us to the case at hand. No one took the letters of Paul and reshaped them to make room for episodes of the Gospels or aphorisms attributed to Jesus. Precisely what Paul's letter to Christians in Rome, for example, might have become, had later authorships amplified the document with citations of the Gospels—what shape the letter would have gained had others inserted exemplary events out of Jesus' life and teachings—these are questions we cannot answer. Nor do we know how Paul's message in the book of Romans would have been reshaped through the amplification of stories and sayings (for the medium and the message do converse). But in the movement from The Fathers to The Fathers According to Rabbi Nathan, we can see how an authorship did such work, receiving out of antiquity and revising in the light of its own sense of taste and judgment the medium and method by which the received document would make its statement. In this book I show in acute detail precisely how that work of revision and renewal took place.

Narrative as a Medium for Making a Religious Statement

Vast tracts of the Hebrew Scriptures—Genesis, much of Exodus, Joshua, Judges, Samuel, and Kings, form a sustained narrative. Episodic stories play a role in Numbers and in some of the prophetic writings, for example,

Jeremiah 36. A quasi-narrative framework sets the stage for the legal portions of Exodus, Leviticus, Numbers, and Deuteronomy. Nonetheless, while the use of narrative to convey religious truth strikes us as routine, to framers of Judaic religious systems in antiquity, the appropriateness of that mode of sacred discourse was by no means self-evident. The authorships of diverse kinds of writings, for example, exegeses of Scripture, law codes, accounts of heavenly journeys, and the like, chose other-than-narrative means of expressing their viewpoints. The Judaism of the Dead Sea Scrolls is one example. The so-called *pesher* rests on an implicit narrative, a history of events, but then the narrative is not realized, merely alluded to. Philo, for his part, developed a Judaic system in which narrative scarcely served as a medium for religious truth.

Once we understand that the resort to narrative is not to be taken for granted and treated as routine, the question I answer in this book makes its point: How, for what purpose, and with what result did an authorship within the ongoing tradition of documents of the Judaism of the Dual Torah introduce narratives of various kinds into its repertoire of discourse? For two reasons The Fathers According to Rabbi Nathan, a document whose closest affinities place it in the circle of the Talmud of Babylonia (ca. sixth century), provides a remarkably apt opportunity to investigate in the context of religious literature the entry of the story as an important medium for presenting a message in Judaism. First, that document contains an unusually rich selection of stories about sages. Hence its authorship (or editorship) clearly saw narrative in the form of stories as a principal mode of expressing its ideas and making its points. Second, The Fathers, a mid-third-century collection of aphorisms attributed to sages of the late second-century Mishnah, which is the document that The Fathers According to Rabbi Nathan serves as exposition and supplement, does not contain stories about sages and has very few narratives of other types. In other words, the base document does not resort to a mode of discourse that the secondary and dependent document deems critical. The Fathers According to Rabbi Nathan therefore may testify to the role of narrative in the delivery of the religious message at hand specifically because its authorship employed in abundance a mode of discourse for which the authorship of The Fathers had no use. In the movement from the one to the other we can see how the framers of the later work of exegesis gave an important place to a genre of materials not found appropriate for use as a paramount medium by prior framers or authorships of canonical documents.

What is at stake is insight not into the literary form of religious expression but into theological framework and message. We shall follow not merely the formation of a fresh genre of writing in the unfolding of a document from its prime text, The Fathers, to its amplification and exegesis, The Fathers According to Rabbi Nathan; as I shall demonstrate, the fresh message of the later document makes its appearance in the new medium of the sage-story. Specifically, what is new in The Fathers According to Rabbi Nathan is a doctrine concerning the sage on the one hand, and history and eschatology on the other. The medium that bears this new message is the story about the sage, which is quite different in narrative form from the story about the biblical hero, the parable, and the narrative setting for a saying, which are three other species of narrative that I have located in our document. As my argument unfolds, therefore, we shall increasingly focus upon the sage-story as a critical literary and religious issue in the unfolding of the Judaism of the canon of the rabbis of late antiquity—hence the title of this book, *Judaism and Story.*

The Sage-Story and the Advent of the Sage

The Judaism portrayed in the writings of the sages, or rabbis, of late antiquity (from the first to the seventh century) at first took slight interest in the lives and persons of those sages. By the end of that period, the canonical writings of Judaism drew upon a rich corpus of stories about the beginnings (meaning of Torah study), sagacity, historical power, and endings (meaning death while engaged in Torah study) of those same figures. Just as the holy man in Christianity from the third century forward served to mediate between heaven and earth, so the sage in the Judaism of the Dual Torah marked the passage from the supernatural to the natural world. The interest in holy men and their lives did not yield biographies of holy men (documents that Christians would reasonably classify as Gospels or lives of saints). We have to wait until the seventeenth-century Sabbatians and the eighteenth-century Hasidim for lives of sages. In the two Talmuds, which serve as exegesis of the Mishnah, and in the contemporary midrash-compilations, which provide exegesis of Scripture, the sage-story did not play a prominent role.

There is, however, our document, The Fathers According to Rabbi Nathan, in which the story about the sage became the paramount and critical medium for the presentation of what was extraordinary and new in the message of its framers. The use of the sage-story as a principal mode of communication would have surprised the compilers of earlier compositions in the unfolding canon of the Judaism of the Dual Torah. For the authorship of the Mishnah, to which The Fathers had itself been attached as the first and most important apologetic, took slight interest in telling stories about sages. That is not to say that the Mishnah does not include narratives, for it assuredly does, particularly to illustrate a law or to provide a setting for the presentation of a saying. But many centuries later, the authorship of The Fathers According to Rabbi Nathan made extensive use of the story about the sage, his origins, sagacity, historical importance, and mode of dying. In doing so, it supplied The Fathers with an added layer of narrative in the genre of the sage-story.

My analysis rests upon a taxonomy of narrative, generated by the document under close analysis here. As we shall see in detail, I find five kinds of narrative—five species of the genus narrative—in The Fathers According to

Rabbi Nathan. I classify these as (1) parable, (2) precedent, (3) narrative setting for a saying, (4) scriptural story, and (5) sage-story. We shall see that the sage-story forms the largest proportion, by far, of the narratives in this document. Moreover, the proportion of the species sage-story in The Fathers According to Rabbi Nathan forms a larger component of the narratives used in that document than it does in the counterpart sector of any other document. The importance of this fact has already been introduced: the fresh messages of The Fathers According to Rabbi Nathan, in contrast to the statement of The Fathers, find their expression in a newly important medium, the sage-story.

There is an additional fact of consequence: among the stories of The Fathers According to Rabbi Nathan, we find that stories which appear *only* in this document conform to narrative conventions that are not followed in stories which appear *both* here and in other documents.[1] The conventions exhibited in the stories in our document require movement—something must actually happen—so that a problem and its solution are recorded through an account of what people not only said but also did (sometimes, to be sure, stated implicitly and not through detailed description). I therefore mean by *sage-story* a narrative with the following distinctive and indicative traits:

1. A beginning, middle, and end.

2. Tension and resolution.

3. Characterization accomplished through an account of motivation.

4. Focus on a particular person and what that person said and did on a distinct and important occasion.

5. Omission of close attention to citations of Scripture as a main focus of discourse. A Scripture-story not only focuses upon a scriptural theme or hero, it also encompasses vast explosions of allusions to or verbatim citations of verses of Scripture.

I derive the catalogue of these traits from an inductive analysis of the sage-stories in The Fathers According to Rabbi Nathan that have no parallels or counterparts in other writings. In comparing the version of the origin of Aqiba, which is unique to our document, and the version of the origin of Eliezer, which appears both in our document and elsewhere, as well as the two stories of the destruction of Jerusalem (the one in our document, the other in the Talmud of Babylonia, both of them involving Yohanan ben Zakkai), I was able to distinguish our document's sage-stories from counterpart narratives elsewhere by resorting to the stated criteria for the definition of a sage-story. For these distinctive and indicative traits do not characterize other stories, for example, ones about scriptural heroes, let alone parables, settings for sayings (in which nothing much happens), or legal precedents and illustrations of the law through concrete accounts of circumstance.

---

1. Those same conventions also characterize some stories about sages in other documents, but not in equivalent proportion. The comparative studies that are required for further progress will have to await their turn.

These four other narrative kinds do not tell us about motivation and characterization; none of them portrays a situation with movement provided by tension and resolution; none has beginning, middle, and end. Ordinarily, the narrative other than the sage-story portrays a stationary tableau. The one exception, the parable, speaks of paradigms, not persons, and illustrates a teaching in a manner that is rhetorically similar to, if more affecting than, the narrative setting for a saying. It is only the authorship of The Fathers According to Rabbi Nathan that employs the story about the sage to make its two new and critical points: the one about the supernatural character of the Torah-sage, the other about the eschatological character of the teleology of the Judaism of the Dual Torah contained within the canonical writings before us.

Part One

Rhetoric and Topic:
The Comparison of Literary and Programmatic Traits

1

The Structure of The Fathers and of The Fathers According to Rabbi Nathan

From Aphorism to Story: The Transformation of The Fathers

The work before us unfolds in stages and requires attention to countless details. Consequently, we may not always recall, in the middle of a sustained sorting out of details, the main point we seek to pursue. Let us therefore set our sights upon it here. We want to know how a document that made its initial statement without resorting to narratives became the medium for the work of storytellers. We also want to understand how the entry of stories conveys a message that was not conveyed by the original document. Answers to these questions will tell us why the framers of The Fathers According to Rabbi Nathan revised the materials they received in The Fathers as they did. Seeing each document whole, we can discern how a secondary expansion has profoundly reshaped the primary text. Then we can relate medium to message, accounting for the interplay of the mode of conveying propositions—narrative, not merely aphoristic and philosophical—and the message to be delivered.

These general remarks bring us to the first of the five specific exercises before us. The answers to our questions require analysis of the two documents by three fundamental criteria. An *authorship* (a group of sages responsible for a piece of unattributed writing) faced decisions on three principal questions concerning rhetoric, topic, and logic. It had to decide what kind of rhetoric to use in conveying its message. That matter affected judgments on what would persuade an audience of readers or listeners to accept the points the authorship proposed to make. It had to determine what topic it wished to treat. That consideration affected the points the authorship wished to make and dictated the program—subject-matter and proposition concerning subject-matter—of the writing. Finally, it had to choose a mode of discourse that would find a hearing in the audience it wished to address. That is, the authorship had to frame its message so that it would appear cogent and comprehensible.

Each of these criteria for the framing of a statement affected the others, of course, since an authorship would have seen a particular fit between a given topic and a particular rhetoric. It may have found that a comprehensible argument was facilitated by one mode of cogent discourse and impeded by another. It would carry us far afield to survey the choices available to the authorships of the canon of the Judaism of the Dual Torah. It suffices to note that any authorship had to make choices; with the repertoire of writings before us, we can compose a catalogue of what people might have done. Comparing one writing to another, furthermore, allows us to specify what they did choose to do—and why they chose to do it.

A glance at The Fathers (given verbatim in appendix 1) answers all three questions concerning principles of composition. The rhetoric is dictated by aphoristic style, producing wise sayings presented as a list. The topic, over all, derives from the realm of wisdom: right conduct with regard to God, society, and self. The logic of cogent discourse derives from the notion that a list of sages constitutes a principle of coherent composition, and the diverse sayings fit together within the sustaining logic of a list of authorities. The list holds together because everything on it is part of a chain of formulation and transmission—tradition—beginning at Moses on Sinai. So one sentence joins the next because all the sentences enjoy the same status, that imparted by the Torah. That logic deriving from authority makes it possible for the audience of the document to see relationships of order, proportion, and sustained discourse, where we see merely a sequence of essentially discrete sayings. The rhetorical device rests upon the same principle of cogent discourse: listing authorities suffices both as a principle of composition and of persuasion. The topical program—with its recurrent emphasis on Torah study and the social, intellectual, and personal virtues required for Torah study—is equally compatible with the logical and rhetorical decisions made by the authorship of the whole. But what about The Fathers According to Rabbi Nathan? How has the later authorship responded to the plan and program of the earlier one? To what degree has it accepted the authority of The Fathers, and how has it determined to imprint upon the received document its conceptions concerning the Torah, what it contains, how it is to be studied, and above all, the manner in which its heroes and saints are to be represented? For example, The Fathers finds a mere name sufficient; The Fathers According to Rabbi Nathan does not. The compilers of The Fathers do not think it necessary to relate events—history—to the Torah. The compositors of The Fathers According to Rabbi Nathan differ; they insert a variety of historical narratives.

We now compare the later document with the earlier for a single purpose: to determine the choices regarding how to compose, out of The Fathers, a greater and more encompassing statement, one that stands in relationship to the earlier writing but does not merely repeat through paraphrase what the earlier writing has said. In general, one piece of writing among the canonical documents of the Judaism of the Dual Torah may stand in one of three relationships to another: autonomy, connection, or continuity. An *autonomous* document does not systematically relate to any other but makes its statement—at least, in formal terms—essentially on its own. It may cite information, but it does not set forth its ideas in the form of a commentary. It contains no systematically inserted evidence of subordination to any other (prior) writing. A writing that is essentially *continuous* with a prior writing, in contrast, systematically gives indications of that fact, for example, by citing a prior writing and amplifying it. Such an essentially subordinated writing does not strike out on its own, except by indirection, that is, by tacking what is fresh onto what is received and accepted. But what of documents that are *connected* but not continuous? That middle relationship is somewhat more difficult to define. In general, we expect to discover two kinds of composition in the second of two connected documents: first, free-standing writing, and second, exegetical statements. The second of two connected documents cites prior materials and amplifies them, as does the second of two documents that are continuous, but it also contains quite distinct materials that are not related in any formal or external manner to anything that has gone before.

    The intent of the authorship of an autonomous writing is clear; it takes as its task the presentation on its own authority of whatever it chooses to say. Paul's letters in general are fine examples of autonomous writings. Writings that are continuous with some prior document continually draw our attention not to themselves but to some prior, authoritative statement. The vast literature of commentary (e.g., the two Talmuds to the Mishnah, the *pesher*-exegeses of the Essene community of Qumran) typify in their form (though not necessarily in their program) this kind of writing. Writings that are connected but not continuous are exemplified by the synoptics, with their utilization of Q, and by The Fathers According to Rabbi Nathan. The intent of these authorships proves more complex to determine. The effect of their literary program is to establish strong links to prior authority in behalf of writers who clearly have their own statement to make. In this context, the comparison of Paul and The Fathers, Q and the Synoptic Gospels, and The Fathers According to Rabbi Nathan, while inexact, proves more than merely adventitious. It should now be clear to the reader what is at stake when we ask how the authorship of The Fathers According to Rabbi Nathan has chosen to relate its writing to The Fathers.

The Principles of Composition: Comparison and Contrast

Since I have used the category *authorship,* and have undertaken to compare and contrast the work of two *authorships,* I owe the reader a clear definition of the term and an explanation of my reason for using it. The Fathers According to Rabbi Nathan is the work not of an author but of an authorship; that is, no single person wrote everything from beginning to end. Rather, our document was composed through the selection and arrangement of available writings. The work of selection and composition, and the determination of proportion and cogency derives from what I call an *authorship:* an indeterminate category that includes any number of individuals. An authorship, by definition, comprises the person or persons who have created the final version of a document that derives from cogent decisions and a coherent plan. Anything less—a set of discrete and unrelated materials, bearing no evidence of adhering to a cogent literary plan but exhibiting traits of chaos—comes to us as a scrapbook, which is the work not of an authorship but of a compiler or group of compilers.

We know that we have a coherent document when we can show that it follows a systematic topical program, resorts to a few (among many available) formal and rhetorical patterns, and rests everywhere upon the premise of a logic of intelligible discourse and cogency. We turn therefore to the issue of structure, which defines the most basic and superficial question at hand. For the principles of structure, or composition, tell an authorship what types of materials to collect and how to arrange and proportion each of the chosen types so as to yield a cogent statement.

We work out the matter of structure in two ways: first by reference to the primary document, The Fathers, and then by comparison of that generative structure and its rules to the structural principles that govern the connected secondary document, The Fathers According to Rabbi Nathan. The structural program of The Fathers is transparent: (1) a list of names, together with (2) wise sayings. Some of these wise sayings are subjected to secondary explication or amplification; most are left as simple gnomic statements. So the authorship of The Fathers has chosen to present us with lists of names joined to sayings, some of them amplified, most not. An equally simple account of the generative structure of The Fathers According to Rabbi Nathan will come only at the end of an inductive study of that document, based on a systematic and complete comparison of The Fathers According to Rabbi Nathan to The Fathers.

Once we have established the way in which the authorship of The Fathers According to Rabbi Nathan chose to select and organize its materials, we identify and classify in chapter 2 the formal patterns of those materials. In this way we may test our theory of the structural principle by asking whether the forms or patterns of language used in the one document and not the other correspond to the principles of composition that dictate choices and arrangements in the one document and not the other. In these two complementary and reciprocal tests—the one of principles of composition, and the other of recurrent formal patterning of language—we may differentiate on purely formal grounds between the primary document and the secondary and (supposedly) derivative connected document.

Comparing The Fathers to The Fathers According to Rabbi Nathan

The Fathers According to Rabbi Nathan presents two types of materials and sets them forth in a fixed order. The document contains (1) amplifications of sayings in The Fathers as well as (2) materials unrelated to anything in the original document. The taxonomy that yields these two general types, of course, will be subject to much refinement. The arrangement of the types of material in The Fathers According to Rabbi Nathan becomes immediately clear. First, our authorship presents amplifications of the prior document; only after that does it tack on its own message. In terms of our earlier classification of relationships between documents, The Fathers According to Rabbi Nathan presents itself first of all as continuous with the prior document, and then shows itself to be connected to it. The compositions that are essentially new in rhetoric, in logic, and in topic are found in that second set of materials. At no point do I find a systematic effort on the part of the later authorship to make its work autonomous, no evidence of a desire to show total independence of prior tradition, whether we invoke rhetorical, logical, or topical criteria. But, as we shall see, that is deceptive. Our authorship does have a new message and does make use of a fresh medium, and in the nature of things, the innovative topic and rhetoric draw in their wake a new logic of intelligible discourse as well. But we reach that conclusion only after a considerable journey.

Let me spell out matters as they will soon be clarified. Where the authorship of the later document has chosen to cite and amplify sayings in the earlier one, that exercise comes first. There may be additional amplification, and what appears to augment often turns out to be quite new and to enter the second of our two categories, in the form of (1) proof texts drawn from Scripture; (2) parables; (3) other sorts of stories, sometimes involving named sages, that illustrate the same point; and (4) sequences of unadorned sayings, not in The Fathers, that make the same point. These come later in a sequence of discourses in The Fathers According to Rabbi Nathan. Where an appendix of secondary materials on a theme introduced in the primary discourse occurs, it is inserted in the later document directly after the point at which that theme appears in the counterpart to the passage in the earlier document; only afterward does the exposition of the saying in The Fathers proceed to a further point. This general order predominates throughout.

To ease the burden on the reader, I have placed the detailed comparisons in appendix 2, and here present only the results. Readers who wish to see how I have reached the characterizations of relationships that I present here will find them fully spelled out there; those who want to know only the result for the unfolding argument will find them in what immediately follows.

Down through The Fathers 1 : 15, we have a clear program of citation and gloss. The plan of the authorship is simple. They work along two lines, in succession. First they cite the base saying and amplify it. This they do by providing proof texts: illustrative stories drawn from lives of sages, parables, and exegeses of Scripture found to be pertinent to the sentiment at hand. Second, details in the exegetical materials trigger secondary accretions; for example, exegeses of a proof text are supplied; names mentioned in a story serve as the framework for the inclusion of further stories, none of them pertinent to the point of the original; or a vast anthology on a theme may be inserted because the theme has made an appearance in another context altogether. With these two principles of aggregation we can explain the entire composition at hand. Why The Fathers 1:16–18, which take up the immediate ancestry of the patriarchate, are not dealt with in the exegesis of successive clauses I do not know. The further materials having to do with the patriarchate are also skipped, and the next passage to receive sustained attention is The Fathers 2:8ff., on Yohanan ben Zakkai and his disciples. The framers of The Fathers According to Rabbi Nathan therefore bypass the important sequence of patriarchal sayings and jump right to the sages' counterpart.

From The Fathers 2:8 through The Fathers 2:15 we follow the pattern of the treatment of chapter 1, that is, a close exegesis and amplification of the sayings of The Fathers. This is made up of materials of two types as before: stories and sayings directly relevant to the materials of The Fathers, and secondary appendices, attached because they intersect at some point, however tangential. Section XIV works its way through Yohanan ben Zakkai's sayings, and then the following units of The Fathers According to Rabbi Nathan, through XVII, stand in the same relationship to the sayings of the first three disciples. My guess is that XVIII should be regarded as an appendix on the theme of masters giving names to disciples. It is not a counterpart of The Fathers 2:1 to 2:8–10. I am not sure why Tarfon's sayings are not dealt with in the present context.

What is clear in chapter 3 is that the authorship has shifted its program. There is slight pretense at interest in the systematic exegesis of The Fathers, such as clearly defined the formal and programmatic plan of the treatment of chapters 1 and 2. Let us first review the facts of the matter and then turn to the broader issues. At 3:1/XIX:I–II, we follow the plan of exegesis, citing and then adding first proof texts, then parables, and finally stories about sages in illustration of the sayings of The Fathers. We then ignore a sizable clump of materials, down through The Fathers 3:10B/The Fathers According to Rabbi Nathan XXI. But the program for Dosa's saying is standard: citation and gloss of a clause, followed by proof texts and then pertinent examples drawn from the lives of the sages. The Fathers 3:9 is treated in the same way at The Fathers According to Rabbi Nathan XXII, and then we move from The Fathers 3:11 to the end of the chapter in The Fathers without any systematic plan of exegesis. So it is clear that The Fathers has not provided the redactional framework for the treatment of the materials pertinent to chapter 3, that is, The Fathers According to Rabbi Nathan XIX–XXII. In other words, if we wish to understand The Fathers According to Rabbi Nathan beyond XVIII, we must read the pertinent chapters as an autonomous statement and address the plan and program of those chapters. This we do in the next part of the present chapter.

Chapter IV of The Fathers According to Rabbi Nathan begins with a familiar pattern, citing a saying in The Fathers and then glossing through verses of Scripture; thus XXIII:I. But then The Fathers 4:2–13, 15–22 play no role whatsoever in the organization of the materials pertinent to The Fathers According to Rabbi Nathan chapter IV. Whatever the principle of selection and composition, it does not derive from that chapter in the way in which The Fathers chapters 1, 2, and (as we shall see) 5 dictate the organization of The Fathers According to Rabbi Nathan. What is interesting, on the other hand, is that the chapter contains a sizable selection of sayings presented in the formal pattern that characterizes Avot itself: name plus connective plus saying, with little or no amplification.

The Fathers chapter 5 serves as the fundamental structure for The Fathers According to Rabbi Nathan chapters XXXI–XLI, with important exceptions. The Fathers 5:1–5, 7–8, 15, and 16–17 provide the organizing principle for The Fathers According to Rabbi Nathan chapters XXXI–XXXV; XXXVII: XI–XXXVIII; XL:VIII–X, XVIII–XX; and XLI. The Fathers According to Rabbi Nathan chapters XXXVI–XXXVII:I–X, XXXIX, and XL:I–V seem to me to be thematic appendices, and The Fathers 5:6, 9, and 10–14 play no role in the structure of the later document. So, by comparison, the treatment of chapter 5 follows the basic program established for The Fathers chapters 1 and 2, but it is not executed as thoroughly. The principle of selection and organization is essentially the same as before, however, and The Fathers chapters 1, 2, and 5 assuredly do serve in a way different from The Fathers chapters 3 and 4, whose principles are not utilized as the means of organizing discourse in The Fathers According to Rabbi Nathan.

Comparing The Fathers According to Rabbi Nathan XXIV–XXX to The Fathers

We have found that The Fathers chapters 1, 2, and 5 provide the structure for The Fathers According to Rabbi Nathan, and that The Fathers chapters 3 and 4 do not. We now know where the problems are. Here we must examine the texts of both documents in detail, since we want to know whether the sections of the later document that do not appeal to the earlier one for structure have some new message as well. The reader will want to examine the details, not merely review the result, since here both substance and structure are important.

We therefore take up those chapters of The Fathers According to Rabbi Nathan in which sizable sequences deal with The Fathers chapters 3 and 4 or ignore The Fathers altogether (since there is no difference). At issue is the relationship of The Fathers According to Rabbi Nathan chapters XXIV–XXX to The Fathers; thus, those chapters now serve as the base structure, with The Fathers as the variable. I give enough of The Fathers According to Rabbi Nathan so that the reader can follow the topical program of that document, but do not cite the entirety of the chapters under analysis.

Once more, we wish to uncover the principles of structure guiding the authorship, with special reference to whether or not the choices characteristic of the chapters that serve as exegeses of The Fathers find a counterpart in those that serve some other purpose.

Before proceeding, I have to explain my use of different typefaces. In order to make clear the way in which the later document takes up the earlier one, I differentiate by typefaces, which permits an immediate recognition of the various sorts of materials and how they are put together.

1. **Boldface type:** At issue is the relationship of The Fathers According to Rabbi Nathan to The Fathers. The Fathers therefore serves as the base structure, and The Fathers According to Rabbi Nathan as the variable. Sayings of The Fathers are given in **boldface type,** and the outline of the contents of The Fathers According to Rabbi Nathan in regular type.

2. SMALL CAPS: Where a saying in The Fathers undergoes no treatment in The Fathers According to Rabbi Nathan, it is given in its proper place and order, but printed in SMALL CAPS. (That clear identification of what is ignored by The Fathers According to Rabbi Nathan lays the foundation for the discussion in chapter 3 of how the two documents differ in content.) Furthermore, where a saying in The Fathers is treated in The Fathers According to Rabbi Nathan at a location other than the normal sequence of the exposition of The Fathers, I present that saying also in small caps. In this way we see precisely the points at which The Fathers has governed the expository structure of The Fathers According to Rabbi Nathan, and where the order and program of the sayings of The Fathers have been ignored. It follows that sayings in small caps do not serve the redactor for the ordering and exposition of the composition at hand.

3. *Italics:* Italics serve a special purpose. Because The Fathers According to Rabbi Nathan contains a fair amount of supplementary material (e.g., appendices inserted because they intersect with a theme introduced by the exegetical discourse), I indicate what is supplementary by *italics.* In this way the reader can readily distinguish what I deem primary from what I take to be a secondary enrichment.

Again, to ease the burden on the reader, I give only part of the exercise here and the rest in appendix 3.

THE FATHERS ACCORDING TO RABBI NATHAN
CHAPTER XXIV (NO COUNTERPART IN THE FATHERS)

XXIV:I.1.   A. Elisha b. Abuyah says, "One who has good deeds to his credit and has studied the Torah a great deal—to what is he to be likened?"

XXIV:II.1.   A. He used to say, "One who has good deeds to his credit and has studied the Torah a great deal—to what is he to be likened?"

XXXIV:III.1.   A. He used to say, "One who has good deeds to his credit and has studied the Torah a great deal—to what is he to be likened?"

XXIV:IV.1.   A. He used to say, "One who has good deeds to his credit and has studied the Torah a great deal—to what is he to be likened?"

XXIV:V.1.   A. He used to say, "He who studies the Torah in his youth—the words of the Torah are absorbed in his blood and come out of his mouth fully spelled out."

XXIV:VI.1.   A. He used to say, "The teachings of the Torah are as hard to acquire as golden vessels and as easy to destroy as glass ones."

XXIV:VII.1.   A. He used to say, "A person can study the Torah for ten years and forget it in two years."

XXIV:VIII.1.   A. He used to say, "Whoever prevails on his fellow to carry out a religious duty is credited by Scripture as if he himself had done it personally."

What we have is a sequence of names of authorities plus connective plus wise sayings. This chapter could as well have found a comfortable niche for itself in The Fathers. There are stories concerning this authority's apostasy. Perhaps the authorship of our document did not know them, or rejected them. Here Elisha is simply another sage. More important, differentiating his sayings from others in the same place is not possible. We have a sequence of variations on a single theme, restatements in diverse ways of one implicit proposition. We shall now see the same phenomenon, which we may call simply restatement by the later authorship of the points made in the earlier document, that is, a relationship of continuity. I refer the reader to appendix 3 for the remainder of this exercise and turn immediately to the result of the work. The rather elaborate exercise begun here and concluded in appendix 3 produces two simple conclusions.

First, the contrast between the materials of The Fathers According to Rabbi Nathan that serve The Fathers chapters 1, 2, and 5 and those that serve The Fathers chapters 3 and 4 justifies the conclusion proposed at the outset; that is, The Fathers chapters 1, 2, and 5 do indeed dictate the order and plan of The Fathers According to Rabbi Nathan chapters I–XXIII and XXXI–XLI but The Fathers chapters 3 and 4 do not exercise equivalent influence on their counterpart chapters in The Fathers According to Rabbi Nathan.

Second, while The Fathers chapters 3 and 4 do not provide for the authorship of The Fathers According to Rabbi Nathan chapters XXIV–XXX the order of sayings for consideration, that fact makes no difference to the principles of composition of the specified chapters of The Fathers According to Rabbi Nathan. The reason is simple: those chapters, which we originally isolated as different in their relationship to The Fathers, follow precisely the same basic plan and program as do the other chapters (I–XXIII and XXXI–XLI) of The Fathers According to Rabbi Nathan. This brings us back to the differentiating criteria of rhetoric, topic, and logic.

First and most interesting, with regard to rhetoric: if they do not cite sayings from The Fathers, they *do* cite gnomic apothegms. Where the sayings come from we do not know. But the principles of rhetoric and also of cogent composition are identical: present the sayings, and explain them. That these sayings are of the same apothegmatic character as the ones that appear in The Fathers is easy to prove by a simple mental experiment. Had we found them in The Fathers, would we have been able to differentiate them from other sayings in the same locale and identify them as originating in The Fathers According to Rabbi Nathan? In my judgment, we would not. As to cogency, the same notion of what joins one saying to another in The Fathers also explains what joins one saying to another in the counterpart materials examined here and in appendix 3.

Second, with regard to topic: the sayings *not* drawn from The Fathers are treated in exactly the same way as those taken from The Fathers. We find a quotation of a saying; amplification, low-level exegesis, or exemplification; then an interest in proof texts and the secondary exegesis of those proof texts; and an occasional appendix, tacked on because of a point of thematic intersection.

Consequently, we must conclude that one and the same overall structure—organization and program of discourse—has governed the composition of the entire tractate, and that is without regard to the diverse relationships of the designated parts of the tractate to the base text at hand. Furthermore, we may easily define the generative structure of both The Fathers and The Fathers According to Rabbi Nathan. It is the same for both documents, with two important exceptions: first, the addition of vast appendixes of unrelated materials; second, the inclusion of enormous biographical narratives, ordinarily also having the character of appendixes in that they rarely illustrate in a precise way the apothegm that is under discussion in the base document (or even in the complementary one). Thus far, all we see is a later authorship that wishes to continue the work of the earlier writers and to conform to the pattern and model defined by the ancients. But that is far from the truth.

One Program of Composition: The Shared Structure of The Fathers and The Fathers According to Rabbi Nathan

We now know the principles of composition of The Fathers According to Rabbi Nathan, and we may define them very simply. Given a saying of an apothegmatic character, *whether or not that saying is drawn from The Fathers,* the authorship of the Fathers According to Rabbi Nathan does the following:

1. Gives a secondary expansion, including an exemplification, of the wise saying at hand.
2. Cites a proof text of Scripture in that same connection.

3. Provides a parable to illustrate the wise saying (as often as not instead of the proof text).

These principles for selecting materials and organizing them in a systematic way were learned from the framers of The Fathers. In addition the authors of The Fathers According to Rabbi Nathan contributed two structural principles of their own:

4. Add a sizable group of materials that intersect with the foregoing, either by amplifying on the proof text without regard to the wise saying it serves or by enriching discourse on a topic introduced in connection with the base saying;

5. Append a protracted story of a sage and what he said and did, which may or may not exemplify the teaching of the apothegm at hand.

This final discovery brings us closer to our original point of departure, for the two sorts of material fall into a single category, which is an essentially autonomous body of material pertinent to a given theme or topic; hence, *topical appendix* is the appropriate name for the category. The point of the discourse to which the materials are appended, however, rarely affects their selection and arrangement, nor does it appear in the composition they constitute. Viewed on the surface, the biographical narratives do not differ in type from the vast compositions on, for example, the first man, except in subject-matter. In later analyses we shall differentiate sage-stories from scriptural stories. It suffices here to note that they work out their own internal proposition and give no evidence that the authorship responsible for them is aware of the proposition that forms their host setting in The Fathers According to Rabbi Nathan. The stories about Yohanan ben Zakkai's escape from Jerusalem and Eliezer's and Aqiba's beginnings, for example, were made up independently and not in connection with the passage in The Fathers According to Rabbi Nathan in which they now find their position.

Thus the authorship of The Fathers According to Rabbi Nathan bears responsibility in two ways for making up principles of structure and composition. The first and more obvious principle is simply that of choosing appropriate materials and arranging them in a pattern meant to explain and amplify gnomic apothegms ordinarily (but not only) found in the collection of The Fathers. The second is the selection and inclusion of vast compositions focused not on gnomic apothegms but on lives of sages—viewed as interesting on their own, not solely as important exemplifications of available principles cast as wise sayings. There are no other important differences between the basic structural program of The Fathers and The Fathers According to Rabbi Nathan. Having seen how the document at hand was composed, we turn now to the forms it comprises.

2

The Matter of Rhetoric:
The Forms of The Fathers and of
The Fathers According to Rabbi Nathan

Consensual Authorship and Formalized Rhetoric

Rhetoric is what guides an author in the composition of sentences, paragraphs, and chapters that yield an intelligible, cogent, and persuasive
statement. Rhetoric may derive from individual choice and preference, or it
may—within a given document—characterize the consensus of the community, the authorship of the document. Not a single document in the canon of
the Judaism of the Dual Torah contains the marks of an individual, recognized
author. Some of them carry names, as does our document, but all imputations
of authorship (e.g., the Mishnah to Judah the Patriarch, the Tosefta to Hiyya)
are post facto and extrinsic to the writing. The publication of a book without a
named author serves an important purpose: it is meant to secure for the book
the authority of the community as a whole. What speaks for one person bears
his name, but then enjoys only his authority; what speaks for everyone bears
no name. That is why named legal opinions carry no authority and why the
canonical writings carry no evidence of individual hands. The absence of a
distinctive author's taste and judgment is conveyed in an aesthetic way as well
in these writings. Few documents contain extensive evidence that a private
person's choice of style—how to say things, as much as what to say—dictates
the characteristics of the document as a whole. On the contrary, a certain uniformity of style imparts to sayings attributed to individuals a prevailing
sameness, a consistency in all matters but specific opinion on a single matter.
Here too we see how a given authorship obliterates the marks of private taste
and personal judgment and gains for all of its participants that authority and
standing that only the collectivity—the consensus of the group—can supply.
   The fact that writings derive from collective consensus explains the importance of analyzing the formal traits of a document's rhetoric. Specifically, all
rabbinic writings produced in late antiquity closely adhere to repeated forms
and literary conventions, and none makes room for or expresses individual
preferences as to style and aesthetics. The single persistent literary trait of all

documents of the canon of the Judaism of the Dual Torah is their highly formalized character. Set patterns of rhetoric, sentence structure, syntax, word choice, and the like dominate each document. These patterns, of course, vary from one document to the next, but in each one the patterning of language and syntax runs uniformly throughout. That makes it easy to compare one document to another and to ask how a later authorship has responded to the formal choices made by an earlier one. Knowing how the basic structure of The Fathers was adopted but also vastly revised by the authorship of The Fathers According to Rabbi Nathan, we now want to find out how that authorship framed the language and syntax that it chose to convey its intended message. In order fully to understand the profound formalization of language at hand, we have to ask why the documents of this canon are formalized and what that set of choices concerning the traditionality of language tells us.

Let us begin with the most basic question: Why does the canon of this particular Judaism choose language that effaces all marks of individual choice and distinctive personal traits of speech? How does that prevailing aesthetic affect the treatment of narrative and our understanding of the characteristics and uses of stories in particular? Answers to these questions will illuminate the road ahead. Let me provide an overview, however, so that we may see in the larger context of the Christianity and Judaism of antiquity the details we are about to examine.

Once more we begin with the simple matter of whether or not writers signed what they wrote. In Christianity they did; in Judaism, they did not. In general Christian writers signed their works, and overall, with noteworthy exceptions, the individuality of the author always shines forth and rarely is obliterated. Even the work of more than a single figure—for example, the Gospels—bears the claim of individual authorship, (e.g., not the school of Matthew, but Matthew; not only the *we,* but even the *I,* in Luke–Acts). By contrast, I cannot point to a single document of the Judaism of the Dual Torah written by an *I.* Uniformity of aesthetic theory in general and of style (syntax, word-choice, and ordering and patterning of language) in particular characterizes the documents, both individually and overall. Storytelling in a given document or for a distinctive purpose (e.g., concerning one theme rather than some other) conforms to conventions so pervasive that the marks of the contribution, taste, and judgment of the individual storyteller (if there ever was one) are invariably obliterated. This difference between the general traits of Christian and of Judaic-rabbinic writers seems to me to account, also, for the phenomenon we examine here, that is, the way in which those who thought stories important inserted them into a document received from the past that omitted them. As we grasp in detail the full weight of the phenomenon at hand, we realize that in the literary dimension, we perceive the encompassing traits of not merely canon but system. To state matters in general terms (requiring much refinement), Christianity in all its forms began with the figure of a single individual, the generative symbol of Christ on the cross, and the model of that individuality left ample place for the development of other individualities, whether in writing or in piety. The Judaism of the Dual Torah began with the figure of the holy community, Israel, serving as the generative symbol served. Sanctity here and now, salvation in time to come—both dealt not with the private person but the sacred society.

A structure that began with a unique individual found place for the individuality of authorship, including distinctive modes of telling discrete tales. A structure that began with the unity and uniformity of a holy community, by contrast, expected from the individual the virtue of exemplification, asking the individual to serve not for distinctive but for exemplary traits. When it came to storytelling, the use and value of stories in the latter structure depended upon the storyteller's ability to efface traits of personal choice and preference, on the one side, and to make the hero of the story into a model, an everyman, on the other. Since the power of the story told in such a way was to give flesh-and-blood meaning to the (prior) aphorism, there was a place for the story in a collection of aphorisms. The story became the medium for the restatement in concrete terms of the general and universally applicable aphorism, and that is why, in my view, the later authorship could carry forward a traditional writing in a thoroughly traditional spirit—and yet innovate in the way that it did. For the innovation masked profound continuity—a new way of stating an old message—and that constituted a profound trait in the nature of the Judaism of the Dual Torah, beginning from Sinai and resting upon the authority of tradition. To state matters simply, both the aesthetics of the literature and its theology conformed to a single deep structure and adhered to a uniform set of definitive preferences. And, by the way, only by telling stories in one way rather than in some other could they serve the larger purposes of the authorship of a document within the system at hand.

What We Learn from Analyzing Rhetorical Form

What I have said explains, once more, the reason that we refer not to an author but to an authorship. It further shows what is at stake, in broad cultural and theological issues, in comparing the work of one authorship with that of an earlier one. Above all, we now understand the invariably anonymous character of the authorships of the canonical writings of the Judaism of the Dual Torah, which arises from the definition of the system at its deepest layers. These facts are of considerable importance in the next stage of our comparison of The Fathers According to Rabbi Nathan with its predecessor, The Fathers. Since traits of formalized speech do characterize a given document, we now compare the forms of public discourse used in the later writing with those that characterize the earlier one. This allows us to ask where and how in matters of rhetorical form the later authorship, in its collective wisdom, has expressed a consensus that is essentially continuous with the one on aesthetics that was paramount for the earlier authorship, and where and how it has chosen to innovate. In this way we can isolate once again those aspects in which the later authorship has separated itself from the earlier one, choosing new rhetorical forms to convey a message that proved to be particular to itself.

A second, quite separate consideration lends importance to the study of the fixed forms of speech. It carries us far afield, but it is critical to our study. Let me explain the problem. In this book I claim to speak of how people wrote books and told stories in a particular period in the unfolding of the Judaism of the Dual Torah, specifically, between the completion of The Fathers, ca. 250 C.E., and the composition of The Fathers According to Rabbi Nathan, at some point between 250 and 600 C.E. All of our manuscripts, however, derive from a much later period; the earliest documents were composed after the rise of Islam in the seventh century, and many of the first manuscripts of the ancient Judaic writings are dated many centuries after that. The manuscript evidence for ancient Judaic writings begins in medieval times, and even then it is not plentiful. Nothing like the plethora of manuscripts of the Gospels going deep into antiquity survived the medieval Christian wars against the Jews' sacred books, which from the burning of the Talmud onward, spread flame to nearly the whole of Israel's patrimony out of antiquity. Given the uncertainty of the texts, with numerous variations in readings not only in detail but even covering entire documents (e.g., the wording not only of sentences, but paragraphs and even chapters), how can I claim to speak of the period in which I place our document? Since the advent of the story where stories were lacking testifies to a shift in the unfolding of the Judaism that rests on one document and continues in the later one, I have to justify my premise about the period to which the two documents attest.

That task carries us by yet another route to the centrality of the formalization of language in the rabbinic writings before us. The Fathers According to Rabbi Nathan reaches us only through a long process of copying and recopying. Accordingly, we cannot be certain that the Hebrew version in our hands is the one originally sent into the world by the authorship of the document. If, therefore, we propose to represent the traits of mind and intellect of the authorship responsible for The Fathers According to Rabbi Nathan, we cannot appeal to any particular detail (e.g., a given paragraph or pericope) because that singleton may or may not have had a place in the original. We do not have the original manuscript that represents what the initial authorship wished to say. We do not even come within a millenium of that original authorship.

As a matter of fact, we do not know that the entirety of the book that we now call The Fathers According to Rabbi Nathan existed in late antiquity. But if I can demonstrate that both that document and its predecessor, The Fathers, conform to a well-defined structure, and that this structure forms the generative foundation of the writing, we may simply sidestep the uncertainty of the details of sentences and paragraphs. We may speak of what is indicative and definitive of the document as a whole, without appealing to the evidence of details that may or may not have been present to begin with. Through analysis of the formal and conventional traits of the document as a whole, we stand on solid ground in maintaining that the cogent discourse that defines the document's rhetoric, topic, and logic marked the document from its original stages. That is to say, The Fathers and The Fathers According to Rabbi Nathan could not have existed without the formal structures we shall uncover. The sole premise, then, is that the document existed, even if not as we now know it, prior to the closure of the Talmud of Babylonia in ca. 600 C.E., and that premise is the point of departure for all studies of our document.

It must follow that if we are able to assign The Fathers According to Rabbi Nathan to a single point of origin, we gain out of the definitive paradigm of rhetoric, topic, and logic a clear picture of the sustaining position of the authorship at hand *ab origine*. Others, joining the creative work of handing on the document, added what they chose, but (as we recognize) solely in line with the established principles of public discourse. The uniformity of rhetoric, topic, and logic justifies the claim to treat the document in two ways: first as testimony—in basic structure, preference of formal rhetoric, and aesthetic choice—to the age in which it originated, and second as cogent, even though later tradents joined the process of formulation and formation. When in due course I relate the indicative traits of the document to the circumstance within the unfolding canon that I believe to be definitive for the document, I refer to no single passage of either document, let alone to a statement within one. To the contrary, I point solely to the definitive and indicative traits of the whole— logic, rhetoric, and topic alike—and these in the larger context of the canonical program of the framers of the Dual Torah in the late fourth, fifth, and sixth centuries. Let me spell out the considerations set forth here.

The state of manuscript evidence, whether rich or impoverished, settles few important questions as to the original intent and statement of the responsible authorship. If we wish to know anything at all about the document as its authorship created it, we must appeal not to particular statements but to the character of the document as a whole, as evidenced in each of its parts. General and ubiquitous traits of rhetoric and logic can be imitated by later copyist-authors, who add their own messages to the document as it passes through their hands, but they cannot be invented, and by definition they do represent the intent and plan of the original authorship. We may even appeal to overall traits of the topical plan and program of the document for evidence of the initial program, even though one or another subject or specific proposition cannot be reliably imputed to the original authorship. The way we solve the problem of the parlous character of the manuscript tradition and evidence of any rabbinic document of late antiquity is to analyze the traits of the whole: What defines, in all of the parts, the indicative character of rhetoric, logic, and topic? When we can answer these questions, we may introduce our document;

that is, we can answer basic questions about the classification and definition of the writing that permit us to understand and make sense of it.[1]

The Forms of The Fathers

To pick up the thread of argument from the end of chapter 1, we now know how the structure of the later document differs from that of the earlier one. Accordingly, we move on to a second critical point of analysis, that of rhetoric. When we arrive at a rhetorical definition of the first document, we shall recognize in what ways the authorship of the second has innovated, finding fresh modes of discourse and a distinctive manner of expressing its propositions. So we continue to peel back the layers of the onion, so to speak. The present exercise follows the inductive lines established in chapter 1. We start with a single component of the document and proceed to test the rhetorical patterns we find there against the traits of another chapter, finally characterizing the whole in terms of the patterns that emerge.

To state in advance the main result, a catalogue of the forms of The Fathers produces only two forms: (1) name plus attributive (*says*) plus wise saying and (2) the list. The document as a whole is formally simple and repetitive, which is one striking way of producing a uniform and cogent message. Even a cursory glance at The Fathers According to Rabbi Nathan reveals a quite different pattern.

List of Names plus Attributive plus Wise Saying

While the authorship of The Fathers sometimes amplifies a saying (e.g., with a secondary expansion or a scriptural proof text), in the main it shows a clear preference for an unadorned presentation of wise sayings joined to named authorities by the connective, *says*. A random sample of three items makes this point clear:

> 1:1. Moses received the Torah at Sinai and handed it on to Joshua, Joshua to elders, and elders to prophets. And prophets handed it on to the men of the great assembly. They said three things: "Be prudent in judgment. Raise up many disciples. Make a fence for the Torah."
> 3:1A. Aqabiah b. Mehalalel says, "Reflect upon three things and you will not fall into the clutches of transgression: Know (1) from whence you come, (2) whither

---

1. So much for critics who argue that until all manuscript evidence has been collated (which critics call *the making of a critical text*), no work of description, analysis, and interpretation is possible. For twenty years that issue has formed one generative consideration for defining my work as I have. (The other was the impossibility of demonstrating which attributions to named authorities are valid and which not.) We use the best texts we have; when better ones come out, we turn to them. But no claim in this book rests on the priority of one reading over some other, and to my knowledge, no story cited in this book exists only in a fragment of the larger manuscript evidence for the document that now contains it.

you are going, and (3) before whom you are going to have to give a full account of yourself.

3:1B. "From whence do you come? From a putrid drop. Whither are you going? To a place of dust, worms, and maggots.

3:1C. "And before whom are you going to give a full account of yourself? Before the King of kings of kings, the Holy One, blessed be he."

4:4B. R. Yohanan b. Beroqa says, "Whoever secretly treats the Name of Heaven as profane publicly pays the price. All the same are the one who does so inadvertently and the one who does so deliberately, when it comes to treating the Name of Heaven as profane."

4:5A. R. Ishmael, his son, says, "He who learns so as to teach—they give him a chance to learn and to teach. He who learns so as to carry out his teachings—they give him a chance to learn, to teach, to keep, and to do."

We see a single pattern. The first of these samples defines the paradigm for the whole: once we pass the introductory remark, we have *they said* plus *three things*. That pattern governs chapter 1 (as a glance at appendix 1 shows). The pattern of chapter 2 is somewhat varied, since it provides names plus attributive plus a sizable catalogue of things. Chapter 2 has a secondary colloquy (not cited), in which a master tells the disciples to go out and find the answer to a riddle, which they do, in a highly formalized construction. But the colloquy in no way corresponds to a narrative; there is scarcely a narrative component in all of The Fathers. Chapter 3 presents us with a fine, if uncommon, instance of a secondary expansion, with 3:1A worked out by 3:1B–C. Most of the sayings, however, lack even that much amplification. The naked form is at 4:4B, 4:5A, and so on.

List of Items of a Single Classification

Chapter 5 is made up of lists of items that share a common quality, as in the following example.

5:5. Ten wonders were done for our fathers in the Temple: (1) A woman never miscarried on account of the stench of the meat of Holy Things. (2) And the meat of the Holy Things never turned rotten. (3) A fly never made an appearance in the slaughter house. (4) A high priest never suffered a nocturnal emission on the eve of the Day of Atonement. (5) The rain never quenched the fire on the altar. (6) No wind ever blew away the pillar of smoke. (7) An invalidating factor never affected the 'omer, the Two Loaves, or the show bread. (8) When the people are standing, they are jammed together. When they go down and prostrate themselves, they have plenty of room. (9) A snake and a scorpion never bit anybody in Jerusalem. (10) And no one ever said to his fellow, "The place is too crowded for me" (Is. 49:20) to stay in Jerusalem.

The list before us collects information of a single classification. I see no point that the collection, on its own, proposes to establish. There is no hierarchy, for example, nor do the diverse items on the list make a point all together that none makes by itself. So we may not call the list, on its own, a propositional one.

The list of chapter 5 accords with a different principle of conglomeration and composition. The point of difference is merely that the earlier chapters list names of authorities; these by themselves make no point I can discern, beyond the chain of tradition in chapter 1. To the names, then, as a secondary matter, wise sayings are affixed, but these in the aggregate make no point beyond themselves any more than do the collected items in the list of chapter 5. The final chapter lists a *set* of items—that is, we move from the list of attributions, which makes no point through the list itself, to the list of items that bear a common trait.

The Forms of The Fathers According to Rabbi Nathan

When we compare the basic structure of The Fathers and The Fathers According to Rabbi Nathan, we ask a simple question: Has the earlier document dictated the traits of organization and balance characteristic of the later one, or does the new composition depart from the choices made by the earlier authorship?

The answer is clear. The framework of The Fathers According to Rabbi Nathan derives not from The Fathers but from an independent plan involving a number of components, some drawn from The Fathers, some derived from a response to The Fathers, and some altogether independent of The Fathers. The authorship of The Fathers According to Rabbi Nathan accepted the basic scheme of listing names and assigning sayings to those names, but it followed the received lists only in part; the authorship exercised freedom of choice in dropping or ignoring what it wished. Furthermore, the authorship of The Fathers provided sayings that demanded amplification and a model for working out that secondary expansion. The case of Aqabyah's saying (3:1A–3:1C, preceding section) presents us with a fine instance of that model. But while the authorship of The Fathers expanded only occasionally, that of The Fathers According to Rabbi Nathan does so as a matter of fixed practice. Finally, the authorship of The Fathers According to Rabbi Nathan drew upon a variety of materials not included in The Fathers. In a purely formal framework, we may point to those fresh materials as the source for what is new in the later work not only in a formal but also in a programmatic and substantive sense.

To begin, we take the simplest question: Has the authorship of The Fathers According to Rabbi Nathan adhered closely to the fundamental structural trait of The Fathers, namely, the order of names, and has that authorship furthermore concentrated on amplifying the sayings assigned to those names? The forms of The Fathers are these:

1. List of names plus attributive plus wise saying
   a. Secondary amplification of a wise saying:
      (1) *How so?*
      (2) *This teaches that*

> (3) Scriptural proof text
> (4) Parable
> 2. List of items of a single classification

As usual, I proceed inductively, analyzing the formal preferences of a single chapter of The Fathers According to Rabbi Nathan in order to form a theory of the formal repertoire of the document as a whole. We then examine two other chapters as a broader sample. If it turns out that our formal repertoire suffices to define their structure, no further test is required, as in the case of The Fathers.

THE FATHERS ACCORDING TO RABBI NATHAN, CHAPTER VI

VI:I.1.   A. **Yosé ben Yoezer says: Let your house be a gathering place for sages. Let your house be a gathering place for sages. And wallow in the dust of their feet, and drink in their words with gusto.**

B. **Let your house be a gathering place for sages:** how so?

C. This teaches that a person's house should be designated for sages and disciples and disciples of their disciples,

D. such as when someone says to a friend, "Lo, I'll watch for you in such and such a place."

We find the citation and gloss of a saying of The Fathers. We shall designate this form in the simplest possible language: **citation and gloss.** The formal treatment will sometimes include *how so* or, as in the present instance, *this teaches.*

VI:II.1.   A. Another teaching: **Let your house be a gathering place for sages:** how so?

B. When a disciple of a sage comes to you to say to you, "Repeat a tradition for me," if you have something to repeat for him, do so, and if not, bid him an immediate farewell.

Citation and gloss

VI:II.2.   A. And let a disciple sit before you not on a bench or on a pillow or a stool but let him sit in your presence on the ground.

B. And every word that comes out of your mouth let him accept upon himself in awe, fear, trembling, and signs of anguish,

C. just as our ancestors accepted [the Torah] at Mount Sinai in awe, fear, trembling, and signs of anguish,

D. so every word that comes out of your mouth let him take upon himself in awe, fear, trembling, and signs of anguish.

The second amplification of the base saying shifts the meaning and the focus. Formally I see no distinctive pattern or traits. This is just a set of sayings of an apothegmatic character. That is to say, what we have can as well have fit into The Fathers, so we may call the present form—so far as it is a form at all—*apothegm.* In fact the formal pattern is identical to the dominant one of The Fathers.

VI:III.1.   A. **And wallow in the dust of their feet:** how so?

B. When a disciple of a sage comes to town, do not say, "What do I need him for?" But go to him,

C. and do not sit before him on a bench or on a pillow or a stool but sit in his presence on the ground.

D. And every word that comes out of his mouth take upon yourself in awe, fear, trembling, and signs of anguish,

E. just as your ancestors accepted [the Torah] at Mount Sinai in awe, fear, trembling, and signs of anguish

Citation and gloss

VI:IV.1.   A. Another comment on the statement, **And wallow in the dust of their feet:**

B. This refers to R. Eliezer.

C. **. . . and drink in their words with gusto:**

D. This refers to R. Aqiba.

Formally, we have here another citation and gloss. This pericope serves as a prologue to the vast stories to follow, first on Aqiba, then on Eliezer. These stories are the one kind of composition in The Fathers According to Rabbi Nathan that is unknown to the framers of The Fathers: the extended narrative of a biographical character. It is not accurate to consider that biographical narrative highly formalized, for the narrative as a whole does not uniformly adhere to a single pattern or set of patterns. It is, in fact, not a form but a genre of writing. Nevertheless, that genre proves characteristic of The Fathers According to Rabbi Nathan. The first protracted instance is spelled out in detail; the others simply indicated in a brief way. Since in a later chapter I cite and analyze what follows, it suffices to give only a small sample:

VI:V.1.   A. How did R. Aqiba begin [his Torah study]?

B. They say, "He was forty years old and had never repeated a tradition. One time he was standing at the mouth of a well. He thought to himself, 'Who carved out this stone?'"

C. They told him, "It is the water that is perpetually falling on it every day."

D. They said to him, "Aqiba, do you not read Scripture, 'The water wears away stones' (Job 4:19)?"

E. On the spot R. Aqiba constructed in his own regard an argument *a fortiori:* "Now if something soft can [Goldin:] wear down something hard, words of Torah, which are as hard as iron, how much the more so should wear down my heart, which is made of flesh and blood."

F. On the spot he repented [and undertook] to study the Torah.

G. He and his son went into study session before a childrens' teacher, saying to him, "My lord, teach me Torah."

H. R. Aqiba took hold of one end of the tablet, and his son took hold of the other end. The teacher wrote out for him *Alef Bet* and he learned it, *Alef Tav* and he learned it, *the Torah of the Priests* [the books of Leviticus and Numbers] and he learned it. He went on learning until he had learned the entire Torah.

I. He went and entered study sessions before R. Eliezer and before R. Joshua. He said to them, "My lords, open up for me the reasoning of the Mishnah."

J. When they had stated one passage of law, he went and sat by himself and said, "Why is this *alef* written? why is this *bet* written? Why is this statement made?" He went and asked them and, in point of fact, [Goldin:] reduced them to silence.

What follows is indicated by reference only to the opening saying of a unit of discourse.

VI:V.2.   A. R. Simeon b. Eleazar says, "I shall make a parable for you. To what is the matter comparable? To a stonecutter who was cutting stone in a quarry. One time he took his chisel and went and sat down on the mountain and started to chip away little sherds from it. People came by and said to him, 'What are you doing?'"

VI:V.3.   A. Said R. Tarfon to him, "Aqiba, in your regard Scripture says, 'He stops up streams so that they do not trickle, and what is hidden he brings into the light' (Job 28:11)."

VI:V.4.   A. Every day he would bring a bundle of twigs [Goldin: straw], half of which he would sell in exchange for food, and half of which he would use for a garment.

VI:V.5.   A. In time to come R. Aqiba is going to impose guilt [for failing to study] on the poor [who use their poverty as an excuse not to study].

VI:V.6.   A. It was at the age of forty that he went to study the Torah. Thirteen years later he taught the Torah in public.

VI:VI.1.   A. How did R. Eliezer ben Hyrcanus begin [his Torah study]?

VI:VI.2.   A. On the way he saw a rock. He picked it up and took it and put it into his mouth.

VI:VI.3.   A. He went and entered study session before Rabban Yohanan ben Zakkai in Jerusalem.

VI:VI.4.   A. Hyrcanus, his father, heard that he was studying the Torah with Rabban Yohanan ben Zakkai. He decided, "I shall go and impose on Eliezer my son a vow not to derive benefit from my property."

Section VI:IV.1 serves only as a preface to the autonomous materials collected on the theme of how two famous masters began their studies late in life, having had no prior education. Rather than by form, we may classify the present set of materials simply by genre: **biographical narrative.** I have cited these materials at length, so that the difference between the narrative genre and the formal patterns of The Fathers and of other passages of The Fathers According to Rabbi Nathan may be made completely clear. In what follows I drastically abbreviate.

VI:VI.1.   A. Why was he called *Sisit Hakkesset?*

B. Because he reclined on a silver couch at the head of all the great men of Israel.

VI:VIII.1.   A. They tell concerning the daughter of Naqdimon b. Gurion that she had a bedspread worth twelve thousand golden denars.

VI:IX.1.   A. Why was he called Naqdimon ben Gurion?

B. Because the sun's rays penetrated for his sake [a play on the root NQD which occurs in both the name and in the verb for penetrate through].

C. [Explaining the reference to the sun's shining for his sake, the following story is told:] One time the Israelites went up to Jerusalem for a pilgrim festival, but they had no water to drink. [Naqdimon b. Gurion] went to an official and said to him, "Lend me twelve wells of water from now until such-and-such a day. If I do not pay you back twelve wells of water, I shall pay you twelve talents of silver," and they agreed on a due date . . .

Biographical narrative

VI:X.1.   A. Why was he called Ben Kalba Sabua [sated dog]?>

B. Because whoever came into his house hungry as a dog went out of his house sated.

VI:X.2.   A. When Caesar Vespasian came to destroy Jerusalem, the zealots wanted to burn up all of [Ben Kalba Sabua's] goods.

B. Kalba Sabua said to them, "Why do you want to destroy this city and seek to burn up all those goods? Hold up for me until I can go into the house and see what I have in the house."

VI:X.3.   A. [But ultimately] what did the men of Jerusalem have to do? They boiled straw and ate it.

B. And all the Israelites stationed near the walls of Jerusalem said, "Would that someone would give me five dates—I would go down and cut off five heads."

Biographical narrative

We have now isolated the following forms and genres: (1) citation and gloss, including *this teaches, how so,* parable, and proof text from Scripture; (2) the genre of biographical tale, following diverse formal patterns or no clear pattern at all. This may include a parable, a secondary restatement as a proposition of a lesson originally conveyed as a story. We now examine another chapter to see whether we can classify everything else within the two designated forms and genres.

THE FATHERS ACCORDING TO RABBI NATHAN, CHAPTER XXI

XXI:I.1.   A. **R. Dosa b. Harkinas says, "Sleeping late in the morning, drinking wine at noon, chatting with children, and attending the synagogues of the ignorant drive a man out of the world."**

B. **Sleeping late in the morning:** how so?

C. This teaches that a person should not intend to sleep until the time of reciting the Shema has passed.

D. For when someone sleeps until the time for reciting the Shema has passed, he turns out to waste time that should be spent studying the Torah.

E. As it is said, "The lazy one says, 'There is a lion in the way, yes, a lion is in the streets. The door is turning on its hinges and the lazy man is still in bed'" (Prov. 26:13–14).

1. Citation and gloss, including *this teaches, how so,* parable, and proof text from Scripture.

XXI:II.1.   A. **Drinking wine at noon:** how so?

B. This teaches that someone should not plan to drink wine at noon.

C. For when someone drinks wine at noon, he turns out to waste time that should be spent studying the Torah.

D. As it is said, "Woe to you, O land, when your king is a boy and your princes feast in the morning" (Qoh. 10:16).

E. And further: "Happy are you, O land, when your king is a free man, and your princes eat in due season, in strength and not in drunkenness" (Qoh. 10:17).

> 1. **Citation and gloss,** including *this teaches, how so,* parable, and proof text from Scripture.

XXI:II.2.   A. What is the meaning of *in due season?* One must say, this refers to the coming age, as it is said, "I the Lord will hasten it in its time" (Is. 60:22).

B. And further: "After a lapse of time like this shall it be said of Jacob and of Israel, O what God has done" (Num. 23:23).

C. So did the Holy One, blessed be he, say to the wicked Balaam, "After a period of time *like this*—but not now, not while you are standing among them, but at the time that I am going to carry out redemption for Israel [Goldin: will their king be free and prophecy be restored]."

> 1. **Citation and gloss,** including *this teaches, how so,* parable and proof text from Scripture.

XXI:III.1.   A. **Chatting with children:** how so?

B. This teaches that a person should not plan to sit by himself and repeat [traditions at home].

C. For if someone sits by himself and repeats traditions at home, he chats with his children and dependents and turns out to waste time that should be spent in the study of the Torah.

D. For it is said, "This book of the Torah shall not depart out of your mouth, but you shall meditate in it day and night" (Josh. 1:8).

> 1. **Citation and gloss,** including *this teaches, how so,* parable and proof text from Scripture.

XXI:IV.1.   A. **And attending the synagogues of the ignorant drive a man out of the world:** how so?

B. This teaches that a person should not plan to join with the idle in the corners of the market place.

C. For if someone sits around with the idle in the corners of the market place, he turns out to waste time that he should spend in studying the Torah.

D. For so it is said, "Happy is the one who has not walked in the counsel of the wicked, stood in the way of the sinners, or sat in the seat of the scornful. . . . But his delight is in the Torah of the Lord" (Ps. 1:1–2).

XXI:IV.2.   A. R. Meir says, "What is the meaning of the statement, *sat in the seat of the scornful?*"

B. "This refers to the theaters and circuses of the gentiles, in which people are sentenced to death,

C. "as it is said, 'I hate the gathering of evildoers and will not sit with the wicked' (Ps. 26:5).

D. "The word *evildoers* refers only to the wicked, as it is said, 'For the

evildoers shall be cut off, and yet a little while and the wicked is no more'
(Ps. 37:9–10).

E. "And what will be the form of the punishment that is coming to them in time
to come?

F. " 'For behold the day comes, it burns as a furnace, and all the proud and all
that do wickedness shall be stubble' (Ma. 3:19).

G. "And the proud are only the scorners, as it is said, 'A proud and haughty
man—scorner is his name' " (Prov. 21:24).

> 1. **Citation and gloss,** including *this teaches,
> how so,* parable and proof text from Scripture.

XXI:V.1.   A. There was the case of R. Aqiba who was in session and repeating
teachings for his disciples. He remembered something that he had done in his youth.

B. He said, "I give thanks for you, O Lord my God, that you have placed my
portion among those who sit in the house of study and have not placed my portion
with those who sit idly in the market place."

This is not really a biographical narrative but a statement given a narrative
setting, not much different from the story of Hillel's seeing a skull and saying,
"Because you drowned others, you were drowned, and those who drowned you
will be drowned." That sort of narrative setting for an apothegm does not form
a counterpart to the biographical narrative. I regard the item as anomalous.

We may return now to the main point in this protracted examination of a
complete chapter. The forms and genres of The Fathers According to Rabbi
Nathan are these:

1. Citation and gloss, including *this teaches, how so,* parable, and proof
text from Scripture.

2. The genre of the biographical tale, following diverse formal patterns or
no clear pattern at all. This may include a parable, a secondary restatement as
a proposition of a lesson originally conveyed as a story.

The Forms of The Fathers According to Rabbi Nathan Compared to The Forms of The Fathers

We may now sum up what we have found. The forms of The Fathers are these:

> 1. List of names plus attributive plus wise saying
>   a. Secondary amplification of a wise saying:
>   (1) *how so?*
>   (2) *this teaches that*
>   (3) Scriptural proof text
>   (4) Parable.
> 2. List of items of a single classification

The forms of The Fathers According to Rabbi Nathan differ in only one
way: The appendix with its subdivision, the genre of biographical tale, following diverse formal patterns or no clear pattern at all. This may include a

parable, a secondary restatement as a proposition of a lesson originally conveyed as a story. The appendix is not a form, of course, but the appendixes are highly formalized. Ordinarily they follow a familiar pattern: citation of a verse of Scripture, followed by secondary expansion of the cited verse. Thus, the form that follows the pattern of citing a statement of The Fathers and then saying, *how so?* or *this teaches that* finds its counterpart in the entirely familiar formal pattern of citation and gloss of Scripture. Indeed, we may say that The Fathers According to Rabbi Nathan serves the Fathers much as the two Talmuds serve the Mishnah and the several compilations of scriptural exegeses serve Scripture. What makes the appendix different in its formal traits is solely the subdivision, *the story*. The principal point at which the framers of The Fathers According to Rabbi Nathan have innovated is therefore clear.

Comparison and Contrast in the Literary Programs of the Two Documents

It remains to provide a complete catalogue of the forms of The Fathers According to Rabbi Nathan, so that the claims of this chapter will rest not on a random sample only, but on a full sifting of the evidence. I omit from the catalogue the instances in which the component of The Fathers According to Rabbi Nathan consists of a citation and gloss of a saying in The Fathers. That exegetical form has already been shown to be fundamental to the structure of The Fathers According to Rabbi Nathan as a whole. The form of citation and gloss or expansion (e.g., *how so?*, or *this teaches that*, or the inclusion of a proof text or a parable) is listed only where a passage *not* in The Fathers is cited and amplified. I give the complete catalogue in appendix 4 and simply record the main points here.

The classifications in appendix 4 yield an interesting point, which is the size and importance of list 5—the list of items with no counterpart in The Fathers. We note that The Fathers According to Rabbi Nathan supplies a sizable share of sayings of the sort that predominate in The Fathers (list 1). It likewise goes over familiar forms in lists 2 and 6. The contribution of a form consisting of the citation of a verse of Scripture followed by a systematic exposition of that verse scarcely attracts our attention; it is a commonplace. What is especially interesting is the contrast between list 3 and list 5. Here the distinction is mine, but I believe a comparison of any of the examples (e.g., XLI:II.1 and XLI:III.1) will make the point.

The point is that we can distinguish stories meant to *illustrate* wise sayings that are not particular to their setting from stories made up to *prove propositions contained solely within themselves* and not supplied by the document in which they make their appearance. The former type refers either to a biblical figure or to no named person; the latter type is always told about a named sage. These stories about sages, when they occur in The Fathers According to

Rabbi Nathan, invariably unfold within their own logic and perspective; they do not ordinarily serve to illustrate the teaching to which the redactor has appended them, and therefore always serve as an appendix, pure and simple. In fact, the bulk of the appended materials consists precisely of those stories. What is formally fresh in The Fathers According to Rabbi Nathan as compared to The Fathers is the story told for a purpose distinct from that of the redactors of a text, that is, the items in list 5 in contrast to those in list 3.

The result of form analysis for the purpose of this inquiry is easy to state—it is the same result we achieved earlier. We now realize that the genre of the story distinguishes The Fathers According to Rabbi Nathan from The Fathers in both structure and form. The work of comparing the two documents leads us next to ask what is like and unlike in their content. Only when we have a clear picture of the ways in which the later exegetes received and reworked the earlier document can we grasp the position and importance of the story in the new document.

3

The Matter of Topic: The Topical Program of The Fathers and of The Fathers According to Rabbi Nathan

From Style to Substance

The comparison of the structure and rhetoric of the later to the earlier piece of writing directs our attention to a simple fact. The authorship of The Fathers According to Rabbi Nathan stands in a relationship of tradition to the prior composition. That is, the later writers have taken over and faithfully replicated the earlier document. At the same time, it is clear, they also wished to add to the tradition. For had they merely copied the prior document and contributed sayings to it, using lists of names and fresh aphorisms to repeat the same basic point, we should have had nothing to report regarding alterations of structure. And had the rhetorical forms chosen by the earlier writers sufficed for their purposes, the authorship of The Fathers According to Rabbi Nathan should have done nothing to enrich the received repertoire. But they did both, reshaping the structure and recasting the forms of discourse. That fact defines what is logically the next question: Do these changes accomplish a genuine alteration of the received text's message, or do they merely provide new ways to say familiar things?

Points in Common, Points of Difference

Let me state the simple syllogism at hand, which has three parts:

1. If we find a passage not treated in The Fathers According to Rabbi Nathan that bears ideas amply attested in the later writing, we have every reason to point toward a continuity of intent and meaning.

2. If, however, we find passages in The Fathers that repeatedly make a single point, and that point does not occur in The Fathers According to Rabbi Nathan, then we may claim that the later authorship wants to say not this but something else.

3. Finally, if we find themes and conceptions in The Fathers According to

Rabbi Nathan that are in no way related to those of The Fathers, we have still more interesting evidence that the later authorship proposes to make its own points.

Let me spell out what is at stake, and why I have framed the question in this simple way. My aim is to avoid subjectivity in defining what the later authorship has chosen for its topical and propositional program. The problem, as to method, is self-evident. Recognizing the differences in the formal preferences of the authorship of the Fathers According to Rabbi Nathan requires little exercise of taste or subjective judgment. Matters are clear on the surface. When we turn to the more difficult but critical issue of changes in opinion and sensibility, however, we find that our own perspective intervenes. Yet here too, if we survey the surface of matters and rely mainly on facts visible to the naked eye, we shall not err. What we now wish to know is precisely what views characterize the later, exegetical document but not the original, apothegmatic one.

We therefore continue to emphasize formalities, and in search of proposition and logic, we follow the path defined by our interest in rhetoric and topic. The bridge from topic to logic and proposition requires only objective description of superficial facts. My ultimate claim, that the later authorship has a distinctive message to deliver and has chosen a particular means—the story—through which to deliver it, rests on the obvious and uninterpreted facts turned up by such description. As before, the pertinent facts are presented in detail in appendices. I refer the reader to appendix 6 for topics treated in The Fathers and not in The Fathers According to Rabbi Nathan, and to appendix 7 for topics treated in The Fathers According to Rabbi Nathan and not in The Fathers. The differences between these catalogues are classified in the following section.

Comparison and Contrast in the Topical Programs of the Two Documents

The authorship of the earlier document speaks only of the individual, who prepares in this world for the life of the world to come. The teleology of the system outlined by The Fathers, then, calls for the individual to prepare for judgment before God and promises eternal life. The Fathers According to Rabbi Nathan shifts the focus of discourse from the individual to the holy people. Its fresh materials prove consistent and one-sided in focusing not so much upon the individual as the nation. The later authorship is equally consistent in its contributions, which time and again promise the age to come for Israel, as against this age, which belongs to the nations.

In this shift of mythic categories of the social entity under discussion—from the individual in The Fathers to the nation in The Fathers According to Rabbi Nathan—the later writers and compositors redefine the earlier teleology and focus it upon historical and social categories, rather than those that emerge from the life and death of the individual. We rapidly refine that rather general statement, however, for when the later authorship wishes to speak of the social rather than the individual category, they find a particular type of individual to represent the society. They turn to history of a very particular kind—namely, biography, episodes in the lives of saints—to encapsulate that whole and to state its purpose and direction.

Topics in The Fathers and Not in The Fathers According to Rabbi Nathan

The data of appendix 6 includes six propositions important in The Fathers and neglected in the later, exegetical document.

1. Working for a living along with study of Torah, at Avot 2:2, has no counterpart in The Fathers According to Rabbi Nathan, the authorship of which tends to insist on the opposite: If you give your best energies to the study of the Torah, the other side of things will work itself out on its own. This treats the study of the Torah in a supernatural way. Note also that R. Sadoq says, "Do not make [Torah teachings] a crown in which to glorify yourself or a spade with which to dig." So did Hillel say, "He who uses the crown perishes." One should not make a living from Torah study, but should both study the Torah and work for a living. The later framing of matters, which represents the sage as a supernatural figure in general, and the sage's study of Torah as yielding supernatural power and also reward in particular, would have surprised the framers of these apothegms.

2. Make His wishes into your own wishes, so that He will make your wishes into His wishes. Put aside your wishes on account of His wishes, so that He will put aside the wishes of other people in favor of your wishes. The statement of Judah the Patriarch, "Whatever is an ornament to the one who follows it, and an ornament in the view of others . . ." belongs in this same category. The stress in both sayings on accommodating others occurs also in another statement neglected by The Fathers According to Rabbi Nathan: R. Haninah b. Dosa would say, "Anyone from whom people take pleasure, the Omnipresent takes pleasure. And anyone from whom people do not take pleasure, the Omnipresent does not take pleasure." Note also that R. Meir says, "Keep your business to a minimum and make your business the Torah. And be humble before everybody."

The notion that a principal task of a person is to please other people and to exercise self-restraint in favor of the will of others, so far as I can see, has no counterpart in The Fathers According to Rabbi Nathan. R. Eleazar Haqqappar says, "Jealousy, lust, and ambition drive a person out of this world." This forms the counterpart of the sayings on the importance of self-abnegation. The following goes over the same ground, emphasizing humility and accommodation: "Anyone in whom are these three traits is one of the disciples of Abraham, our father; but [if he bears] three other traits, he is one of the disciples of Balaam, the wicked; (1) a generous spirit, (2) a modest mien, and

(3) a humble soul—he is one of the disciples of Abraham, our father. He who exhibits (1) a grudging spirit, (2) an arrogant mien, and (3) a proud soul—he is one of the disciples of Balaam, the wicked." I find pertinent the following as well: R. Ishmael says, "(1) Be quick [in service] to a superior, (2) efficient in service [to the state], and (3) receive everybody with joy" (Avot 3:12).

3. R. Hananiah, Prefect of the Priests, says, "Pray for the welfare of the government. For if it were not for fear of it, one man would swallow his fellow alive" (Avot 3:3). This appreciation for the government runs contrary to the tendency of such statements as Avot 2:3, "be wary of the government," which do receive ample discussion in The Fathers According to Rabbi Nathan. Whether or not the period from ca. 250 to ca. 600 marked the entry of sages into the administration of Israel's affairs in both the land of Israel and Babylonia we do not know. We do know that the later documents of the canon of the Dual Torah consistently represent sages as important figures in politics. The shift we note here is consistent with that later representation of the state of affairs.

4. R. Hananiah b. Hakhinai says, "(1) He who gets up at night, and (2) he who walks around by himself, and (3) he who turns his desire to emptiness—lo, this person is liable for his life" (Avot 3:4). I am not entirely sure what this saying means. If the stress is on living in community and fellowship with others—and (1) and (2) seem to intend that point—then it is a commonplace in both documents, which stress the importance of the community's values and interests over the individual's. In addition, The Fathers, as we have just noted, emphasizes the centrality of accommodating the wishes of others.

5. R. Nehunia b. Haqqaneh says, "From whoever accepts upon himself the yoke of the Torah do they remove the yoke of the state and the yoke of hard labor" (Avot 3:5). The contrast of the authority of the Torah as against the authority of the state is not drawn in The Fathers According to Rabbi Nathan. I see no intersection between this statement and the ones that emphasize the importance of both study of the Torah and also labor. They make a different point, which is to keep the two in balance.

6. I have already introduced the distinction between an ahistorical and an eschatological teleology: the one focused upon the individual, this life, and life eternal; the other emphasizing the nation, this age, and the coming age. In my *Messiah in Context: Israel's History and Destiny in Formative Judaism* (Philadelphia: Fortress, 1983), I have shown that, overall, a shift from an ahistorical and individual to an eschatological and national teleology characterizes the unfolding of the canon of the Dual Torah, beginning with the Mishnah, inclusive of Avot, and ending with the Yerushalmi and the Bavli, inclusive of The Fathers According to Rabbi Nathan. Here we see the shift in a concrete way.

For example, R. Jacob says, "This world is like an antechamber before the world to come. Get ready in the antechamber, so you can go into the great hall." He would say, "Better is a single moment spent in penitence and good deeds in this world than the whole of the world to come. And better is a single moment of inner peace in the world to come than the whole of a lifetime spent in this world." The stress in these sayings is on the individual, this life, and the life of the resurrection. It is not on this age and the age to come, and the life of Israel restored to its land and government. Note also the corresponding stress on the individual in the following: R. Jacob would say, "Those who are born are [destined] to die, and those who die are [destined] for resurrection. And the living are [destined] to be judged—so as to know, to make known, and to confirm that (1) he is God, (2) he is the one who forms, (3) he is the one who creates, (4) he is the one who understands, (5) he is the one who judges, (6) he is the one who gives evidence, (7) he is the one who brings suit, (8) and he is the one who is going to make the ultimate judgment."

The Fathers 4:22C goes over the same ground, in the passage indicated: "(1) despite your wishes were you formed, (2) despite your wishes were you born, (3) despite your wishes do you live, (4) despite your wishes do you die, and (5) despite your wishes are you going to give a full accounting before the King of kings of kings, the Holy One, blessed be he." The following once more stresses the judgment of the individual. "The disciples of Balaam the wicked inherit Gehenna and go down to the Pit of Destruction, as it is said, but you, O God, shall bring them down into the pit of destruction; bloodthirsty and deceitful men shall not live out half their days" (Ps. 55:24). He would say, "The shameless go to Gehenna, and the diffident to the garden of Eden." That is not to say the fate of the Temple and of Jerusalem play no role in The Fathers. These eschatological symbols occur: "May it be found pleasing before you, O Lord our God, that you rebuild your city quickly in our day and set our portion in your Torah." Further, at The Fathers According to Rabbi Nathan XLI:XX we do have an extensive discourse on Gehenna in terms of individual judgment. So the point of difference is the absence of national-eschatological discourse in the foundation document.

Topics in The Fathers According to Rabbi Nathan and Not in The Fathers

The materials particular to the exegetical document are catalogued in appendix 7. I do not catalogue the lists given in The Fathers According to Rabbi Nathan but not in The Fathers, corresponding in number of entries (e.g., ten, seven, four) to those in The Fathers, because I cannot see any reason for the omission of one such list or the inclusion of another; none of the lists presents a clearcut hierarchy and provides an implicit statement of a proposition. Here are the topics treated in the later writing that seem to have no counterpart in the earlier one.

1. The first man and woman; general traits of humanity; I:IX–XVIII, large anthology on the first man; IV:VII.1, God diversified human beings in three aspects; XXXI:I, the human being is equivalent to the whole of creation. Note also XXXVII:I–III; on creation: XXXVII:VI.

2. Stories about sages: VI:V–VII; XV:IV, V; XVII:III–V; XVIII:II; XIX:II–III; XXV:I–IV; XXXVIII:V; XLI:II–III.

3. XX: I–VII, Hananiah: Torah study takes away hunger, silliness, libido, impulse to do evil, bad woman, idle nonsense, yoke of mortals. Israel's fate depends on that of the nations: Israel suffers when nations prosper. Israel regains its prosperity when it keeps the Torah. Note also XXVIII: XII, Judah b. Ilai: Treat words of Torah as the main thing and earning a living as trivial.

4. XXIV: I–VIII, Elisha b. Abuyah's sayings: study of Torah along with good deeds is the best combination. [Study Torah when young—sayings are not particular to the exegetical document.] Note also XXIX: V.1: studying in order to teach others is best. XXIX: VI: waking up in the middle of the night on account of words of the Torah is a good omen.

5. XXVI: II–XI, Aqiba: Do not live among gentiles; do not take vows. Get buried in Land of Israel. Simeon b. Eliezer: Israelites living outside of the Land are idolators in all innocence. Aqiba: Marry appropriate to one's status. Note also XXVIII: I–II, superiority of Land of Israel to all other Jewish communities everywhere.

6. XXIX: VII, Eliezer Haqqappar: Honor one's fellow not for the sake of money and treat someone lightly so as to carry out a prior obligation to perform a religious duty.

7. XXIX: VIII, Four types of repentence and their effects. Note also XXXIX: I–II, V; XL: V, nature of repentence.

8. XXX: III–V, Meir: One who might have committed a transgression is treated by the rules of the Torah more strictly than one who has actually done so. Nathan b. Joseph: Whoever inadvertently commits a transgression is regarded by Scripture as though he had done it deliberately. Aqiba: Whoever associates with transgressors, even though not doing what they do, ends up with the punishment that is coming to them. Simeon: The liar is punished by not being believed when he is telling the truth.

9. XXXIII: IV–V, correspondence of Israel's redemption and suffering. Note also eschatological sayings at XXXIV: V: When Israelites do not carry out the will of the Omnipresent, the nations of the world appear to them like a boar out of the forest; XXXV: IV.3, Jerusalem is destined to have all the nations and kingdoms gathered together in its midst; XXXVI: I–VII, who has a portion in the world to come and who does not have a portion in the world to come. Let us now ask what this list of topics, in the aggregate, suggests.

Where The Fathers According to Rabbi Nathan
Differs from The Fathers

We begin with what the authorship of The Fathers According to Rabbi Nathan did not choose to say. Three points of emphasis in The Fathers lack any restatement and development in the Fathers According to Rabbi Nathan.

First, the study of the Torah alone does not suffice; one must also make an honest living through work. In The Fathers According to Rabbi Nathan we find not that point but its opposite: one should study the Torah, and other things will take care of themselves—a claim of a more supernatural character than the one in The Fathers.

Second, the earlier document tells sages to accommodate their wishes to those of the community at large, to accept the importance of the government, to work in community, and to practice self-abnegation and restraint in favor of the wishes of others. The sage here is less a supernatural figure than a political leader, eager to conciliate and reconcile the other.

Third, and most important, the later document imparts to the teleological question an eschatological answer altogether lacking in the earlier one. This constitutes the single important negative point of contrast, so let us expand upon it. If we were to ask the authorship of Avot to spell out their teleology, they would draw our attention to the numerous sayings about this life as a time of preparation for the life of the world to come on the one side, and to judgment and eternal life on the other. The focus is on the individual and how he or she lives in this world and prepares for the next. Commonly in the two documents before us when we speak of the individual, we also tend to find the language of "this world" and "the world to come," *olam hazzeh, olam habbah.* The sayings about this world and the next form a stunning contrast to the ones about this *age* and the "next age," *olam hazzeh, leatid labo.* In general, though not invariably, the shift in language draws in its wake a shift in social category from individual to social entity (group, nation, or people). The word *olam* bears two meanings, "world" and "age." In context, when the word bears the sense of "world," the category under discussion is the private person, and where the required sense in English, is "age," then—as a rough rule of thumb—what is promised is for the nation.

We can tell that the definitive category is social and therefore national when what is at stake is the fate not of the private person but of holy Israel. The concern then is what will happen to the nation in time to come, meaning the coming age, not the coming life of the resurrection. The systemic teleology shifts its focus to the holy people and, alongside, to the national history of the holy people—now and in the age to come. So in the movement from "this world" and "the world to come," to "this age" and "the age to come," often expressed as "the coming future," *leatid labo,* we note an accompanying categorical shift in the definitive context from the individual and the private life of home and family to the society and historical, public life. That shift then characterizes the teleological movement as much as the categorical change, and it is contained both in general and in detail in the differences we have noticed between The Fathers and The Fathers According to Rabbi Nathan.

The stories also contain those fresh points that differentiate the later from the earlier document. That is to say, the national-eschatological interest that is unique to the later document, with its focus on living only in the Land of Israel, and its contrast between this age, possessed by the gentiles, and the age to come, in which redeemed Israel will enjoy a paramount position, emerges not only in sayings but also in stories about the critical issue, the destruction of Jerusalem and the loss of the Temple, along with the concomitant matter about repentence and how it is achieved at this time.

Yet a further point of development lies in the notion that study of the Torah combined with various virtues (e.g., good deeds, fear of sin) suffices, and a concomitant assurance that making a living no longer matters. Here too the new medium of the later document—the stories about sages—bears the new message. For that conviction emerges not only explicitly (e.g., in the sayings of Hananiah about the power of Torah study to take away many sources of suffering, or Judah b. Ilai's that one should treat words of the Torah as principal, earning a living as trivial), but also in the detail that both Aqiba and Eliezer began poor, but through their mastery of Torah ended rich.

We note also that The Fathers According to Rabbi Nathan contains a sizable share of sayings not used in The Fathers, but only one name that occurs only in the later document, Elisha b. Abuyah, produces resonance. That is because of the famous stories about his apostasy, which we should expect to have discouraged inclusion of his wise sayings. This does not seem to me an indicative shift—only an interesting one—but I do not know what to make of it.

The Advent of the Holy Sage and of Episodes in the Lives of the Saints

In our sifting of details, we should not miss the main point. The Fathers According to Rabbi Nathan differs from The Fathers in one aspect so fundamental as to change the face of the base document completely. While the earlier authorship took slight interest in lives and deeds of sages, the later one contributed in a systematic and orderly manner the color and life of biography to the named but faceless sages of The Fathers. Let me state emphatically the simple fact we have turned up: *The stories about sages make points that correspond to statements of viewpoints that are unique to The Fathers According to Rabbi Nathan.*

I conclude, therefore, that the principal point of programmatic difference between The Fathers and The Fathers According to Rabbi Nathan is as follows: The Fathers presents an ideal of the sage as model for the everyday life of the individual, who must study the Torah and also work, and prepare now, through the good life, for life after death, while The Fathers According to Rabbi Nathan has a different conception of the sage, of the value and meaning of the study of the Torah, and of the center of interest, and has also selected a new medium for the expression of its distinctive conception. To spell this out:

1. The sage in the Fathers According to Rabbi Nathan is not a judge and teacher alone but also a supernatural figure.

2. Study of the Torah in preference to making a living promises freedom from the conditions of natural life.

3. Israel as the holy people seen as a supernatural social entity takes center stage.

And these innovative points are conveyed not only in sayings but in stories about sages.

What follows is that the medium not only carries a new message *but also forms a component of that new message.* The sage as a supernatural figure now presents Torah teachings through what he does, not only through what he says. Therefore telling stories about what sages did and the circumstances in which they produced their sayings forms part of the Torah, as it clearly did not in the earlier document. The interest in stories about sages therefore proves to be not merely literary or formal; it is more than a new way of conveying an old message. Stories about the sages are told because sages stand for a message that can emerge only in stories, not in sayings alone. So we turn to a close reading of the stories themselves to review that message and find out why it now emerges through stories in particular. What we see is nothing short of a new mode of revelation, that is, of conveying and imparting God's will in the Torah. Judaism (our term and category) requires stories because the Torah (their term and category) reaches Israel not merely through what the sage says but through what he is and does.

We have now seen that the stories about sages portray a burden of values distinct from those expressed in the sayings of The Fathers. Those stories commonly are attached to portions of The Fathers According to Rabbi Nathan that serve as exegeses of sayings in The Fathers, on the one side, or in Scripture, on the other. The framers of The Fathers According to Rabbi Nathan thus imputed to The Fathers (as well as to Scripture) the messages that they themselves proposed to deliver.

The Sage, the Story, and the Advent of History

People told stories because they wanted to think about history, and in their setting history emerged in an account of what happened, with an implicit message of the meaning of events conveyed in the story as well. They further conceived of the social entity, Israel, as an extended family, children of a single progenitor, Abraham, and his sons, Isaac and Jacob. Consequently, the stories they told centered on family history. That accounts in general for the details of what the authorship of The Fathers According to Rabbi Nathan chose to add to the topical program of The Fathers.

The sage in the system of The Fathers According to Rabbi Nathan constituted the supernatural father, who replaced the natural one; events in the life of the sage constituted happenings in the history of the family-nation, Israel. So, as we shall see, history blended with family, and family with Torah study. The national, salvific history of the family-nation, Israel, took place in such events as (1) the origins of the sage, that is, his beginnings in Torah study;

(2) the sagacity of the sage, the counterpart to what we should call social history; (3) the doings of the sage in great turnings in the family's history, including, especially, the destruction of the Temple, now perceived (presumably after the fiasco of the emperor Julian's aborted plan, in ca. 361 to rebuild the Jerusalem Temple) as final and decisive; and (4) the death of the sage, while engaged in Torah study. These form the four classifications of story in our document.

Part Two

Logic and Proposition:
Narratives in
The Fathers According to Rabbi Nathan

4

The Matter of Logic and Proposition: The Burden of Narrative in The Fathers According to Rabbi Nathan

The Three Logics of Intelligible Discourse and the Importance of Narrative

When people wish to communicate their ideas, they present propositions to others. These propositions evoke a shared logic, one that makes the thought of one person intelligible to another. One sentence generates another; a statement follows from a prior one. These form intelligible discourses, turning facts into statements of meaning and consequence. Discourse shared by others begins when one sentence joins to another to frame a proposition in such a way that others understand the connection between the two sentences.

This we know, in the West, as a *syllogism,* which conveys and also proves a proposition; for example:

1. All Greeks are philosophers;
2. Demosthenes is a Greek;
3. therefore Demosthenes is a philosopher.

The sentences standing by themselves convey not a proposition but merely a statement of a fact, which may or may not be true, and which may or may not bear sense and meaning beyond itself. Sentences 1 and 2 by themselves state facts but announce no proposition. But the logic of syllogistic discourse joins the two into No. 3, which does indeed constitute a proposition and also (by the way) shows the linkage between No. 1 and No. 2. But there are other ways to set forth propositions, make points, and thus undertake intelligible discourse besides the philosophical and syllogistic one with which we are familiar in the West.

In the canonical writings of the Judaism of the Dual Torah, authorships present their propositions in ways that are familiar to us, as well as in one way that we do not usually encounter in our own intellectual world. Overall, writers rely upon one of three means of linking sentence to sentence in paragraphs. They make propositions that rest upon philosophical bases, for example, through the proposal of a thesis and the composition of a list of facts that prove the thesis. This familiar, Western mode of scientific expression through the classification of data, which we may call *the science of making lists* (*Listenwissenschaft*), is best exemplified by the Mishnah, but it dominates also in such profoundly philosophical-syllogistic documents as Leviticus Rabbah. Within the idiom of the canonical writings of the Dual Torah, those documents bring us closest to familiar modes of thought.

A second logic derives from narrative, which sees cogency in the order of events and conveys a proposition through the setting forth of happenings in a sequence that makes a point; that is, it establishes not merely the facts about what happens, but the teleology that explains those facts. Then we speak not only of events but their relationship, claiming to account for that relationship in the sequence and order of happenings. That second logic predominates in the parts of The Fathers According to Rabbi Nathan that appeal to narrative in general, and storytelling in particular, to convey messages that prove fresh and particular to the later document.

The third logic is the one that is not familiar to us in the West. It draws upon the premises of an established text to link otherwise unrelated statements to one another and to form of them all an intelligible proposition. This third logic is represented in The Fathers. Only when we see how the logic perceived (by sages at least) as a given, in an established and received text, permits intelligible discourse to take place shall we grasp how profound an innovation is the amplification of The Fathers through the inclusion of an entirely different mode of intelligible discourse. Let us examine a small passage of The Fathers (1:1–3), so that the point will be entirely clear. I present in italics the things that people say, which would correspond to the propositions of a syllogistic, philosophical discourse.

> 1:1. Moses received the Torah at Sinai and handed it on to Joshua, Joshua to elders, and elders to prophets. And prophets handed it on to the men of the great assembly. They said three things, *"Be prudent in judgment. Raise up many disciples. Make a fence for the Torah."*
>
> 1:2. Simeon the Righteous was one of the last survivors of the great assembly. He would say, *"On three things does the world stand: On the Torah, and on the Temple service, and on deeds of loving-kindness."*
>
> 1:3. Antigonus of Sokho received [the Torah] from Simeon the Righteous. He would say, *"Do not be like servants who serve the master on condition of receiving a reward, but [be] like servants who serve the master not on condition of receiving a reward. And let the fear of Heaven be upon you."*

Now if we ask ourselves what the italicized words have in common, how they form a cogent discourse, the answer is clear. They have nothing in common and, standing by themselves, do not establish a proposition in common. They do not form an intelligible discourse. But—and this must stand as a premise of all argument—in the mind of the authorship of The Fathers, which has set matters forth as we see them, those same words serve intelligible discourse. The principle of cogency, however, upon which intelligibility rests, does not derive from what is said. Since we find no syllogistic statement or other philosophically formulated proposition, and since we find no narrative of any sort, we address a mode of intelligible discourse that falls into a different classification from either philosophical or narrative logic. What holds the several sentences together is the list of named authorities, and the premise that Rabbi X is linked on a common list—a text, a canon of names—with Rabbi Y, and linked in that order—first X, then Y—accounts (for the authorship at hand) for the intelligibility of the writing. That is to say, the logic of The Fathers derives from the premise of an established text—in this case, a list of names— that joins together otherwise unrelated statements. What makes The Fathers an intelligible statement overall (or in its principal parts) is not what is said but who does the saying. The list of those canonical names, in proper order, holds together an otherwise unintelligible sequence of statements (any one of which, to be sure, is as intelligible as the statement, "All Greeks are philosophers"). The coherence is formal and extrinsic.

The upshot is that a statement that relies for intelligibility upon the premise of an established text (whether a list of names; a passage of Scripture; the known sequence of events, as in the *pesher* writings; or the well-known sequence of events in the life of a holy man) differs in its fundamental logic from one that relies for intelligibility upon either narrative or philosophical and syllogistic thought. To state the matter very simply, the movement from the Fathers to The Fathers According to Rabbi Nathan represents a shift not only of structure and organization, as we saw in chapter 1, rhetorical form, as we noted in chapter 2, and topical program, as we realized in chapter 3. The change is still more profound, since it involves the introduction of a mode of thought not present in the earlier writing.

Narrative as Mode of Thought, Medium, and Message

The new messages of The Fathers According to Rabbi Nathan concerning the nation, enduring this age, and waiting for the age to come, occur not only or primarily in sayings but also in stories. A medium not utilized in The Fathers carries a new message. Of greatest consequence, as I have now explained, the medium and the message appeal to a mode of thought different from the logic that dominates in The Fathers. My task is now to define with some care what I mean and do not mean by narrative in general and by a story in particular, and also to specify the diverse species of the genus narrative. This I propose to accomplish by the inductive classification of the diverse narratives that occur in The Fathers According to Rabbi Nathan. Once we recognize the types of narratives at hand, we may compare them and point to what is unlike the diverse species of the common genus. Let us begin with the genus narrative, all the while remaining within the limits of our document (for I cannot claim to contribute in any way to narratology, but only hope to clarify how the recognition of types of narrative helps us to understand a certain shift within the history of a religious system).

An Inductive Taxonomy of Narrative
in The Fathers According to Rabbi Nathan

A narrative conveys a message by telling a sequential tale of things that happened, rather than by framing a message in general and abstract language. The sequence by which things happen is what joins one detail to another, one sentence or paragraph to the next. There is a logic, a sense, order, proportion, and lesson, conveyed through narrative, and these, properly understood, present a proposition, just as much as a logic, sense, required order, proposition, and structure will produce, in philosophical discourse, an entirely intelligible statement. The narrative mode of logical discourse, of course, encompasses a variety of styles, and appropriate indicators instruct us on how to classify the types of narratives. Focusing upon one document in particular, we may readily distinguish one type of narrative from another.

But one trait must characterize all narratives, or we have something other than narrative (in the context of the single document under discussion here): A narrative contains some action, even if only implicit. *Someone came and said* does not constitute a narrative; *he said to him . . . he said to him . . .* does not form the substrate of implicit action, for what is said is ordinarily a position in logical analysis and practical reason. But *someone came and did, and the rabbi, seeing the action, ruled* does constitute a narrative, though of a different sort from one in which a sequence of sustained actions, with beginning, middle, and end, constitutes the account and bears the main message. So too, *walking along one day, he saw a skull in the water and said* forms a narrative, even though the narrative serves only to provide a setting for the saying.

So the trait that characterizes all sustained narrative discourse, but is absent in all non-narrative discourse, is that a point is made through a description of action, not merely a report of a position or principle that is established through what is said. I emphasize that the description of action may be implicit in what is said, for example, "Why did you do such and so?" "Because I wanted . . ." Implicit action is different from the statement of a principle; for example, "Why do you maintain so and so?" "Because the verse says . . . ," or, "Because the established principle is . . ." That mode of discourse reports on a conversation, to be sure, but does not portray an event, tell a tale, evoke a pictorial tableau of completed action, or indicate something that someone has done.

The genus narrative may encompass diverse modes of the concrete portrayal of a message, of which I find four in our document:

1. The parable
2. The precipitant: the narrative setting for, or formal precipitant of, a saying
3. The (ordinarily legal, but sometimes moral) precedent
4. The story furthermore is divided into two subspecies:
    a. Scriptural, or Scripture-story
    b. Sagacious, or sage-story

I shall show that in The Fathers According to Rabbi Nathan these are sufficiently different from one another in narrative technique to justify separate classifications. Other classifications of narrative and further subdivisions of the taxa I have specified will not detain us for the purpose of the present inquiry. In the next two chapters, when I compare the narratives of our document with their counterparts elsewhere (chapter 6) and the use of various types of narrative, in proportion, in other important canonical writings of the Judaism of the Dual Torah (chapter 7), I invoke only the preceding taxonomy.

The Parable

A parable unfolds through resort to narrative: "There was a king who had such and so, who said such and such, who did so and so, with the result that such and such happened." The parable is a narrative in that the appeal for cogency is to teleology, and the proposition of the parable emerges (whether made explicit or not) as a self-evident exemplification of the teleology at hand. So the explanation, the principle of cogency, derives from the order of events: "Do this with that result; say this with that consequence." As we shall see later on, stories exhibit the same indicative traits as parables; thus, a brief comparison is in order.

A parable is like a story, in that the narrative is centered on what people do rather than on what they say, and the message is carried by the medium of described action, commonly with a point of tension introduced at the outset and resolved at the end.[1] A parable is different from a story, in that its author presents a totally abstract tale, not mentioning specific authorities, placing the action in concrete time and setting, or invoking an authoritative text (e.g., a proof text of Scripture). Like a story, a parable will not serve to prove a point of law or supply a precedent. As to the sage-story in particular, it centers on a sage's exemplary actions as the point of tension and resolution, while a parable ordinarily focuses on wisdom or morality, which the parable's narrator will propose to illustrate. A parable teaches its lesson explicitly; a story about a sage is rarely explicit in specifying its lesson, and the implicit lesson is always the exemplary character of the sage and what he does—whatever it is, whatever its verbal formulation as a lesson. So there is a very considerable difference between the parable and the story.

One example of a parable (so labeled) in our document follows:

I:XIII.2.   A. R. Simeon b. Yohai says, "I shall draw a parable for you. To what may the first man be compared? He was like a man who had a wife at home. What did that man do? He went and brought a jug and put in it a certain number of dates

---

1. The literature on the parable—cited at length in Davis's bibliography, which serves this book—has not helped me in my inquiry, because the parable is treated as a constant among the diverse documents at hand. (See Joseph M. Davis, "Literary Studies of Aggadic Narrative: A Bibliography," in J. Neusner, ed., *New Perspectives on Ancient Judaism* [Lanham, Md.: University Press of America, 1987], 3:185–218.) I do not know of a study that differentiates the form and use of the parable in one document from its form and use in some other. The literary form (if that is what it is) is treated as uniform throughout. But the failure to undertake any sort of sus-

and nuts. He caught a scorpion and put it at the mouth of the jug and sealed it tightly. He left it in the corner of his house.

B. "He said to her, 'My daughter, whatever I have in the house is entrusted to you, except for this jar, which under no circumstances should you touch.' What did the woman do? When her husband went off to market, she went and opened the jug and put her hand in it, and the scorpion bit her, and she went and fell into bed. When her husband came home from the market, he said to her, 'What's going on?'

C. "She said to him, 'I put my hand into the jug, and a scorpion bit me, and now I'm dying.'

D. "He said to her, 'Didn't I tell you to begin with, "Whatever I have in the house is entrusted to you, except for this jar, which under no circumstances should you touch."' He got mad at her and divorced her.

E. "So it was with the first man.

F. "When the Holy One, blessed be he, said to him, 'Of all the trees of the garden you certainly may eat, but from the tree of knowledge of good and evil you may not eat, for on the day on which you eat of it, you will surely die' (Gen. 2:17),

G. "on that day he was driven out, thereby illustrating the verse, 'Man does not lodge overnight in honor'" (Ps. 49:24).

Simeon's point is that by giving man the commandment, God aroused his interest in that tree and led man to do what he did. So God bears a measure of guilt for the fall of man.

The trait of the parable that draws our attention is its impersonality: the details of the narrative point toward the lesson to be drawn, not to specific things like the name of the man, the day of the week, and the place of the event. These have no bearing, obviously, because the parable is parabolic, intended to state in a concrete narrative a general point. The parable in its narrative traits is the opposite of a historical story, such as we find told about sages. The former is general, universal, and pertinent to humanity wherever and whenever the narrated event takes place; the latter is specific, particular, relevant to a concrete circumstance, situation, and person.

The Precipitant: The Narrative Setting for a Saying

What I call the *formal setting,* or *precipitant,* for a saying merely portrays a situation to which a setting pertains, for example, *He saw a skull and said.*[2] That hardly adds up to a substantial narrative, let alone a sustained story, since nothing happens to draw out the significance of the event (he saw), but it does demand classification as a narrative, because something has happened, not merely been said. Such a formal setting for a saying may be substantial, but it does not constitute a narrative in the way that a parable, a sage-story, or some other kind of story does, because the saying, not the action, forms the focus of

---

tained analysis and differentiation leaves open to question all the conclusions and propositions about the parable that have been laid forth. (I do not know that there is such a thing as *the* parable.)

2. The Fathers contains a few examples of this kind of narrative.

interest, and the potentialities of tension and resolution constituted by the precipitating action (one day he saw a skull and said . . .) are never explored. The precipitant is like a parable in its generality and exemplary character, but it is unlike a parable in that the burden of the narrative is carried not by what is done, as in the parable, but only by what is said.

In the following example I provide only enough of Eleazar's speech to indicate that the setting (the narrative) has no bearing upon the substance of the saying (the speech).

XVIII:I.4.   A. R. Eleazar b. Azariah he called a peddler's basket . . .

XVIII:II.1.   A. When R. Joshua got old, his disciples came to visit him. He said to them, "My sons, what was the new point that you had today in school?"

B. They said to him, "We are your disciples, and your water [alone] do we drink."

C. He said to them, "God forbid! It is impossible that there is a generation of sages that is orphaned [and without suitable guidance]. Whose week was it to teach?"

D. They said to him, "It was the week of R. Eleazar b. Azariah."

E. He said to them, "And what was the topic of the narrative today?"

F. They said to him, "It was the passage that begins, 'Assemble the people, the men and the women and the children'" (Deut. 31:12).

G. He said to them, "And what did he expound in that connection?"

H. They said to him, "This is how he interpreted it. 'The men come to learn, the women to listen, but why do the children come? It is to provide the occasion for the gaining of a reward for those who bring them.'"

I. He said to them, "You had a good pearl in your hands, and you wanted to make me lose it! If you had come only to let me hear this one thing, it would have been enough for me."

XVIII:II.2.   A. They said to him, "There was another exposition today, concerning the following verse: 'The words of the wise are as goads and as nails well fastened are those that sit together in groups; they are given from one shepherd'" (Qoh. 12:11).

B. "'Just as a goad guides the cow in its furrow, so the words of the Torah guide a person to the ways of life."

What follows works out the speech and never refers back to the narrative setting, which has no impact upon the point of what is portrayed; from the viewpoint of the message, it is simply a formality. I include the taxon here because this kind of narrative does occur, but it bears no burden of proposition and cannot figure in any sustained discussion of the story in particular.

A Precedent or Illustration of a Law

A precedent narrates a case, often enough in the form of a tale of something done, not merely said. The setting is always discourse on the law, but what distinguishes the narrative as precedent from the narrative as story is not its setting but the definitive narrative convention that pertains in the precedent alone. Specifically, the precedent portrays a tableau of *completed action,* in which the tension is established not by the action but by the (sage's) ruling, and in which the resolution of the tension is accomplished solely by the same component, the decision of the sage. In line with this convention that nothing really happen, the precedent rarely includes a beginning, middle, and end, such as we always find in parables and stories. The precedent or illustration is concrete and specific, as a story is, but not to a distinctive person, time, and place, as a story is. The precedent, unlike a story, is paradigmatic and makes a general point, rather than historical and particular to a distinctive situation. A precedent or illustration of the law is like a parable in that it presents no concrete details that allow us to identify a particular place or actor.

A subspecies of the species precedent in The Fathers According to Rabbi Nathan is the illustrative tale, invoked not to prove a point but only to make one concrete. The illustrative tale differs from the parable not only in that it is not called a parable; more decisive, the narrative of the illustration is laconic and narrowly descriptive of known, this-worldly circumstances. What marks the parable, its enchanted setting (e.g., a king in an indeterminate place or time), never makes an impact on the illustration.

The precedent is readily recognized, since in the Mishnah and related documents it is commonly marked by the word *ma'aseh,* which, in the context of legal discourse, routinely points toward a story that bears legal weight as a precedent. The illustration is not always so designated, but is readily identified. I have translated the word *ma'aseh* as "precedent" in the following story, which bears upon sages' teaching to build a fence around the law by observing stricter rules than the law on its own demands. I give the whole of the narrative, because its traits of exposition do contribute to our inquiry into the story. Specifically, we are interested in how the narrative qualities of a story differ from those of the precedent.

II:I.2.   A. There is the precedent of a man who studied much Scripture, repeated much Mishnah, extensively served as a disciple of sages, but died when his years were only half done, and his wife took his *tefillin* and made the circuit of synagogues and school-houses, crying and weeping, saying to them, "My lords, it is written in the Torah, 'For it is your life and the length of your days' (Deut. 30:20).

B. "On what account did my husband, who studied much Scripture, repeated much Mishnah, extensively served as a disciple of sages, die when his years were only half done?"

C. No one knew what to answer her. But one time Elijah, of blessed memory, was appointed to deal with her, saying to her, "My daughter, on what account are you crying and weeping?"

D. She said to him, "My lord, my husband studied much Scripture, repeated much Mishnah, extensively served as a disciple of sages, but died when his years were only half done."

E. He said to her, "When you were in your period, on the first three days of your period, what was your practice?"

F. She said to him, "My lord, God forbid, he never touched me, even with his little finger. But this is what he said to me, 'Do not touch a thing, perhaps you may come into doubt about something.'"

G. "As to the last days of your period, what was your practice?"

H. She said to him, "My lord, I ate with him, drank with him, and in my clothing slept with him in the same bed, and, while his flesh touched mine, he never had the intention of any inappropriate action [such as sexual relations before the period had fully ended]."

I. He said to her, "Blessed be the Omnipresent, who killed him. For so is it written in the Torah: 'To a woman during the unclean time of her menstrual period you shall not draw near'" (Lev. 18:17).

This is a highly formal and well-articulated narrative, introducing the question with great clarity and repeating the circumstance at A, B, and D, setting up a crisis or point of narrative tension at C (*no one knew . . .*), then invoking the supernatural, also at C, to resolve the tension. So there are really two narratives, A–B, and C and following, which prepares the way for the detailed articulation of the point the storyteller wishes to make, which is at H–I in the conclusion that things have worked out just as they should.

A more usual kind of precedent ties a story to a legal ruling, as in the following item. Here the narrative includes the name of the authority, as it must, but the personality and role of the named authority make no impact, since the narrative points toward J, the ruling, which occurs also at M. The boldface type is cited verbatim from B.Q. 8:7.

III:III.1.   A. There was a man who violated the instructions of R. Aqiba by pulling off a woman's hair-covering in the marketplace.

B. She brought complaint before R. Aqiba and he imposed on the man a fine of four hundred *zuz*.

C. The man said to him, "My lord, give me time [to pay up this substantial sum]."

D. He gave him time.

E. When the man left court, his friend said to him, "I'll tell you how you won't have to pay her even something worth a penny."

F. He said to him, "Tell me."

G. He said to him, "Go and get yourself some oil worth an *issar* and break the flask at the woman's door."

H. [He did so.] What did that woman do? She came out of her house and let her hair down in the marketplace and mopped up the oil with her hands and wiped it on her hair.

I. Now the man had set up witnesses and came back to R. Aqiba's court and said to him, "Should I pay off four hundred *zuz* to this contemptible woman? Now because of a mere *issar*'s worth of oil, this woman could not forego the dignity owing to herself, but rather came out of her house and let her hair down in the marketplace and mopped up the oil with her hands and wiped it on her hair."

J. He said to him, "You have no legitimate claim at all. For **if a person [who] inflicts injury on herself, even though one is not permitted to do so, is exempt**

from penalty, others who do injury to that person are liable, she who does injury to herself is exempt from penalty, while you, who have done injury to her [are liable]. Go and pay her the four hundred *zuz.*"

The narrative points toward the ruling at J, and the details of the tale are so formed as to provide a concrete illustration for the abstract ruling. The narrator sets up the point of tension by the device of having the defendant ask for and be granted time, with E–H providing the incident and the action. Then I works out the consequence and makes the point, and everything finds resolution at J. The difference between this narrative-precedent and the foregoing is less than meets the eye, since the composition of the former also points toward the climactic ruling.

Another kind of narrative, within the same species as the precedent, serves the related purpose of illustrating the law. It differs from the foregoing example only in that the narrative that illustrates the law does not serve as a precedent in a concrete case, while the one involving Aqiba does. We noticed, however, that Aqiba's precedent simply illustrates the abstract law in a concrete way, and so does the story that follows. Thus I perceive no intrinsic difference (e.g., in the formation of the narrative), but only a difference in function, and that is on account of the redactors' selection and use and not the tale's intrinsic characteristics. Here is a self-evidently valid example of how a narrative illustrates a rule:

VIII:IV.1.   A. **And give everybody the benefit of the doubt:** how so?

B. [By way of illustrating the importance of giving the benefit of the doubt, we tell] the case of a girl who was taken captive for ransom. Two pious men went after her to ransom her.

C. One of them went into the whore house. When he came out, he said to his fellow, "Of what did you suspect me?"

D. He said to him, "To find out how much was the going price for buying her back."

E. He said to him, "By the Temple service, that is just how it was!"

F. He said to him, "Just as you have given me the benefit of the doubt, so may the Holy One when he judges you give you the benefit of the doubt."

VIII:V.1.   A. [By way of illustrating the importance of giving the benefit of the doubt, we tell] another case of a girl who was taken captive for ransom. Two pious men went after her to ransom her.

C. One of them was arrested as a bandit and imprisoned.

D. Every day his wife brought him bread and water. One day he said to her, "Go to Mr. So-and-so and tell him that I am imprisoned on a charge of prostitution, while he is happily sitting at home and paying no mind to the girl."

E. She said to him, "Is it not enough for you that you are imprisoned, but you are getting involved in nonsense!"

F. She did not go, but she just kept herself busy with nonsense.

G. He said to her, "Please, please go and tell him."

H. She went and told him.

I. What did that man do? He went and brought silver and gold and reliable men with him and retrieved both [the man and the girl held for ransom].

J. When the man got out, he said to them, "Give me this girl, so that she will sleep with me in bed, but in her clothing."

K. In the morning, he said to them, "Allow me to immerse."

L. They immersed him. [in Goldin's translation: "Let her immerse herself." They had her immerse herself.]

M. He said to those who presided at the immersion, "As to this act of immersion of mine, on what account did you suspect me?"

N. They said to him, "We said to him, all the time you were in prison, you were hungry and thirsty [and therefore felt no sexual urge at all], and now that you have gotten out into the free air, you once again feel desire, on which account you may have produced a seminal emission."

O. He said to them, "As to the immersion of the girl, on what account did you suspect her?"

P. They said to him, "All that time that she was held among gentiles, she ate their food and drank their drink, now you have instructed us to immerse her so that she may regain a state of purity."

Q. He said to them, "By the Temple service, that is just how it was. Just as you have given me the benefit of the doubt, so may the Holy One, when he judges you, give you the benefit of the doubt."

Now that we see how a narrative may serve as a precedent or an illustration, we come to the story, the nearest neighbor to the illustration.

A sequence of stories on the importance of philanthropy underlines the distinction just now introduced between the narrative's intrinsic traits of exposition and the extrinsic uses to which a narrative may be put. All of the stories that follow make the same point, but all are different from one another. They serve as illustrations that are different from the precedent involving Aqiba but like the two stories about giving everybody the benefit of the doubt in one substantial way. The precedent in a legal context always invokes the name of a specific authority—for obvious, functional reasons—while precedents that serve only as illustrations and not for legal purposes usually involve not sages but ordinary folk, ordinarily unnamed. The tale that is told, moreover, rings the changes on a common theme. To show the diversity of the tale told as an illustration of a common theme—the power of philanthropy to secure desired benefits—I reproduce the complete narratives.

III:V.1. A. There was the case of a pious man who gave a *denar* to a poor man during the time of famine. His wife criticized him [for giving away what little they had in need], so he went and spent the night in the graveyard. He heard two spirits gossiping with one another, saying to one another, "My friend, come on and let's fly around the world and see what sort of disaster is coming into the world."

B. The other said to her, "I can't go forth, because I am buried in a wrapping made of a reed mat, but you go, and whatever you hear come and report to me."

C. The other went and came back, and the former said to her, "My friend, have you heard anything from [following Goldin:] beyond the veil about what sort of disaster is coming upon the world?"

D. She said, "I heard that whoever sows in the time of the earlier rains [will lose out, because] hail will hit his crops."

E. The man went and sowed in the second, not in the first rain. The crops of everybody were hit by hail, but his crop was not smitten.

F. The next year the man went and spent the night in the graveyard.

G. He heard two spirits gossiping with one another, saying to one another, "My friend, come on and let's fly around the world and see what sort of disaster is coming into the world."

H. The other said to her, "Didn't I tell you, I can't go forth, because I am buried in a wrapping made of a reed mat, but you go, and whatever you hear come and report to me."

I. The other went and came back, and the former said to her, "My friend, have you heard anything from [following Goldin:] beyond the veil about what sort of disaster is coming upon the world."

J. She said, "I heard that whoever sows in the time of the later rains [will lose out, because] blast will hit his crops."

K. The man went and sowed in the first rain. The crops of everybody were hit by blast, but his crop was not smitten.

L. His wife said to him, "How come when the disasters came upon everyone in the world, the crops of everybody were hit by hail and smitten by blast, but yours were not hit by hail or smitten by blast." He told her the whole story.

M. Some time later the pious man's wife had a fight with the mother of the girl [who had been buried in a cheap matting of reed as her shroud]. She said to her, "Go and I shall show you how your daughter is buried in a cheap matting of reed as a shroud."

N. The next year the man went and spent the night in the graveyard.

O. He heard two spirits gossiping with one another, saying to one another, "My friend, come on and let's fly around the world and see what sort of disaster is coming into the world."

P. The other said to her, "My friend, leave me alone. The words that have passed between you and me have now been heard among the living."

The formal characteristics of this story are blatant: the three sequences of action, the careful matching of details, first one way, then the opposite way, and the resolution that makes the point. What is striking is the indirection of the storyteller, who first introduces his real theme—the power of philanthropy—then tells the tale without reverting to the theme, and in the end even concludes without ever getting back to the theme. And yet the setting of the stage is everything, and the story, without the man's overhearing what the spirits say, simply cannot be told. So the point is made with considerable subtlety. The narrative power is attained by the sequence of action, then matched but with opposite action, then the resolution in a cessation of action. The following story has no narrative points in common with the preceding.

III:VI.1. A. There was the case of a pious man who regularly gave charity. Once he took his place on a ship, a strong wind came, and his ship sank in the sea.

R. Aqiba saw [that this had happened to] him [and wished to make certain that testimony of the man's death was provided in court, so that the man's widow would be free to remarry].

B. He came to court to give testimony in behalf of the man's widow, so that she might wed. But before the sage had taken the stand, the man himself came and stood before him.

C. [Aqiba] said to him, "Are you the man who sank into the sea?"

D. He said to him, "Yes."

E. "And who dredged you up from the sea?"

F. He said to him, "It is the charity that I carried out that brought me up from the sea."

G. He said to him, "How do you know?"

H. He said to him, "When I had descended to the depths of the ocean, I heard the great thunder coming from the waves of the ocean, with this one saying to that, and that one to the other, 'Run and let us raise up this man from the sea, who has carried out acts of charity for his entire life.'"

I. At that moment R. Aqiba commenced discourse, "Blessed is God, the God of Israel, who has chosen the words of the Torah and the words of sages.

J. "For the words of the Torah and the words of sages endure for ages and ages to come.

K. "For it is said, 'Cast your bread upon the waters, for you shall find it after many days' (Qoh. 11:1), and, 'Charity delivers from death'" (Prov. 109:2).

I cannot think of a tale that has less in common with the tripartite drama about the spirits than the one at hand. It has a single line from beginning to end, and the substance of the tale is told not by the external narrator, but by the principal actor, the man who was saved. Aqiba then states the lesson to be learned, just as he did in the legal precedent. We may conclude that where a named sage appears, he ordinarily takes the role of stating the point of the narrative and does not appear in the narrative except as a kind of deus ex machina.

III:VII.1. A. There was the case of Benjamin, the righteous man, who was appointed in charge of the charity fund. A woman came before him and said to him, "My lord, feed me."

B. He said to her, "By the Temple service! There is nothing in the charity fund to give you."

C. She said to him, "My lord, if you do not feed me, you will turn out to have killed a widow and her seven children."

D. He went and provided for her from his own funds.

E. After a while Benjamin the righteous man fell sick and lay in bed in distress. [This indicates a decree had been issued against him in heaven.]

F. The ministering angels said before the Holy One, blessed be he, "Lord of the world, you have said that whoever saves a single life in Israel is as if he had saved the entire world. Benjamin the righteous, who kept alive a widow and her seven children, how much the more so, and now he is suffering in bed on account of this illness."

G. Forthwith they sought mercy for him, and the decree against him was torn up, and he was given twenty-two more years in addition to the years that had been allotted to him.

This story reverts to the narrative technique in which the external, anonymous voice of the narrator carries the burden of the tale. The action of Benjamin saves the woman's life, and thus the powerful passage of *F–G* follows. I see nothing in common, as to narrative program and technique, between this narrative and the preceding one, and I find little in common among these three tales on the same topic. Their common traits are clear: what unites them is the theme, on the one side, and the paradigmatic purpose of the narrative, on the other. The exposition and argumentation in behalf of the theme leaves no room for characterization of individuals. The absence of a shared narrative program (e.g., the tale of the two spirits differs in literary convention from the tales about the miraculous effects of philanthropy) should not obscure the fundamental difference between the narrative as illustration and the narrative as story, to which we now turn. A story is different from a parable, a precipitant, and a precedent in some ways, but like them in others.

The Story (Scriptural or Sage)

Among narratives, we may always distinguish a story from any other type of narrative in one fundamental and definitive way: *While meaning to provide a good example of how one should behave, the teller of a story always deals with a concrete person and a particular incident.* The person is concrete in that he (our document contains not a single story about a woman) is always specified by name. It concerns a particular incident in that the viewpoint of the narrator makes clear the specific nature of the event that is reported. The story always happens in historical time, and its point is subordinate to the description of action—the development of a point of tension, at which the story commences, and its resolution, at which the story concludes: beginning, middle, and end. This is not to suggest that a story's traits are not shared with any other kind of narrative. A story is like an illustration in its presentation of a narrative (such and such is what happened) and in its interest in the concrete and specific way of framing a point. But the differences are more striking. Let me now make this point clear, first abstractly, then concretely, since it forms the centerpiece of the taxonomy at hand.

Let me first distinguish the story from its closest analogue, the illustration. Both of these modes of narrative deal with a concrete person and a particular incident, even though the illustration may not invoke the name of a sage, while a story commonly does. A particular set of materials, in which a story-as-illustration and a story in the classic and definitive sense occur together, will make this point abundantly clear. The difference between the species story and the illustration, which I categorize as a subspecies of the species precedent, emerges in the striking contrast between the treatment of two sayings in the same pericope of The Fathers by The Fathers According to Rabbi Nathan Chapter XXXVIII.

XXXVIII:III.1.   A. **Pestilence comes to the world on account of** neglect of the requirement to leave in the fields the defective grape, the forgotten sheaf, and the corner of the field, as well as to separate tithe for the poor person.

XXXVIII:IV.1.   A. There is the case of a woman who lived in the neighborhood of a landlord, and her two sons went out to gather [the crops that are to be left for the poor], but did not find any produce in the field.

    B. Their mother said, "When my sons come from the field, perhaps I'll find something in their hands to eat."

    C. For their part, they were saying, "When we get home, perhaps we'll find something in mother's hands to eat."

    D. She found nothing with them, nor they with her, to eat. They put their heads on their mother's lap and all three of them died on one day.

    E. The Holy One, blessed be he, said to them, "You people have exacted from them their lives! By your lives! I shall exact from you your lives."

    F. And so Scripture says, "Do not rob from the weak, because he is weak, nor crush the poor in the gate, for the Lord will plead their cause and take the life of those who despoil them" (Prov. 22:22–23).

We see that the saying about pestilence coming to the world because of neglect of the provision of the gifts to the poor is illustrated in a concrete way. Yet the case of the woman is not particular to the rule, because *E–F* do not refer back to pestilence. Two facts are important in our classification of narratives: first, the use of the narrative of the woman and her children as a means of amplifying the general point (if not its particular expression), and second, the narrator's disinterest in concrete details (e.g., the woman's name, where and when she lived, and the like). This brings us to a fine example of the story in the sense in which, in this typology of narratives, I wish to define it. From the contrast and the example, we see the components of the encompassing definition.

The story, told in the same setting as the preceding illustration and concerning precisely the same proposition, differs as follows:

1. In contrast to the illustration, the story is exceedingly concrete and specific.

2. The story itself is redactionally autonomous and always ignores the main point the redactor has introduced the story to amplify.

The second trait seems to me nearly universal. Let me explain in abstract terms and then provide ample illustration. The storyteller in our document is never bound by the requirements of a larger redactional purpose and intent. From a redactional perspective, the story always appears to have descended from on high. I do not know whether or not that redactional trait means that the story is told for its own sake, since I cannot define the traits of a story told for its own sake, but the generative and definitive power of the story derives from internal interests, not extrinsic ones. The context in which the story is evoked plays no role in its formation. The storyteller composes the narrative along lines required by the generative tension of the story at hand, not those imposed by the redactional purpose supplied by its (planned) setting. The power of the story—its definitive function—is intrinsic to the narrative and self-evident within the narrative. Any further point that the story serves to prove or illustrate lies outside of the imaginative framework. This last observation will become clear in concrete terms when we consider the story set in juxtaposition with the illustration we have just read.

In what follows we are told that war ("a sword") comes because of perversion of justice or failings of the Torah teachers. The story that is told takes up this second point, but now the "sword" becomes specific to the story: one of the authorities has his head cut off by a sword. Yet a good illustration (or precedent) for the saying about "those who teach the Torah not in accord with the law" would tell us that a given master rejected the decided law and imposed his own heretical or dissenting view instead. The story at hand does not imagine such a point; rather it has the holy rabbi put to death for taking pride in his office. But who mentioned that sin at all? It is a failure that hardly pertains to "teaching the Torah not in accord with the law," except, perhaps, in a most recondite setting. Thus, while the illustration just cited adequately relates to the teaching it is meant to illustrate, in the following story the point of the saying and the narrative focus do not intersect.

XXXVIII:V.1.   A. **A sword comes into the world because of the delaying of justice and perversion of justice, and because of those who teach the Torah not in accord with the law.**

XXXVIII:V.2.   A. When they seized Rabban Simeon b. Gamaliel and R. Ishmael on the count of death, Rabban Simeon b. Gamaliel was in session and was perplexed, saying, "Woe is us! For we are put to death like those who profane the Sabbath and worship idols and practice fornication and kill."

C. Said to him R. Ishmael b. Elisha, "Would it please you if I said something before you?"

D. He said to him, "Go ahead."

E. He said to him, "Is it possible that when you were sitting at a banquet, poor folk came and stood at your door, and you did not let them come in and eat?"

F. He said to him, "By heaven [may I be cursed] if I ever did such a thing! Rather, I set up guards at the gate. When poor folk came along, they would bring them in to me and eat and drink with me and say a blessing for the sake of Heaven."

G. He said to him, "Is it possible that when you were in session and expounding [the Torah] on the Temple mount and the vast populations of Israelites were in session before you, you took pride in yourself?"

H. He said to him, "Ishmael my brother, one has to be ready to accept his failing. [That is why I am being put to death, the pride that I felt on such an occasion.]"

I. They went on appealing to the executioner for grace. This one [Ishmael] said to him, "I am a priest, son of a high priest, kill me first, so that I do not have to witness the death of my companion."

J. And the other [Simeon] said, "I am the patriarch, son of the patriarch, kill me first, so that I do not have to witness the death of my companion."

K. He said to him, "Cast lots." They cast lots, and the lot fell on Rabban Simeon b. Gamaliel.

L. The executioner took the sword and cut off his head.

M. R. Ishmael b. Elisha took it and held it in his breast and wept and cried out: "O holy mouth, O faithful mouth, O mouth that brought forth beautiful gems, precious stones, and pearls! Who has laid you in the dust, who has filled your mouth with dirt and dust?

N. "Concerning you Scripture says, 'Awake, O sword, against my shepherd and against the man who is near to me'" (Zech. 13:7).

O. He had not finished speaking before the executioner took the sword and cut off his head.

P. Concerning them Scripture says, "My wrath shall wax hot, and I will kill you with the sword, and your wives shall be widows, and your children fatherless" (Ex. 22:23).

XXXVIII:V.3.   A. Since it is said "I will kill you with the sword," do I not know that "your wives shall be widows"?

B. They will be widows but not really widows, for they will not find witnesses [that you have died, so as] to permit them to remarry.

C. The example is Betar, from which not a single one escaped so as to give testimony that someone has died and his wife may remarry.

D. Since it is said, "your wives shall be widows," do I not know that "your children will be fatherless"?

E. But they will be fatherless and not fatherless [for the same reason as before], so that the property they are to inherit will remain in the domain of their father, with the result that they will not be permitted to inherit and to transact business with that property [being unable to settle the estate].

The tacked-on passage shows where the redactor enters in and the narrator of the story pulls out. The proof text, Ex. 22:23, bears its own amplification, and that is given at XXXVIII:V.3. The contrast to the foregoing is self-evident.

The story about the execution by the sword of the two great rabbis surely cannot illustrate the notion that they were responsible for a delay of justice or the perversion of justice or taught the Torah not in accord with the law. It is simply tacked on as a story about how people died by the sword. The power and nobility of the story testify to the narrator's intent, which is not to tell us how a rabbi took pride in his public reception. That is why I distinguished intrinsic narrative purpose from extrinsic use. The broader redactional plan requires assembling thematically relevant but substantively autonomous materials around a tangential topic: death by the sword, in this case. The storyteller has told the story for his own purpose, involving the moving action within, not merely the illustrative tableau pointing to an external truth. The interchange, the search for the hero's motive, the soul's honesty in recognizing its guilt, yield a quite powerful polemic in favor of God's ultimate and perfect justice. The story vindicates God's justice—nothing less. It furthermore portrays affecting heroes. These are given personality, character, even the ele-

ments of biography. In these indicative aspects the story clearly differs from
the illustration, the precedent, the parable, and other modes of narrative. (The
secondary expansion of the exegesis of the proof text points to that same conclusion.) With regard to the classification of diverse narratives, comparing the
narrative about the widow and her children to the story about the execution of
the two rabbis yields solid reason for treating the two as distinct species of the
genus narrative.

An Inductive Taxonomy of the Story
in The Fathers According to Rabbi Nathan

Now that we recognize differences among the four species of narrative, noting
in particular what makes the story different from the other three, we turn to a
classification of the instances of the story in The Fathers According to Rabbi
Nathan. Our particular point of interest remains what it was: Does the new and
different mode of intelligible discourse, realized in a fresh medium, bear a
message that also proves distinct from that of the other kinds of narratives? A
survey of the stories at hand yields ample justification for the claim that as the
medium is different, so too is the message.

The stories of The Fathers According to Rabbi Nathan break down in a
number of ways. One division, which further analysis justifies, separates
stories about scriptural topics from those about sages. The former I call
simply *Scripture-stories,* the latter, *sage-stories.* We review the exempla of
both and establish the fact that they are, as exercises of narrative, two distinct
subspecies of the species story. No subjectivity is required to notice that one
kind of story concerns the topic of biblical heroes or themes, and the other
sages and their doings. That is why the differentiating indication is valid: anyone may replicate my classification of stories and determine whether or not
the differences I discern between stories on one type of topic and those on the
other in fact yield different traits of narrative and other conventions. Critical
to my case concerning the entry of the story into Judaism, that is, into the
canon of the Dual Torah, is the distinction between stories about scriptural
topics and those about sages; thus I dwell on this matter.

Two questions define our reading of stories on scriptural figures. First, we
wish to find out whether the subject-matter—scriptural themes rather than
sages' lives and deeds—imposes narrative literary conventions that differ
from those that guide writers of stories about sages. Second, we want to know
what points emerge from stories about scriptural themes and how these propositions relate to those of stories about sages. The Fathers According to Rabbi
Nathan contains stories on two fundamental themes: creation, encompassing
the first man and woman, and Moses and Israel. We examine these two distinct themes separately.

Scripture-Stories Concerning the Creation

All stories about the first man and woman, as well as creation, occur in a single vast anthology in the Fathers According to Rabbi Nathan chapter I. What we see at the outset is the reason for our authorship's inserting the anthology. They meant to make specific "the fence" that the first man "made around his words," to which the amplification of Avot 1:1 alludes. Then a good example of the matter is given, I:VIII.1C–D, which is given its own amplification at I:VIII.5. Afterward, the entire composition follows. Let us first review the whole, with some comments on the components, then account for the arrangement of the parts, and finally turn to broader issues of narrative in general and the story in The Fathers According to Rabbi Nathan in particular.

I:VIII.1.   A.   What is the fence that the first man made around his words?

B.   Lo, Scripture says, "And the Lord God laid a commandment on Man, saying, Of all the trees of the garden you may certainly eat, but from the tree of knowledge of good and evil you may not eat, for on the day of your eating of it you will surely die" (Gen. 2:17).

C.   Man did not want to state the matter to Woman as the Holy One, blessed be he, had stated it to him, but rather he said to her, "Of the fruit of the tree which is in the midst of the garden God has said, 'You may not eat and *you may not touch it* lest you die'" (Gen. 3:3). [He made a fence around his words by extending the matter from eating to merely touching.]

D.   At that moment the wicked snake thought to himself, saying, "Since I cannot make Man stumble, I shall go and make Woman stumble." He went and entered discourse with her and had a long conversation with her, saying to her, "If it was as to not touching the tree that you say the Holy One, blessed be he, has laid a commandment on us, lo, I am going to touch it, but I shall not die. You too may touch it and you will not die."

E.   What did the wicked snake do at that moment? He went and touched the tree with his hands and feet and shook it until its fruit fell to the ground.

F.   But some say he did not touch it at all. But when the tree saw [the snake], it said, "Wicked! wicked! don't touch me!" For it is said, "Let not the foot of pride overtake me and let not the hand of the wicked shake me" (Ps. 36:12).

I:VIII.2.   A.   Another interpretation of the verse, "Let not the foot of pride overtake me and let not the hand of the wicked shake me" (Ps. 36:12).

B.   This refers to the wicked Titus, may his bones be pulverized, for, with wand [penis] in hand he hit the alter saying, "Wolf, wolf! you are a king and I am a king, come and make war against me! How many oxen were slaughtered on you, how many fowl were killed on you, how much wine was poured out on you, how much incense was burned up on you. You are the one who consumes the entire world," as it is said, "Oh Ariel, Ariel, the city where David encamped, add year to year, let the feasts come around" (Is. 29:1).

I:VIII.3.   A.   [Continuing I:VIII.1.D:] And the snake further said to her, "If it was as to not eating of the tree that you say the Holy One, blessed be he, has laid a commandment on us, lo, I am going to eat of it, but I shall not die. You too may eat of it and you will not die."

B. Now what did Woman think to herself? "All the things that my lord [Man] has taught me from the very beginning are lies." (For Woman would call the first Man only "my lord.")

C. So she went and took of the fruit and ate it and gave it to Man and he ate, as it is said, "And the woman saw that the tree was good for eating and an appealing sight" (Gen. 3:6).

I:VIII.4.   A. At that moment Eve was assigned ten curses [below: three decrees, cf. I:XIV.3], as it is said, "To the woman he said, 'I will greatly multiply your pain and your travail; in pain you shall bring forth children; and your desire will be to your husband; and he shall rule over you'" (Gen. 3:16).

B. "I will greatly multiply your pain" refers to the two kinds of blood that a woman discharges, one the pain of menstrual blood, the other that of hymeneal blood.

C. "and your travail" refers to the pain of pregnancy.

D. "in pain you shall bring forth children" bears the obvious meaning [and refers to the pain of giving birth].

E. "and your desire will be to your husband" refers to the fact that a woman lusts after her husband when he goes off on a journey.

F. "and he shall rule over you" refers to the fact that a man asks explicitly for what he wants, while a woman just aches in her heart for it, cloaked as in mourning, imprisoned, cut off from all men [other than her husband].

I:VIII.5.   A. [Reverting to our opening proposition:] Now what is it that led to the woman's touching the tree? It was the fence that the first Man erected around his words.

B. On this basis they have said: "If someone puts too much of a fence around what he says, he will not be able to [Goldin:] stand by his words."

C. On this basis they have said: "A person should not embellish [a report, when repeating] what he hears."

D. R. Yosé says, "Better a fence ten handbreadths high that stands than one a hundred handbreadths high that falls down."

Fence here is an embellishment or an addition to what one says, aimed at adding to effect. That is something one should not do, rather than something one should do. So when at I:VI.1.B we were told that the first man made a fence around his words, we expected that we should emulate that action. But as we see, the point is just the opposite. The first man embellished the instructions that God had given to him, with the result that is spelled out. It seems to me that this composition is singularly inappropriate to the present context. At least part of it, a systematic collection conglomerated around Ps. 36:12, surely took shape before insertion here. Then there is an independent exegesis of Gen. 3:16. I:VIII.5 pretends to carry us all the way back to our opening proposition. As we already realize, however, that is an error, since the opening proposition was that one should set up a hedge around one's statements, but the closing one—quite appropriate to the large and complex composition before us—is that one should not do so too much, a separate and essentially contradictory position.

We now go on to a further exposition of the topic that has made possible this treatment of the proposition, that is, the fall of man and woman.

I:IX.1.   A. At that time, the wicked snake reflected, "I shall go and kill Man and marry his wife and be king over the whole world and walk upright and eat all the gourmet foods of the world."

B. Said to him the Holy One, blessed be he, "You have said, 'I shall kill Man and marry Woman.'" Therefore: "I shall put hatred between you and woman" (Gen. 3:15).

C. "You have said, 'be king over the whole world.'" Therefore: "You are most cursed of all cattle" (Gen. 3:14).

D. "You have said, 'I shall walk upright.'" Therefore: "On your belly you shall walk" (Gen. 3:15).

E. "You have said, 'I shall eat all the gourmet foods of the world.'" Therefore: "You will eat dirt all the time you live" (Gen. 3:15).

The systematic exegesis of Gen. 3:14–15, reasoning backward from God's curse to the original motivation of the snake, simply serves as a thematic supplement to the foregoing. In no way does it advance the argument concerning setting up (or not setting up too high) a fence around one's words. This same thematic miscellany continues.

I:X.1.   A. R. Simeon b. Menassia says, "What a loss of a great servant, for if the snake had not been cursed, every Israelite would have had two snakes in his house, one to send westward, the other eastward, to bring back good sardonix, jewels, pearls, every sort of desirable thing in the world, and no one could do them any harm.

B. "Not only so, but they would have served as beasts of burden in place of camels, asses, mules, bringing manure out to the fields and orchards."

The principle of aggregation is simple: more on the same theme as before.

I:XI.1.   A. R. Judah b. Bathera says, "The first Man was reclining in the Garden of Eden, with the ministering angels serving as his retinue, roasting meat for him, cooling wine for him.

B. "The snake came and saw all this glory and was filled with envy."

I:XII.1.   A. What was the order of the creation of the first Man? [The entire sequence of events of the creation and fall of man and woman took place on a single day, illustrating a series of verses of Psalms that are liturgically utilized on the several days of the week.]

B. In the first hour [of the sixth day, on which man was made] the dirt for making him was gathered, in the second, his form was shaped, in the third, he was turned into a mass of dough, in the fourth, his limbs were made, in the fifth, his various apertures were opened up, in the sixth, breath was put into him, in the seventh, he stood on his feet, in the eighth, Eve was made as his match, in the ninth, he was put into the Garden of Eden, in the tenth, he was given the commandment, in the eleventh, he turned rotten, in the twelfth, he was driven out and went his way.

C. This carries out the verse: "But Man does not lodge overnight in honor" (Ps. 49:13).

D. On the first day of the week [with reference to the acts of creation done on that day], what Psalm is to be recited? "The earth is the Lord's and the fullness thereof, the world and they who dwell in it" (Ps. 24:1). For [God] is the one who owns it and transfers ownership of it, and he is the one who will judge the world.

E. On the second day? "Great is the Lord and greatly to be praised in the city of our God" (Ps. 48:2). He divided everything he had made [between sea and dry land] and was made king over his world.

F. On the third day? "God is standing in the congregation of the mighty, in the midst of the mighty he will judge" (Ps. 82:1). He created the sea and the dry land and folded up the land to its place, leaving a place for his congregation.

G. On the fourth day? "God of vengeance, O Lord, God of vengeance, appear" (Ps. 94:1). He created the sun, moon, stars, and planets, which give light to the world but He is going to exact vengeance from those who serve them.

H. On the fifth? "Sing aloud to God our strength, shout to the God of Jacob" (Ps. 81:2). He created the fowl, fish, mammals of the sea, who sing aloud in the world [praises of God].

I. On the sixth? "The Lord reigns, clothed in majesty, the Lord is clothed, girded in strength, yes, the world is established and cannot be moved" (Ps. 93:1). On that day he completed all his work and arose and took his seat on the heights of the world.

J. On the seventh? "A Psalm, a song for the Sabbath day" (Ps. 92:1). It is a day that is wholly a Sabbath, on which there is no eating, drinking, or conducting of business, but the righteous are seated in retinue with their crowns on their heads and derive sustenance from the splendor of God's presence, as it is said, "And they beheld God and ate and drank" (Ex. 24:11), like the ministering angels.

K. And [reverting back to B] why [was man created last]?

L. So that [immediately upon creation on the sixth day] he might forthwith take up his Sabbath meal.

The order of creation is worked out at A, B. The sizable insertion, D–J, then goes over the order of creation as it is celebrated in Psalms recited in the cult. Only K–L take up where B has left off. That D–J has been composed in its own terms we need not doubt, and the entire complex has been tacked on for essentially the same reason as the foregoing: an enormous thematic supplement to what was, to begin with, irrelevant to the exposition of the matter at hand.

I:XIII:1.   A. R. Simeon b. Eleazar says, "I shall draw a parable for you. To what may the first Man be compared? He was like a man who married a proselyte, who sat and gave her instructions, saying to her, 'My daughter, do not eat a piece of bread when your hands are cultically unclean, and do not eat produce that has not been tithed, and do not profane the Sabbath, and do not go around making vows, and do not walk about with any other man. Now if you should violate any of these orders, lo, you will be subject to the death penalty.'

B. "What did the man himself do? He went and in her presence ate a piece of bread when his hands were cultically unclean, ate produce that had not been tithed, violated the Sabbath, went around taking vows, and with his own hands placed before her [an example of what he had himself prohibited].

C. "What did that proselyte say to herself? 'All of these orders that my husband gave me to begin with were lies.' So she went and violated all of them."

I:XIII.2. A. R. Simeon b. Yohai says, "I shall draw a parable for you. To what may the first Man be compared? He was like a man who had a wife at home. What did that man do? He went and brought a jug and put in it a certain number of dates and nuts. He caught a scorpion and put it at the mouth of the jug and sealed it tightly. He left it in the corner of his house.

B. "He said to her, 'My daughter, whatever I have in the house is entrusted to you, except for this jar, which under no circumstances should you touch.' What did the woman do? When her husband went off to market, she went and opened the jug and put her hand in it, and the scorpion bit her, and she went and fell into bed. When her husband came home from the market, he said to her, 'What's going on?'

C. "She said to him, 'I put my hand into the jug, and a scorpion bit me, and now I'm dying.'

D. "He said to her, 'Didn't I tell you to begin with, "Whatever I have in the house is entrusted to you, except for this jar, which under no circumstances should you touch."'" He got mad at her and divorced her.

E. "So it was with the first man.

F. "When the Holy One, blessed be he, said to him, 'Of all the trees of the garden you certainly may eat, but from the tree of knowledge of good and evil you may not eat, for on the day on which you eat of it, you will surely die' (Gen. 2:17),

G. "on that day he was driven out, thereby illustrating the verse, 'Man does not lodge overnight in honor'" (Ps. 49:24).

I am puzzled by the point of Simeon's statement at I:XIII:1. I do not see how the parable is relevant to Adam as the story has been expounded here. For it was Eve who violated Adam's instructions, and the one error Adam made was stated above, "Man did not want to state the matter to Woman as the Holy One, blessed be he, had stated it to him, but rather he said to her, 'Of the fruit of the tree which is in the midst of the garden God has said, "You may not eat and *you may not touch it* lest you die."'" That has no bearing on Adam's violating his *own* instructions, which is the point of the story before us. Clearly, the point of pertinence comes at C, which intersects explicitly with the following: "Now what did Woman think to herself? All the things that my lord [Man] has taught me from the very beginning are lies." But that is on account of the exaggeration of man's statement of God's instruction; that is, man had built too high a fence around God's words, and that point has no bearing here. The upshot is that the parable intersects with but does not illustrate the materials before us. That forms a still stronger argument for the proposition that the person who has collected these materials as a thematic appendix had very little role in making the materials up, and also had no strong theory of what he wished to say through the compilation of the document, beyond the mere development of a scrapbook on certain themes.

The pertinence of the second parable, I: XIII.2, is clear. Simeon's point is somewhat odd, however, since what he wishes to say is that by giving man the commandment, God aroused his interest in that tree and led man to do what he did. So God bears a measure of guilt for the fall of man. F–G are clearly tacked on and out of place, since they do not revert to the parable at all and make their own point, Ps. 49:24.

I: XIV.1.   A. On the very same day Man was formed, on the very same day Man was made, on the very same day his form was shaped, on the very same day he was turned into a mass of dough, on the very same day his limbs were made and his various apertures were opened up, on the very same day breath was put into him, on the very same day he stood on his feet, on the very same day Eve was matched for him, on the very same day he was put into the Garden of Eden, on the very same day he was given the commandment, on the very same day he went bad, on the very same day he was driven out and went his way,

B. thereby illustrating the verse, "Man does not lodge overnight in honor" (Ps. 49:24).

I: XIV.2.   A. On the very same day two got into bed and four got out.

B. R. Judah b. Beterah says, "On the very same day two got into bed and seven got out."

I: XIV.3.   A. On that very same day three decrees were issued against Man,

B. as it is said, "And to Man he said, 'Because you have obeyed your wife, cursed is the ground on your account; in labor you shall eat its produce. . . . Thorns also and thistles it will produce for you, and you shall eat the herb of the field'" (Gen. 3:17–18).

C. When the first Man heard what the Holy One, blessed be he, said to him, namely, "You shall eat the herb of the field," his limbs trembled, and he said before him, "Lord of the world, shall I and my cattle eat in a single crib?"

D. Said to him the Holy One, blessed be he, "Since your limbs have trembled, 'in the sweat of your face you shall eat bread'" (Gen. 3:19).

E. And just as three decrees were issued against the first Man, so three decrees were issued against Woman.

F. For it is said, "To the woman he said, 'I will greatly multiply your pain and your travail; in pain you shall bring forth children; and your desire will be to your husband; and he shall rule over you'" (Gen. 3:16).

G. "I will greatly [multiply] your pain" refers to the fact that, when a woman produces menstrual blood at the beginning of her period, it is painful for her.

H. "I will [greatly] multiply your pain" refers to the fact that when a woman has sexual relations for the first time, it is painful for her.

I. "In pain you shall conceive" refers to the fact that, when a woman first gets pregnant, for the first three months her face is distorted and pale.

No. 1 goes over familiar materials. It is tacked on because it goes over the same proof text as is given earlier. No. 2 carries forward the formulaic pattern of No. 1, and so does No. 3.

I: XV.1.   A. When evening fell, the first Man saw the world growing dark as the sun set. He thought to himself, "Woe is me! Because I turned rotten, the Holy One, blessed be he, on my account brings darkness to the entire world." But he did not know that that is how things are.

B. At dawn when he saw the world grow light with sunrise, he rejoiced. He went and built altars and brought an ox whose horns extended beyond its hooves and offered it up as a whole offering [retaining no parts for his own food],

C. as it is said, "And it shall please the Lord better than an ox whose horns extend beyond its hooves" (Ps. 69:32).

I:XV.2. A. As to the ox that the first Man offered, the bull that Noah offered, and the ram that Abraham, our father, offered in place of his son on the altar, all of them were "beasts in which the horns extended beyond the hooves."

B. For it is said, "And Abraham looked up, and he saw, lo, another ram, caught by its horns in the bush" (Gen. 22:13).

The anthology on the first man runs its course. We have at No. 1 a set piece, which, so far as I can see, does not continue any prior discussion. It is simply inserted whole. No. 2 is attached to No. 1 because of its pertinence to the theme of the particularly desirable animal for sacrifice.

I:XVI.1. A. At that moment three groups of ministering angels descended, with lutes, lyres, and diverse other musical instruments in their hands, and with [the first man] they recited a song.

B. For it is said, "A Psalm, a song, for the sabbath day. It is good to give thanks to the Lord . . . to declare your loving-kindness in the morning and your faithfulness at night" (Ps. 92:1–3).

C. "To declare your loving-kindness in the morning" refers to the world to come, as it is said, "They are new every morning, great is your faithfulness" (Lam. 3:23).

D. "And your faithfulness at night" refers to this world, which is compared to night, as it is said, "The burden of Dumah. One calls to me out of Seir, watchman, what of the night? watchman, what of the night? (Is. 21:11).

The long narrative about the first man on the day of the fall from grace proceeds on its own lines. The rhetorical-formulaic that links one piece to the next, *on that very same day,* or, *at that time,* provides the outline of a reasonably cogent narrative program.

I:XVII.1. A. At that time said the Holy One, blessed be he, "If I do not judge the snake, I shall turn out to destroy the entire world."

B. And he thought to himself, "This one that I crowned and made king over the entire world has gone wrong and eaten of the fruit of the tree."

C. He forthwith turned on him and cursed him,

D. as it is said, "And the Lord God said to the snake" (Gen. 3:14).

E. R. Yosé says, "If the curse concerning the snake had not been stated in Scripture [following Goldin, p. 15:] after theirs [the curse of man and woman], [the snake] would have destroyed the entire world.

The narrative proceeds apace. The reason for including it—the reference to the first man and the fence that he (wrongly) erected around his words—has long since fallen from sight.

I:XVIII:1.   A. When the Holy One, blessed be he, created the first Man, he formed a face on him both in front and in back,

   B. for it is said, "You have fashioned me in back and in front and laid your hand upon me" (Ps. 139:5).

   C. Then the ministering angels came down to destroy him, so the Holy One, blessed be he, took him and placed him under his wings, as it is said, "and laid your hand upon me."

I:XVIII.2.   A. Another interpretation of the clause, "And laid your hand upon me":

   B. Once [the first man] went rotten, the Holy One, blessed be he, took away one of [the two faces he had originally given to man].

I:XVIII.3.   A. On this basis [we derive the fact that] the first Man and the Temple, when they were created, were created with both of God's hands.

   B. How do we know that [when man was created,] he was created with both hands?

   C. As it is said, "Your hands have made me and formed me" (Ps. 119:73).

   D. How do we know that the Temple was created with two hands?

   E. As it is said, "The sanctuary, O Lord, which your hands have established" (Ex. 15:17); "And he brought them to his holy border, the mountain, which his right hand had gotten" (Ps. 78:543); "The Lord shall reign for ever and ever" (Ex. 15:18).

The long narrative on the creation of the first man reaches its conclusion with a final miscellany. Pertinent verses, Nos. 1–2, are adduced to provide a further fact. No. 3 follows as an appropriate appendix.

Let me conclude by answering the questions with which we began. First, does the subject-matter—scriptural themes—generate its own narrative literary conventions, which differ from those that guide writers of stories about sages? On the surface, the answer is clearly yes. Stories about the first man make profligate use of verses of Scripture. These predominate and govern, and the amplification of the sense of those verses proves a dominant interest. When we come to stories about sages, by contrast, we shall locate few proof texts and slight concern for the exposition of the meaning of verses of Scripture. The focus is on the sage and the event at hand, and exegesis of a verse of Scripture, where it occurs, takes a subordinate position. Further differences will soon make their appearance.

Second, do we find propositions emerging from stories on scriptural themes? Clearly we do, but these do not on the surface relate to large historical questions, such as we shall locate in the stories about sages. I postpone further generalization until we have examined the second important group of Scripture-stories, those that concern Moses.

Scripture-Stories Concerning Moses and Israel

Moses is called *our rabbi,* and he serves as the model and paragon of the sage. At the same time, of course, he is a scriptural hero, and thus forms a bridge between the model of virtuous hero deriving from Scripture, the written Torah, and the counterpart deriving from the world of sages, that is, the realm of the oral Torah. The figure of Moses allows us to find out whether merely because a sage derives from Scripture, that is, the written Torah, stories about him will differ from stories about sages of the oral Torah. We wish to know whether stories about Moses exhibit traits characteristic of stories about scriptural figures or those that are characteristic of stories about sages. The answer to that question will tell us whether the point of origin of the theme of a story—the written Torah, or Scripture; the oral Torah, or the life of the sage of the Mishnah—imposes different narrative conventions upon the narrative and doctrinal program of the story itself. We proceed to the repertoire supplied by The Fathers According to Rabbi Nathan.

XII:I.5. A. And there are those who say that for this reason it is said "every member of the house of Israel wept for Aaron for thirty days:"

B. Whoever can see Eleazar and Phineas, sons of high priests, standing and weeping, and not join in the weeping?

XII:II.1. A. At that moment Moses asked for a death like the death of Aaron,

B. for he saw the bier of Aaron lying in state in great honor, with bands of ministering angels lamenting for him.

C. But did he ask for such a death in the presence of some other person? Was it not in the privacy of his own heart? But the Holy One, blessed be he, heard what he had whispered to himself.

D. And how do we know that Moses asked for a death like the death of Aaron and [the Holy One, blessed be he,] heard what he had whispered to himself?

E. As it is said, "Die in the mountain to which you go up, and be gathered to your people as Aaron your brother died in Mount Hor" (Deut. 32:50).

F. Thus you have learned that Moses asked for a death like the death of Aaron.

XII:II.2. A. At that time [the Holy One, blessed be he] said to the angel of death, "Go, bring me the soul of Moses."

B. The angel of death went and stood before him, saying to him, "Moses, give me your soul."

C. Moses grew angry with him and said to him, "Where I am sitting you have no right even to stand, yet you have said, 'Give me your soul'!" He threw him out with outrage.

D. Then the Holy One, blessed be he, said to Moses, "Moses, you have had enough of this world, for lo, the world to come is readied for you, for a place is prepared for you from the first six days of creation."

E. For it is said, "And the Lord said, 'Behold a place by me, and you shall stand upon the rock'" (Ex. 33:21).

F. The Holy One, blessed be he, took the soul of Moses and stored it away under the throne of glory.

G. And when he took it, he took it only with a kiss, as it is said, "By the mouth of the Lord" (Deut. 34:5).

XII:II.3. A. It is not the soul of Moses alone that is stored away under the throne of glory, but the souls of the righteous are stored away under the throne of glory,

B. as it is said, "Yet the soul of my Lord shall be bound in the bundle of life with the Lord your God" (1 Sam. 25:29).

C. Is it possible to imagine that that is the case also with the souls of the wicked?

D. Scripture says, "And the souls of your enemies, those he shall sling out as from the hollow of a sling" (1 Sam. 25:29).

E. For even though one is tossed from place to place, it does not know on what to come to rest.

F. So too the souls of the wicked go [Goldin:] roving and fluttering about the world and do not know where to come to rest.

XII:II.4. A. The Holy One, blessed be he, further said to the angel of death, "Go, bring me the soul of Moses."

B. The angel of death went in search of him in his place but did not find him. He went to the Great Sea and said to it, "Has Moses come here?"

C. The sea replied, "From the day on which the Israelites passed through me, I have not seen him."

D. He went to the mountains and hills and said to them, "Has Moses come here?"

E. They replied, "From the day on which Israel received the Torah on Mount Sinai, we have not seen him."

F. He went to Sheol and Destruction and said to them, "Has Moses come here?"

G. They said to him, "His name we have heard, but him we have never seen."

H. He went to the ministering angels and said to them, "Has Moses come here?"

I. They said to him, "God understands his way and knows his place [Goldin: cf. Job 28:23]. God has hidden him away for the life of the world to come, and no one knows where."

J. So it is said, "But wisdom, where shall it be found? and where is the place of understanding? Man does not know its price, nor is it found in the land of the living. The deep says, 'It is not in me,' and the sea says, 'It is not with me'. . . . Destruction and death say, 'We have heard a rumor thereof with our ears'" (Job. 28:13–15, 22).

XII:II.5. A. Joshua too was seated and grieving for Moses,

B. until the Holy One, blessed be he, said to him, "Joshua, why are you grieving for Moses? 'Moses, my servant, is dead'" (Joshua 1:2).

The narrative begins at XII:II with the now familiar *at that moment,* which serves to introduce a narrative effect for the statement of a proposition on a scriptural theme or passage. Section XII:II then does not tell a story at all; it simply makes the point that Moses asked to die the way Aaron had. That proposition is proved by reference to the indicated proof texts. But XII:II.2 (complemented by No. 3) does seem to me a fine example of a story. The narrative has a beginning, middle, and end: the angel of death is told to go and get Moses's soul, but Moses refuses to hand it over until God tells Moses that he has to do so. We cannot point to the story as an example of dramatic art, but it is more than a mere setting for a wise saying, on the one side, or proof or illustration of a proposition, on the other.

Section XII:II.4 forms a far more powerful story on precisely the same theme. Now we have a sequence of stunning conversations, within a narrative framework that makes its impact upon what is said. This second story makes the same point as the first—Moses's soul is hidden God knows where—but it makes it in a massive, dramatic framework, invoking heaven and earth, the sea, the mountains, and so on. Yet, if we ask once again if the story at hand exhibits dramatic intent, the answer is negative. Still more consequential, the story unfolds through what is said, rather than both through what is said and through what is done. No described action serves to carry a part of the burden of the story. In fact, in the several stories we note that nothing much happens: no one gets killed, no building gets burned. These stories have only the thinnest narrative core of action, explicit or implicit.

XVII:II.1.   A.   **And get yourself ready to learn Torah, for it does not come as an inheritance to you:** how so?

XVII:II.2.   A.   When Moses, our master, saw that his sons had no knowledge of the Torah which would qualify them to succeed him in the leadership, he cloaked himself and stood in prayer.

B.   He said before him, "Lord of the world, tell me who will go in [and] who will come out at the head of all this people?"

C.   For it is said, "And Moses spoke to the Lord, saying, 'Let the Lord, the God of the spirits of all flesh, set a man over the congregation, who may go out before them and who may come in before them'" (Num. 27:15ff).

D.   Said the Holy One, blessed be he, to Moses, "Moses, take Joshua" (Num. 27:15).

E.   Said the Holy One, blessed be he, to Moses, "Go and act as his voice so that he may give an exposition in your presence at the head of all the great men of Israel [and that will signify that he is heir]."

F.   At that moment Moses said to Joshua, "Joshua, as to this people that I am handing over to you, I am giving you not goats but kids, not sheep but lambs, for as yet they are not much experienced in the practice of religious duties, and they have not yet reached the growth of goats and sheep."

G.   So it is said, "If you do not know, O you fairest among women, go your way forth by the footsteps of the flock and feed your kids beside the shepherds' tents" (Song 1:8).

The base clause is illustrated by the case of Moses' sons, but only in a rather general way, for the focus of the story is Moses' leaving the people in Joshua's hands and warning Joshua that they are still in an immature state. This story has nothing to do with the exposition of the notion that the Torah is no one's inheritance, although the story does intersect with that notion. What follows is tacked on because it invokes the proof text, Song 1:8. The same narrative traits characterize the materials at hand as mark the earlier stories about Moses. That is to say, very little actually happens, and the narrative framework serves only to define the arena for dialogue. The story, such as it is, makes its point through that dialogue. Moses realizes that his sons will not inherit, and God tells him to choose Joshua. Moses does that and gives him some advice: end of the tale.

Indicative Traits of the Scripture-Story

I see four definitive traits of the Scripture-story, as exemplified in those concerning the first man.

1. The first and paramount trait is the profligate use of verses of Scripture. These predominate and govern, and—more to the point than mere quantity—the amplification of the sense of those verses proves a dominant interest. Indeed, more often than not, the point of a scriptural story is to clarify the scriptural verse or its broader narrative. The sage-story, in contrast, never takes as its point of tension and departure the clarification of the meaning of a verse of Scripture, and citation of verses of Scripture is economical and tangential to the sequence of action and narrative thrust.

2. A second indicative trait is the invariably dominant role of the narrator (unseen, unidentified). The story is told not through dialogue alone or principally, but through the narrator's constant intervention: he tells us what the snake was thinking (I: VIII.1) as well as what he did. The interest in describing action is subordinate to interest in ascertaining motivation and describing the consequence of improper deeds resulting from inappropriate motivation.

3. A third (already familiar) trait is the redactor's insistence upon including along with a story other important exegeses of a verse of Scripture cited in the story. That accounts for the intrusion of I: VIII.2, interrupting the flow from I: VIII.1D to I: VIII.3. The redactor's point of interest is clearly the verse and *its* exposition—whether through concrete narrative or through abstract paraphrase and amplification. Stories about sages do not ordinarily bear the freight of (to us intruded) exegeses of the verses they cite. They run their course, beginning to end, without so sizable an interruption as is represented by I: VIII.2 and its counterparts. Another instance is at I: VIII.4, continuing I: VIII.3. *At that moment* provides the narrator with the form of a story, but the substance is a set-piece exegesis of Gen. 3:16. In terms of our original classification, I: VIII.4 constitutes nothing more than a precipitant. Section I: IX.1 follows suit; once more *at that time* makes up whatever narrative we are going to be given; I: X.1 does not change the picture. Section I: VIII.5 does not present us with anything like a story. It is important, however, and serves the principal interest of the ultimate redactor of the entire composition.

4. A fourth trait is the striking absence of movement, the lack of a beginning, middle, and end, of tension and resolution, not to mention sustained interest in characterization. The cardboard characters ordinarily serve to compose a tableau, which, frozen and at rest, makes its point in the aggregate. Stories about sages, in contrast, make their point not through a fixed and stationary tableau but through the unfolding of action, whether *he said to him . . . , he said to him . . . ,* or the tale of what actually is done.

When we come to I: XII.1 through inductive observation of the unfolding narrative, we therefore begin to realize that what we have in the aggregate before us hardly constitutes a story at all. The ultimate interest of the redactor predominates not only in selection and arrangement, but also in the substance of the narrative. In fact, the narrative tells no story at all but merely serves the purpose of presenting a setting for an exposition. Section I:XII.1 pretends to narrate the order of creation, but in fact proposes to demonstrate the proposition that the liturgical psalms, recited on each day of the week in the Temple, form the counterpart to events that are not events but stages in the unfolding of creation and the fall of man. Section I:XIII.1–2 follows suit. The parables do not constitute stories, for reasons already specified. Section I:XIV.1 presents the illusion of a narrative by beginning with *on the very same day,* which functions as does *at that hour.* In fact we have no narrative at all until I:XIV.3. Then we do have a brief narrative, I:XIV.3C–D, but the narrative contains no action, recounted or implied; it simply allows us to juxtapose two verses, which tell a lesson. What has been said applies to the remainder of the anthology, which contains narratives but little action, making points not through what happens or even through what is said, but through the invocation of verses of Scripture. As a generalization, therefore, we may say that the story on a theme drawn from Scripture is not a story at all.

We thus distinguish both in subject-matter and in narrative technique the story based on Scripture and the story based on the sage, that is, the story within the written Torah, as read by sages, and the story within the oral Torah, as read by the same authorities. Having made this distinction, we need not dwell on the point of these stories. A brief catalogue suffices to show the disparate and random topics.

I:VIII. One should not make too high a fence around one's words, in such a way as to distort the meaning.

I:IX. If one wishes something one should not desire, he gets the opposite of what he wants.

I:X. Had the curse of the snake not taken place, Israel would have had a good servant.

I:XI. The snake envied man.

I:XII. "Man does not lodge overnight in honor."

I:XIII. "Man does not lodge overnight in honor." The further point of the parable, however, is that a commandment may serve to rouse one's interest in sinning.

I:XIV. "Man does not lodge overnight in honor."

I:XV. The course of the natural world brought man reassurance, and he makes a sacrifice to express his gratification.

I:XVI. This world contrasted to the world to come.

I:XVII. The snake was cursed.

I:XVIII. Creation of man and Temple were both done with God's hands.

The opening point ties the entire anthology to the larger setting in which it has been located. It is difficult to see how propositions in particular (as distinct from the larger general theme) join one item to the next, fore or aft. Nor can I explain the order of the propositions. I see a group formed by I:XI–XIV, but otherwise it seems to me nothing more than a set of miscellanies, not spun out around a common proposition or sequence of points, but all joined, more or less randomly, because of an unfolding theme. We see no thematic cogency at all. To broaden that judgment, let me briefly review the points made by the telling of the stories about scriptural heroes:

1. The animals of pious men (Abraham) keep the Torah (this story is given at the beginning of chapter 5).

2. The soul of Moses (among the righteous) is hidden with God.

3. God designated Joshua.

These seem to me random and unexceptional. In conclusion, let us answer the indicative questions that made this analysis necessary:

1. Does the subject-matter—scriptural themes—generate narrative literary conventions that differ from those that guide writers of stories about sages? Chapter 5 will show us that the answer is clearly yes.

2. Do we find propositions emerging from stories on scriptural themes? We do, although these propositions are particular and limited; they do not on the surface relate to large historical questions. We find propositions of greater power when we turn to sage-stories. We close in midstream, proceeding directly to the other of the two topics that require us to differentiate the species story into two subspecies.

5

The Sage-Story in Particular

From Aphorism to Story

The authorship of The Fathers presented the message of sages solely in aphoristic form. Apothegms bore the entire weight of that authorship's propositions, and—quite consistently—what made one saying cogent with others
fore and aft was solely the position of the authority behind that saying: here,
not there. Of the four types of narrative we find in The Fathers According to
Rabbi Nathan—precedent, precipitant, parable, and story (scriptural or saga-
cious)—three are completely neglected in The Fathers. The authorship of The
Fathers fully acknowledged the importance of the past, referring to historical
events of Scripture, but they did not retell in their composition the scriptural
stories of what had happened long ago. They understood that their predeces-
sors lived exemplary lives, but they did not tell stories about sages. They had
every reason to appreciate the power of parable, but they did not think it necessary to harness that power to deliver their particular message, or even to
state their propositions in colorful ways. In the compilation as we know it, the
framers of The Fathers used narrative only as a precipitant, to describe with
great economy the setting in which a stunning saying was set forth. They did
not cite narratives in the form of precedents.

The authorship of The Fathers According to Rabbi Nathan clearly found
inadequate the mode of intelligible discourse and the medium of expression
selected by the framers of the document they chose to extend. The later writers had a message they deemed integral to that unfolding Torah of Moses at
Sinai. They resorted to a mode of intelligible discourse, narrative, that conveyed propositions with great clarity, deeming that medium a vehicle for
conveying propositions from heart to heart. Not only so, but among the narratives they used, they selected the sage-story for closest attention and narrative
development. A sustained reading of their sage-stories shows us how the framers made ample use of formerly neglected matters of intellect, aesthetics,

and theology to construct intelligible discourse in a medium meant to speak with immediacy and power and convey a message of critical urgency.

Accordingly, they found place for all four types of narrative and made use of the sage-story to convey powerful propositions lacking all precedent in The Fathers; in context, they were of an utterly fresh order. But precisely what messages did they wish to convey through the story, and how did the sage-story in particular serve their purposes? The answers to these questions come to us only from a sustained review of the sage-story, its narrative traits, and its propositional foci.

The Scripture-Story and the Sage-Story: Differences in Narrative Convention

We start by demonstrating that the sage-story is fundamentally different from the Scripture-story. To do so, we simply set side by side stories about a scriptural hero and a sage; the authorship of The Fathers According to Rabbi Nathan presents both sorts. The difference is not merely that one speaks of a hero who appears in Scripture, the other of one who derives from the chain of tradition of the oral Torah—much to the contrary. The contrast shows us right at the outset that quite different narrative conventions apply to the two distinct topics, the hero of Scripture and the hero of sagacity. Stories about the archetypal sage, Moses, "our lord," turn out not very different from stories on other scriptural topics. The striking contrast in the narrative qualities of the stories about Hanina's and Abraham's beasts, which follow, tells the whole tale. The first story deals with a hero of the written Torah, Abraham, and the second with one of the oral Torah, Hanina b. Dosa. The same point is made with reference to both figures; thus the important point of difference occurs solely in the distinctive modes of telling.

> VIII:VI.1.   A. Just as the righteous men in ancient times were pious, so their cattle were pious.
>
> B. They say that the cattle of Abraham, our father, never went into a house which contained an idol,
>
> C. as it is said, "For I have cleared the house and made room for the camels" (Gen. 24:31), meaning, "I have cleared the house of teraphim."
>
> D. And on what account does Scripture say, "And made room for the camels"?
>
> E. This teaches that they would not enter Laban the Aramaean's house until they had cleared away all the idols from before them.
>
> VIII:VI.2.   A. There was the case of the ass of R. Hanina b. Dosa, which bandits stole and tied up in the courtyard. They set before it straw, barley, and water, but it would not eat or drink.
>
> B. They said, "Why should we leave it here to die and make a stink for us in the courtyard? They went and opened the gate and sent it out, and it went along, braying, until it came to the house of R. Hanina b. Dosa.

C. When it got near the house, [Hanina's] son heard its braying.

D. He said to him, "Father, it appears to me that the braying is like the braying of our beast."

E. He said to him, "My son, open the gate for it, for it must be nearly dying of starvation."

F. He went and opened the gate for it, and put before it straw, barley, and water, and it ate and drank.

G. Therefore they say, "Just as the righteous men in ancient times were pious, so their cattle were pious."

The contrast between the two stories could not be drawn more sharply. In the story about the biblical hero we have proof text after proof text. In fact we have nothing like a narrative. "They say that so and so did or did not do such and such" hardly tells an engaging story. Then comes a lesson, E. By contrast, the case involving Hanina's ass makes the same point through a fully expounded narrative. The hero is the animal, not the authority. The story works out its message without the need for G, since the point is made within the limits and discipline of the story itself, with its point of tension—the stolen beast that finds its way home after it is released because of its own pious behavior—and the resolution thereof. The juxtaposed stories indicate that where the written Torah supplies the materials for a narrative, the consequent tale hardly qualifies as a story at all.

This brings us back to the questions that define our reading of stories on sages. First, we wish to find out whether the subject-matter—sages' lives and deeds—imposes narrative conventions that differ from those that guide writers of stories about Scriptural figures. On the surface we come across numerous obvious differences in narrative convention. Three seem to be definitive:

1. The story about a sage has a beginning, middle, and end, and it also rests not only on verbal exchanges (*he said to him . . . , he said to him . . .*) but on described action.

2. The story about a sage unfolds from a point of tension and conflict to a clear resolution of the conflict.

3. The story about a sage rarely invokes a verse of Scripture and never serves to prove a proposition concerning the meaning of a verse of Scripture.

What about Scripture-stories? The traits of stories about scriptural figures and themes in retrospect prove opposite:

1. The story about a scriptural hero has no beginning, middle, and end, and little action. The burden of the narrative is carried by *he said to him . . . , he said to him . . .* Described action is rare and plays a minor role in the unfolding narrative. Often the narrative consists of little more than a setting for a saying, and its point is conveyed not through what is told but through the cited saying.

2. The Scripture-story is worked out as a tableau, with description of the components of the stationary tableau placed at the center. There is little movement and no point of tension that is resolved.

3. The Scripture-story always invokes verses from Scripture and makes the imputation of meaning to those verses the center of interest.

Presented with stories taken from our document that lack all indication of their subject-matter, we could readily distinguish those focused upon scriptural heroes from those centered upon sages. When the narrators wish to talk about sages, they invoke a set of narrative conventions deemed appropriate to that topic, and when they present stories on scriptural heroes and topics, they appeal to quite different narrative conventions. When we compare the propositions of one set of stories with those of the other, detailed attention to specific stories supplies further points of differentiation.

The Repertoire of Sage-Stories

Let us proceed directly to the repertoire of sage-stories and conduct an experiment in the description of how these stories are told. The sage-stories in The Fathers According to Rabbi Nathan do not cover a broad variety of topics. Only certain aspects of the lives and doings of sages demanded attention, and then for highly particular purposes. I classify the stories by topics, because the most superficial trait, subject-matter, will present my developing essentially subjective judgments. As we shall see, the sage-stories attend to only four topics: (1) the sage's beginning in Torah study, (2) his character and his deeds in relationship to the Torah, (3) the role of the sage in important historical events, and (4) the death of the sage. A list of the topics that are neglected, for example, the sage's childhood and wonderful precociousness in Torah study, the sage's supernatural deeds, the sage's everyday administration of the community's affairs, the sage's life with other sages and with disciples, could fill many pages, but it suffices to notice that our document includes a restricted list of topics and then differentiates them internally by telling quite diverse stories about different sages. It becomes clear that when the authorship of The Fathers According to Rabbi Nathan resorts to narrative in general and storytelling in particular, with special attention to sage-stories, it has in mind a very particular purpose and message. There is nothing random or episodic in its choice of topics, and, as we shall see, the medium of storytelling served the message conveyed. These claims are substantiated through a detailed survey of the stories of our document. Then, in part 3 of the book, I raise the logically necessary question: How different and how special are the stories of our document in the context of the canonical literature of which The Fathers According to Rabbi Nathan forms a rather minor component? For in claiming special importance for this document's introduction—with spectacular success—of storytelling into the repertoire of the canonical writings of the Judaism of the Dual Torah, I do impute to it a pivotal place and importance.

The method followed here relies upon inductive classification of superficial and therefore positive, factual traits. The description of the sage-story proceeds through the examination of concrete cases. I ask the same questions throughout: What is the point of the story? How is the story told to make its point? Are these points the same as the ones in the stories told about scriptural figures? If they are different, where and how do they go their own way? At the end we shall come to solid generalizations.

The Origins from Nowhere: Aqiba and Eliezer

The Fathers According to Rabbi Nathan contains stories of the origins of two sages, Aqiba and Eliezer. By *origins,* the storytellers mean the beginnings of the Torah study of a famed authority. Life begins at birth, but when we wish to tell sage-stories, beginnings are measured differently: the sage begins life when he begins Torah study. The two sages whose origins are found noteworthy both began in mature years, not in childhood (despite the repeated emphasis of The Fathers upon the unique value of beginning Torah study in childhood). The proposition implicit in origin stories, then, is that a man may start his Torah study at any point in life and hope for true distinction in the Torah community. But that does not account for the germ of the story, the critical tension that creates an event worthy of narrative, that poses a question demanding an answer, a problem requiring a solution through a tale with a beginning, middle, and end.

The critical tension of origins derives from the formation of supernatural (in contrast to natural) relationships. Life begins in the womb. But life in the Torah begins at a supernatural birth, and there must be a tension between the natural beginning and the supernatural one. It is expressed through contrasting natural ties and relationships (to father and mother, brothers and sisters, or to one's wife) with supernatural ties to Torah study. When a man undertakes to study the Torah in the stories before us, he abandons his natural relationships to his family (to his wife or to his father). The point of origin of the sage marks the wedding of the sage to the Torah, with the concomitant diminution of his relationship to his wife, who may be abandoned and even required to support the nascent sage's children as well as herself. The nascent sage furthermore gains a new father, the master or sage, and cuts his ties to his natural father, losing his share in his father's estate. These tensions generate the stories before us.

While told in their own terms and subject to differentiation from each other, the stories make essentially the same points: one can begin Torah study in mature years and progress to the top; when one does so, one also goes from poverty to wealth through public recognition of one's mastery of the Torah —and a range of parallel propositions. The supernatural relationship, which supercedes the natural ones to wife and father, generates honor, riches, and fame for the sage and, through reflection, for the natural family as well; that is the point of these stories, which take up a pressing question and answer it in a powerful way.

What of the redactional question? When the compositors of The Fathers

According to Rabbi Nathan made up or selected these stories (we do not know which), did they invent or revise them to conform to the requirements of a larger setting in which they planned to situate them? The answer—for sage-stories of *all* kinds—is negative. The stories before us are attached to the saying of Yosé b. Yoezer, "And wallow in the dust of their feet, and drink in their words with gusto." The base saying therefore introduces the desired theme, which is Torah study that requires accepting with humility the reduced status of disciple before the master. But once the theme of sages' origins in the Torah is introduced, the entire composition moves in its own direction. Nothing in the redactional structure defined by The Fathers makes an impact upon the structure of the stories at hand, which are autonomous. Section VI:IV.1 serves as a deftly constructed joining block between the already completed materials to follow on Aqiba, then Eliezer, and the rather pointed and germane exegesis of the statements of Avot. Clearly, the authorship has a powerful interest in including stories about sages' lives, and the structure of The Fathers served only as a suitable framework.

VI:IV.1.   A. Another comment on the statement, **And wallow in the dust of their feet:**

B. This refers to R. Eliezer.

C. **. . . and drink in their words with gusto:**

D. This refers to R. Aqiba.

This pericope serves as a prologue to the vast stories that follow on Aqiba and then on Eliezer.

VI:V.1.   A. How did R. Aqiba begin [his Torah study]?

B. They say: He was forty years old and had never repeated a tradition. One time he was standing at the mouth of a well. He thought to himself, "Who carved out this stone?"

C. They told him, "It is the water that is perpetually falling on it every day."

D. They said to him, "Aqiba, do you not read Scripture? 'The water wears away stones'" (Job. 4:19).

E. On the spot R. Aqiba constructed in his own regard an argument a fortiori: now if something soft can [Goldin:] wear down something hard, words of Torah, which are as hard as iron, how much the more so should they wear down my heart, which is made of flesh and blood."

F. On the spot he repented [and undertook] to study the Torah.

G. He and his son went into study session before a childrens' teacher, saying to him, "My lord, teach me Torah."

H. R. Aqiba took hold of one end of the tablet, and his son took hold of the other end. The teacher wrote out for him *Alef Bet* and he learned it, *Alef Tav* and he learned it, *the Torah of the Priests* [the books of Leviticus and Numbers] and he learned it. He went on learning until he had learned the entire Torah.

I. He went and entered study sessions before R. Eliezer and before R. Joshua. He said to them, "My lords, open up for me the reasoning of Mishnah."

J. When they had stated one passage of law, he went and sat by himself and said, "Why is this *alef* written? Why is this *bet* written? Why is this statement made?" He went and asked them and, in point of fact, [Goldin:] reduced them to silence.

Clearly, our opening component in the *magnalia Aqibae* is a narrative. The tone and program establish the mood of narrative: *he was . . . he had . . . he did . . .* But how shall we classify the narrative, and by what criteria? One important criterion is whether the narrative describes a situation or tells about something that happened, with a beginning, middle, and end; the one is at rest, the other in movement.

These constitute questions with objective answers. Do we have a tableau or a story, or, for that matter, a parable or any of those other types of narratives we have already classified? By the simple criterion that a story has a beginning, middle, and end, which dictate points of narrative tension, and a clearly delineated program of action, we have a story. The components do more than merely set up pieces in a static tableau; they flow from one to the next and yield movement—hence narrative action.

What about the parable? Aqiba's origins in no way form or appeal to a parable or serve the purposes of a parable; there is a named authority, a specific hero. The passage also forms more than a dramatization of the (stated) proposition that one can start Torah study late in life, or of an exegesis of Scripture (i.e., a setting that serves to precipitate a comment on a verse of Scripture). If we compare the materials at hand to a statement like "One day he saw a skull floating on the water and said . . . ," we realize the difference.

What about the Scripture-story? The blatant differences require slight amplification. We note that verses of Scripture scarcely intervene, and there is no focus on the exegesis of a verse of Scripture. At D, Aqiba and his interlocutors do not interpret the verse but simply draw upon its statement of fact.

A story, as I said, has a beginning, middle, and end: movement from tension to resolution. In the present story there is a beginning (he had not studied), a middle (he went and studied), and an end, following Goldin's persuasive rendering: "he reduced them to silence." True, the action takes place mainly in what Aqiba thought, rather than in what he did, but in the nature of things, the action of going to study the Torah forms the one genuinely dramatic deed that is possible with the present subject-matter. The beginning is worked out at B–F. The middle is at G–H: Aqiba was so humble as to study with his own son. Then at I–J we have a climax and conclusion: Aqiba proved so profound in asking questions that he reduced the great authorities to silence. That conclusion hardly flows from A–H, but it is absolutely necessary to make the entire sequence into a cogent story. Otherwise we have merely bits and pieces of an uncompleted narrative.

Let us proceed to what follows in the context of the story of Aqiba's origins.

VI: V.2.   A. R. Simeon b. Eleazar says, "I shall make a parable for you. To what is the matter comparable? To a stonecutter who was cutting stone in a quarry. One time he took his chisel and went and sat down on the mountain and started to chip away little sherds from it. People came by and said to him, 'What are you doing?'

B. "He said to them, 'Lo, I am going to uproot the mountain and move it into the Jordan River.'"

C. "They said to him, 'You will never be able to uproot the entire mountain.'

D. "He continued chipping away at the mountain until he came to a huge boulder. He quarried underneath it, and unearthed it, and uprooted it, and tossed it into the Jordan.

E. "He said to the boulder, 'This is not your place, but that is your place.'

F. "Likewise this is what R. Aqiba did to R. Eliezer and to R. Joshua."

The parable without F simply says that with patience one may move mountains. By itself—not applied—it amplifies or at least continues VI: V.1.E, the power of words of Torah to wear down the hard heart of a human being. But the parable proves particular to the preceding story, since the addition, E–F, applies the parable to VI: V.1.J, the humiliation of Joshua and Eliezer. We may wonder whether, without the announcement at A that we have a parable, the parabolic character of the tale would have impressed us. The answer is that the general traits of a parable—an anonymous illustration in concrete and everyday terms of an abstract proposition—do occur in A–D, at which point the parable worked out its proposition: "He continued chipping away . . ." Even E, without F, can remain within the limits of the announced proposition of the parable, that is, the power of patience and persistence. So only F is jarring. It clearly serves the redactor's purpose. It does not transform the parable into a story, since it does not impose upon the prior narrative that particularity and temporal uniqueness that characterize the story.

VI: V.3.   A. Said R. Tarfon to him, "Aqiba, in your regard Scripture says, 'He stops up streams so that they do not trickle, and what is hidden he brings into the light' (Job 28:11).

B. "Things that are kept as mysteries from ordinary people has R. Aqiba brought to light."

He said to him does not make a story, and what is said does not bear the marks of a story, in whole or in part.

VI: V.4.   A. Every day he would bring a bundle of twigs [Goldin: straw], half of which he would sell in exchange for food, and half of which he would use for fuel.

B. His neighbors said to him, "Aqiba, you are killing us with the smoke. Sell them to us, buy oil with the money, and by the light of a lamp do your studying."

C. He said to them, "I fill many needs with that bundle, first, I repeat traditions [by the light of the fire I kindle with] them, second, I warm myself with them, third, I sleep on them."

VI: V.5.   A. In time to come R. Aqiba is going to impose guilt [for failing to study] on the poor [who use their poverty as an excuse not to study].

B. For if they say to them, "Why did you not study the Torah," and they reply, "Because we were poor," they will say to them, "But was not R. Aqiba poorer and more poverty-stricken?"

C. If they say, "Because of our children [whom we had to work to support]," they will say to them, "Did not R. Aqiba have sons and daughters?"

D. So they will say to them, "Because Rachel, his wife, had the merit [of making it possible for him to study, and we have no equivalent helpmates; our wives do not have equivalent merit at their disposal]."

It is hard to classify VI: V.4 as other than a narrative setting for a conversation, but the conversation makes no point by itself. In fact the whole forms a prologue to VI: V.5, which does make a powerful point.

VI: V.6.   A. It was at the age of forty that he went to study the Torah. Thirteen years later he taught the Torah in public.

B. They say that he did not leave this world before there were silver and golden tables in his possession,

C. and before he went up onto his bed on golden ladders.

D. His wife went about in golden sandals and wore a golden tiara of the silhouette of the city [Jerusalem].

E. His disciples said to him, "My lord, you have shamed us by what you have done for her [since we cannot do the same for our wives]."

F. He said to them, "She bore a great deal of pain on my account for [the study of] the Torah."

This item completes the preceding narrative of how Rachel's devotion to Aqiba's study of the Torah produced a rich reward. The *they said to him . . . he said to him . . .* sequences do not comprise a story or even establish much of a narrative framework. The upshot is that for Aqiba we have a sequence of narratives but only one story, the one at the beginning. The composite does not hang together very well, but it does make a few important points.

This brings us to the story of the origins in the Torah of Eliezer:

VI: VI.1.   A. How did R. Eliezer ben Hyrcanus begin [his Torah study]?

B. He had reached the age of twenty-two years and had not yet studied the Torah. One time he said, "I shall go and study the Torah before Rabban Yohanan ben Zakkai."

C. His father Hyrcanus said to him, "You are not going to taste a bit of food until you have ploughed the entire furrow."

D. He got up in the morning and ploughed the entire furrow.

E. They say that that day was Friday. He went and took a meal with his father-in-law.

F. And some say that he tasted nothing from the sixth hour on Friday until the sixth hour on Sunday.

The narrative is rather strange, since none of the actions is given a motivation. That immediately evident difference between Eliezer's and Aqiba's story will prove still more striking later than it does now. It suffices here to note the

points at which the two stories diverge in narrative technique. In the case of
Aqiba, we know why the great master originally determined to study the
Torah, but in the case of Eliezer we do not. All we know is that at the mature age
of twenty-two, he determined to study in the session of Yohanan ben Zakkai.
My judgment is that the storyteller intends to explain Eliezer's origins as
Yohanan's disciple, not to work out his inner motivation. That accounts, also,
for the random details, none of which fits together with the next. I see only a
sequence of unintegrated details: he was twenty-two and decided to study the
Torah. His father said, "Do not eat until you plough the furrow." He ploughed
the furrow. Then he went and ate with his father-in-law. Some say he did not
eat until Sunday. These details, scarcely connected, produce no effect either
of narrative or of a propositional character.

> VI: VI.2.   A. On the way he saw a rock. He picked it up and took it and put it
> into his mouth.
> B. And some say that what he picked up was cattle dung.
> C. He went and spent the night at his hostel.

Even if we read VI: VI.2 as part of VI: VI.1, all we have is more unintegrated
details. Nothing in VI: VI.1 – 2 points to a cogent narrative, let alone a story.
All we have are odd bits of information about what someone said. The whole
conglomerate does serve, however, to set the stage for VI: VI.3. The details
necessary to understand what is coming have now made their appearance, and
the climax is before us: he went and studied, and because he had eaten dung,
produced bad breath. Yohanan recognized the bad breath and said, "Just as
you suffered, so you will enjoy a reward."

> VI: VI.3.   A. He went and entered study session before Rabban Yohanan ben
> Zakkai in Jerusalem.
> B. Since a bad odor came out of his mouth, Rabban Yohanan ben Zakkai said to
> him, "Eliezer my son, have you taken a meal today?"
> C. He shut up.
> D. He asked him again, and he shut up again.
> E. He sent word and inquired at his hostel, and asked, "Has Eliezer eaten any-
> thing with you?"
> F. They sent word to him, "We thought that he might be eating with my lord."
> G. He said, "For my part, I thought that he might be eating with you. Between
> me and you, we should have lost R. Eliezer in the middle."
> H. He said to him, "Just as the odor of your mouth has gone forth, so will a
> good name in the Torah go forth for you."
> VI: VI.4.   A. Hyrcanus, his father, heard that he was studying the Torah with
> Rabban Yohanan ben Zakkai. He decided, "I shall go and impose on Eliezer my
> son a vow not to derive benefit from my property."
> B. They say that that day Rabban Yohanan ben Zakkai was in session and ex-
> pounding [the Torah] in Jerusalem, and all the great men of Israel were in session
> before him. He heard that he was coming. He set up guards, saying to them, "If he
> comes to take a seat, do not let him."

C. He came to take a seat and they did not let him.

D. He kept stepping over people and moving forward until he came to Ben Sisit Hakkesset and Naqdimon b. Gurion and Ben Kalba Sabua. He sat among them, trembling.

E. They say on that day Rabban Yohanan ben Zakkai looked at R. Eliezer, indicating to him, "Cite an appropriate passage and give an exposition."

F. He said to him, "I cannot cite an appropriate passage."

G. He urged him, and the other disciples urged him.

H. He went and cited an opening passage and expounded matters the like of which no ear had ever heard.

I. And at every word that he said, Rabban Yohanan ben Zakkai arose and kissed him on his head and said, "My lord, Eliezer, my lord, you have taught us truth."

J. As the time came to break up, Hyrcanus his father stood up and said, "My lords, I came here only to impose a vow on my son, Eliezer, not to derive benefit from my possessions. Now all of my possessions are given over to Eliezer my son, and all my other sons are disinherited and will have no share in them."

We have a beginning: Hyrcanus plans to go and place Eliezer under a vow of ostracism. That not only begins the story, but it also creates an enormous tension. A dramatic setting is set up: do not let the father sit down at the back, so that the father will sit among the greatest men of Jerusalem (B–D). Yohanan then calls upon Eliezer to speak, and after appropriate urging, he does. The tension is resolved at the climax, which also is the conclusion. I cannot think of a more perfect story, since every detail contributes to the whole, and the storyteller's intent—to underline the reward coming to the disciple, even though his family originally opposes his joining the sage—is fully realized. We note, therefore, that the conglomerate of narratives involving both Aqiba and Eliezer in fact rests on a single story, and that story forms the redactional focus, permitting the aggregation of further materials, not all of them of a finished character, and some of them not stories at all.

Let us now stand back and review the whole composite involving both Aqiba and Eliezer, which makes the point that one can start Torah study in mature years. Section VI:IV.1 serves only as a preface to the autonomous materials collected on the theme of how two famous masters began their studies late in life, having had no prior education. Both Eliezer and Aqiba, moreover, started off poor but got rich when they became famous. There is no clear connection between the materials and the original saying. Perhaps the reference to wallowing in the dust of their feet in connection with Eliezer is meant to link up to the detail that he put a piece of dirt or cow dung in his mouth, but that seems to me farfetched. The work refers first to Eliezer, then to Aqiba, but tells the stories in reverse order. The diverse stories on Aqiba are hardly harmonious, since one set knows nothing of his wife, while the other introduces her as the main figure. The first set, No. 2ff., emphasizes how "slow and steady wins the race." The lesson is that if one persists, one may ultimately best one's masters. No. 3 goes over the same matter, now with a parable to make the point that if one persists, he can uproot mountains. This seems to me appropriately joined to the foregoing, with the notion that Joshua and Eliezer are the mountains, as is made explicit. Tarfon then goes over the same matter in yet another way in No. 4. No. 5 then goes over the theme of studying in poverty. No. 5 seems to me a rather pointless story, but it leads to No. 6, which presents its own message explicitly. I treat No. 6 as distinct from No. 5 because it introduces the distinct theme of Aqiba's wife, and that has nothing to do with studying in poverty, but rather the wife's toleration of the husband's long absences. No. 7 then carries forward the second theme of the foregoing, Aqiba's wealth later on and how he lavished it on Rachel. I find puzzling the failure of the storyteller to take an interest in the source of Aqiba's great wealth. The sequence on Eliezer goes over a recurrent theme, but is as incoherent as the foregoing. No. 1 presents a number of problems of continuity, since 1.A–D are simply gibberish, there being no clear relationship between C and B. How E–F fit in I cannot say. One may make a good case for treating VI:VI.1 and VI:VI.2 as continuous. But because of the detail of 2.A, "on the way he saw a rock," it seems to me that we are on good ground in treating the latter as a fragment of yet another story, rather than as a bridge. Section VI:VI.3 is coherent and complete, a cogent and readily comprehended statement on its own. Section VI:VI.4 also works well, beginning to end. The details given in D then account for the appendix which follows, VI:VII–X.

Supernatural Patience as the Torah's Way of Life

Our attention is drawn next to the consequence of rebirth in the supernatural realm defined by the Torah. Studying the Torah changes one's character and therefore one's relationships with other people, just as it redefines the disciple's relationships with his (natural) family. The supernatural character of the sage finds expression, for instance, in the sage's remarkable—and unnatural—patience. So we turn to the description of traits of personality and character exhibited by those who study the Torah as sages' disciples.

Patience and forebearance, necessary traits of the sage, serve to win people to the Torah and so to give them their share in eternal life. Sagacity attained through discipleship leads to eternal life. Learning not joined to discipleship yields death. The patience of the sage certifies his successful discipleship, his authentic learning of the Torah. The deeper issue—the traits of personality and character that Torah learning is supposed to instill—is worked out through the stories before us. And that is the important point: it is specifically through telling stories about sages, not merely formulating abstract statements of their ideal, that the authorship of The Fathers According to Rabbi Nathan delivers the message at hand.

XV:IV.1.   A. What characterized the patience of Hillel the Elder?
    B. They tell the following case, concerning two people, who went and made a bet with one another for four hundred *zuz*.

C. They stipulated, "Whoever can go and infuriate Hillel will get the four hundred *zuz*.

D. One of them went [to try]. That day was a Friday, toward nightfall, and Hillel was washing his hair. The man came and knocked on the door, saying, "Where is Hillel, where is Hillel?"

E. Hillel wrapped himself up in his cloak and came to meet him. He said to him, "Speak."

F. He said to him, "Why are the eyes of the people of Palmyra [Tadmor] bleary?"

G. He said to him, "Because they live in the sands of the desert and the winds blow and scatter the sand into their eyes. Therefore their eyes are bleary."

H. He went and waited a while and came back and knocked on the door.

I. He said, "Where is Hillel, where is Hillel?"

J. He wrapped himself up in his cloak and came out.

K. He said to him, "My son, what do you need?"

L. He said to him, "I need to ask a matter of law."

M. He said to him, "Go ahead."

N. He said to him, "Why are the feet of the Africans flat?"

O. He said to him, "Because they live by swamps, and every day walk in water, therefore their feet are flat."

P. The man went his way, waited a while, came back, and knocked on the door.

Q. He said, "Where is Hillel, where is Hillel?"

R. He wrapped himself in his cloak and went out.

S. He said to him, "What do you need to ask?"

T. He said to him, "I have to ask a matter of law."

U. He said to him, "Ask." He then wrapped himself in his garment and sat down before him.

V. He said to him, "What do you need to ask?"

W. He said to him, "Is this the way princes reply? May people like you not become many in Israel."

X. He said to him, "God forbid! Watch yourself. What do you want?"

Y. He said to him, "On what account are the heads of the Babylonians long?"

Z. He said to him, "My son, you have asked an important 'law.' It is because over there they do not have smart midwives. When the baby is born, the ones who deal with it are slave-boys and slave-girls. Therefore their heads are long. But here, where we have smart midwives, when a baby is born, they raise it in a cradle and rub its head. Therefore their heads are round."

AA. He said to him, "You have cost me four hundred *zuz*."

BB. He said to him, "Hillel is worth your losing four hundred *zuz* without Hillel's losing his temper."

XV:V.1.   A. What characterized the impatience of Shammai the Elder?

B. They say there was the case of a man who stood before Shammai. He said to him, "My lord, how many Torahs do you have?"

C. He said to him, "Two, one in writing, one memorized."

D. He said to him, "As to the one in writing, I believe you. As to the memorized one, I do not believe you."

E. He rebuked him and threw him out.

F. He came before Hillel. He said to him, "My lord, how many Torahs were given?"

G. He said to him, "Two, one in writing, one memorized."

H. He said to him, "As to the one in writing, I believe you. As to the memorized one, I do not believe you."

I. He said to him, "My son, sit."

J. He wrote for him, *Alef, bet.*

K. He said to him, "What is this?"

L. He said to him, "An *alef.*"

M. He said to him, "This is not an *alef* but a *bet.*"

N. He said to him, "What is this?"

O. He said to him, "*Bet.*"

P. He said to him, "This is not a *bet* but a *gimmel.*"

Q. He said to him, "How do you know that this is an *alef* and this a *bet* and this a *gimmel*? But that is what our ancestors have handed over to us—the tradition that this is an *alef,* this a *bet,* this a *gimmel.* Just as you have accepted this teaching in good faith, so accept the other in good faith."

XV:V.2.   A. There was the case of a gentile who was passing behind a synagogue and heard a child reciting in Scripture: "This is the clothing which they shall make: a breast plate, ephod, and robe" (Ex. 28:4).

B. He came before Shammai and said to him, "My lord, all this honor—for whom is it designated?"

C. He said to him, "It is for the high priest who stands and carries out the service at the altar."

D. He said to him, "Convert me on the stipulation that you make me high priest so that I may carry out the service at the altar."

E. He said to him, "Is there no priesthood in Israel, and do we not have high priests to stand and carry out the acts of service at the altar assigned to the high priest, so that a mere convert who has come only with his staff and wallet may come and take up the service of the high priest?"

F. He threw him out.

G. He came before Hillel and said to him, "My lord, convert me, on the stipulation that you make me high priest so that I may carry out the service at the altar."

H. He said to him, "Sit, and I shall tell you something [of the rules of the office you propose to enter]. For if someone proposes to greet a mortal king, is it not logical that he should learn the rules of going in and coming out?"

I. He said to him, "Yes."

J. "You, who wish to greet the King of kings of kings, the Holy One, blessed be he, surely should learn how to enter the house of the Holy of Holies, how to set up the lamps, how to offer an offering on the altar, how to arrange the table, how to set out the wood."

K. He said to him, "Do what you think appropriate."

L. He first wrote for him, "*Alef, bet,*" and the man learned the letters.

M. Then he presented the *Torah of the Priests* [the books of Leviticus and Numbers], and the man went on learning the words until he came to the verse, "The non-priest who draws near [the altar] shall die" (Num. 1:51).

N. The proselyte constructed an argument a fortiori concerning himself: "If an

Israelite, who is called a son of the Omnipresent, and concerning whom the Presence of God has said, 'And you shall be mine as a kingdom of priests and a holy people' (Ex. 19:6), nonetheless is subject to Scripture's admonition, 'The nonpriest who draws near [the altar] shall die' (Num. 1:51), I, who am a mere proselyte, who has come only with my wallet, all the more so!"

O. The proselyte was reconciled on his own.

P. He came before Hillel the Elder and said to him, "May all the blessings that are in the Torah rest on your head, for if you had been like Shammai the Elder, you would have wiped me out of this world and of the world to come. Your humility has brought me into this world and the coming one."

Q. They say that to that proselyte two sons were born. One he called Hillel, and one he called Gamaliel, and they called them Hillel's converts.

The stories about Hillel and Shammai present in narrative and dramatic form a single proposition: Patience should characterize the sage.

The narrator leaves no doubt concerning his aesthetic power. He begins in each case with a clear beginning, stating the issue at hand and establishing a tension, as in XV:IV.1.C: whoever can infuriate Hillel wins enough money to live for two years. Then there is a triad of action, D–G, H–O, P–Z, with the first two components closely matched, and the third exhibiting points of difference so as to lead to the climax and resolution. Then we have a clear conclusion, AA–BB. The second story, XV:V.1 provides as its generative tension the story about the encounter with Shammai, yielding the meeting with Hillel. It is of course not a story about Shammai at all; that component serves only to establish the point of tension—the doctrine of the two Torahs—and its resolution in the encounter with Hillel. It yields in narrative form the conclusion and the lesson that people have to accept the teachings of the tradition in good faith. Section XV:V.2 matches the preceding story in its narrative pattern, with a beginning supplied by Shammai, a middle and climactic conclusion produced by Hillel. Now the lesson is that one's own reasoning yields the correct reading of the Torah. The conclusion, XV:V.2P–Q, reverts back to the superscription, XV:IV.1, indicating that it is from a single hand that the whole composite has come to us in its final statement.

A further story that conveys the importance of patience as the evidence of conforming to the personality required by the Torah follows.

XLI:III.1.   A. There is the case of R. Simeon b. Eleazar, who was coming from the house of his master in Migdal Eder, riding on an ass and making his way along the sea shore. He saw an unusually ugly man. He said to him, "Empty head! What a beast you are! Is it possible that everyone in your town is as ugly as you are?"

B. He said to him, "And what can I do about it? Go to the craftsman who made me and tell him, 'How ugly is that utensil that you have made!' "

C. When R. Simeon b. Eleazar realized that he had sinned, he got off his ass and prostrated himself before the man, saying to him, "I beg you to forgive me."

D. He said to him, "I shall not forgive you until you go to the craftsman who made me and tell him, 'How ugly is that utensil that you have made!' "

E. He ran after the man for three miles. The people of the town came out to meet him. They said toward him, "Peace be to you, my lord."

F. He said to them, "Whom do you call, 'my lord'?"

G. They said to him, "To the one who is going along after you."

H. He said to them, "If this is a 'my lord,' may there not be many more like him in Israel."

I. They said to him, "God forbid! And what has he done to you?"

J. He said to them, "Thus and so did he do to me."

K. They said to him, "Nonetheless, forgive him."

L. He said to them, "Lo, I forgive him, on the condition that he not make a habit of acting in that way."

M. On that same day R. Simeon entered the great study-house that was his and gave an exposition: " 'One should always be as soft as a reed and not as tough as a cedar.'

N. "In the case of a reed, all the winds in the world can go on blowing against it but it sways with them, so that when the winds grow silent, it reverts and stands in its place. And what is the destiny of a reed? In the end a pen is cut from it with which to write a scroll of the Torah.

O. "But in the case of a cedar it will not stand in place, but when the south wind blows against it, it uproots the cedar and turns it over. And what is the destiny of a cedar? Foresters come and cut it down and use it to roof houses, and the rest they toss into the fire.

P. "On the basis of this fact they have said, 'One should always be as soft as a reed and not as tough as a cedar.' "

This story opens with a striking encounter. There is a meeting, and the sage insults the ugly man, who responds appropriately: Go tell God about it. Simeon realized his error. The narrative relies on considerable action: the sage runs after the man, is met by the townsfolk who great him with honor, the insulted one realizes the state of affairs and curses the sage. Then the sage gives an exposition which makes the point that is required. The narrative that has preceded hardly serves merely as a setting for the exposition. Quite to the contrary, the exposition forms the climax and conclusion of a well-told story, with a beginning and a critical event, a middle, and a conclusion of considerable power and meaning. There are even elements of characterization, movement within the story in the presentation of the personalities of both sage, who learns something, and the opposite party, who is given his just and rightful reward: a lesson he precipitates.

Sagacity and History

The sage plays a public, not only a private role. I have already explained why, within the genealogical theory of Israel as one extended family, the sage as supernatural father forms the critical element in the history of the family, Israel. That history is defined by the encounter with Rome in particular. Rome is represented by its persona, its family hero, counterpart to Abraham, Jacob, or Moses, just as is Israel, and that can only be the emperor. That is why, in addition to the theme of Torah study, the sage-story bears a second important burden, namely, that of history and eschatology, this age and the age to come.

All sage-stories in the Fathers According to Rabbi Nathan that do not deal with the lives and deeds of sages concern the one large historical question facing Israel: its history in this world and destiny in the world to come. History finds its definition in a single event, the encounter with Rome, which involves two aspects: first, the destruction of the Temple and the sages' role in dealing with that matter; second, the (associated, consequent) repression of Torah sages and their study. Israel's history in this world works itself out in the encounter with Rome, Israel's counterpart and opposite, and that history in the world soon to come will see a reversal of roles. The centrality of study of the Torah in securing Israel's future forms the leitmotif of the stories at hand. We begin with the important and protracted story about the destruction of the Temple, which finds its setting in an exegesis of the saying in The Fathers that the world stands on deeds of loving-kindness. These then are found by the exegete at Hos. 6:6, and the intrusion of that verse carries in its wake a narrative—not a story but a precipitant—about Yohanan ben Zakkai and his disciple, Joshua, in the ruins of the Temple. Only at the end of the matter do we find the major historical story of the destruction.

IV:V.1.   A. . . . **on deeds of loving-kindness:** how so?

B. Lo, Scripture says, "For I desire mercy and not sacrifice, [and the knowledge of God rather than burnt offerings]" (Hos. 6:6).

C. To begin with, the world was created only on account of loving-kindness.

D. For so it is said, "For I have said, the world is built with loving-kindness, in the very heavens you establish your faithfulness" (Ps. 89:3).

IV:V.2.   A. One time [after the destruction of the Temple] Rabban Yohanan ben Zakkai was going forth from Jerusalem, with R. Joshua following after him. He saw the house of the sanctuary lying in ruins.

B. R. Joshua said, "Woe is us for this place which lies in ruins, the place in which the sins of Israel used to come to atonement."

C. He said to him, "My son, do not be distressed. We have another mode of atonement, which is like [atonement through sacrifice], and what is that? It is deeds of loving-kindness.

D. "For so it is said, 'For I desire mercy and not sacrifice, [and the knowledge of God rather than burnt offerings]' " (Hos. 6:6).

IV:V.3.   A. So we find in the case of Daniel, that most desirable man, that he carried out deeds of loving-kindness.

B. And what are the deeds of loving-kindness that Daniel did?

C. If you say offering whole offerings and sacrifices, do people offer sacrifices in Babylonia?

D. And has it not in fact been said, "Take heed that you not offer your whole offerings in any place which you see but in the place which the Lord will select in the territory of one of the tribes. There you will offer up your whole offerings" (Deut. 12:13–14).

E. What then were the deeds of loving-kindness that Daniel did?

F. He would adorn the bride and make her happy, join a cortege for the deceased, give a penny to a pauper, pray three times every day,

G. and his prayer was received with favor,

H. for it is said, "And when Daniel knew that the writing was signed, he went into his house—his windows were open in his upper chamber toward Jerusalem—and he kneeled upon his knees three times a day and prayed and gave thanks before his God as he did aforetime" (Dan. 6:11).

This entire construction serves as a prologue to what follows, an account of the destruction of the Temple, which forms the background to IV:VI.1. We have not a story but a narrative that forms a setting for a saying, as in IV:V.2. From "One time . . . ," we are given the occasion on which the colloquy of B–C, took place. Still, there is a narrative side to matters that emerges from the implicit movement from B to C. But classifying the passage as a story does not seem justified. The autonomy of the sage-story is shown once more, for the story that follows, utterly independent of what precedes it, exhibits all of the indicative traits we have defined and demonstrates that the introductory materials have simply provided a proper setting for the stunning account before us.

IV:VI.1. A. Now when Vespasian came to destroy Jerusalem, he said to [the inhabitants of the city,] "Idiots! Why do you want to destroy this city and burn the house of the sanctuary? For what do I want of you, except that you send me a bow or an arrow [as marks of submission to my rule], and I shall go on my way."

B. They said to him, "Just as we sallied out against the first two who came before you and killed them, so shall we sally out and kill you."

C. When Rabban Yohanan ben Zakkai heard, he proclaimed to the men of Jerusalem, saying to them, "My sons, why do you want to destroy this city and burn the house of the sanctuary? For what does he want of you, except that you send him a bow or an arrow, and he will go on his way."

D. They said to him, "Just as we sallied out against the first two who came before him and killed them, so shall we sally out and kill him."

E. Vespasian had stationed men near the walls of the city, and whatever they heard, they would write on an arrow and shoot out over the wall. [They reported] that Rabban Yohanan ben Zakkai was a loyalist of Caesar's.

F. After Rabban Yohanan ben Zakkai had spoken to them one day, a second, and a third, and the people did not accept his counsel, he sent and called his disciples, R. Eliezer and R. Joshua, saying to them, "My sons, go and get me out of here. Make me an ark and I shall go to sleep in it."

G. R. Eliezer took the head and R. Joshua the feet, and toward sunset they carried him until they came to the gates of Jerusalem.

H. The gatekeepers said to them, "Who is this?"

I. They said to him, "It is a corpse. Do you not know that a corpse is not kept overnight in Jerusalem."

J. They said to them, "If it is a corpse, take him out," so they took him out and brought him out at sunset, until they came to Vespasian.

K. They opened the ark and he stood before him.

L. He said to him, "Are you Rabban Yohanan ben Zakkai? Indicate what I should give you."

M. He said to him, "I ask from you only Yavneh, to which I shall go, and where I shall teach my disciples, establish prayer [Goldin: a prayer house], and carry out all of the religious duties."

N. He said to him, "Go and do whatever you want."

O. He said to him, "Would you mind if I said something to you."

P. He said to him, "Go ahead."

Q. He said to him, "Lo, you are going to be made sovereign."

R. He said to him, "How do you know?"

S. He said to him, "It is a tradition of ours that the house of the sanctuary will be given over not into the power of a commoner but of a king, for it is said, 'And he shall cut down the thickets of the forest with iron, and Lebanon [which refers to the Temple] shall fall by a mighty one'" (Is. 10:34).

T. People say that not a day, two, or three passed before a delegation came to him from his city indicating that the [former] Caesar had died and they had voted for him to ascend the throne.

U. They brought him a [Goldin:] catapult and drew it up against the wall of Jerusalem.

V. They brought him cedar beams and put them into the catapult, and he struck them against the wall until a breach had been made in it. They brought the head of a pig and put it into the catapult and tossed it toward the limbs that were on the Temple altar.

W. At that moment Jerusalem was captured.

X. Rabban Yohanan ben Zakkai was in session and with trembling was looking outward, in the way that Eli had sat and waited: "Lo, Eli sat upon his seat by the wayside watching, for his heart trembled for the ark of God" (1 Sam. 4:13).

Y. When Rabban Yohanan ben Zakkai heard that Jerusalem had been destroyed and the house of the sanctuary burned in flames, he tore his garments, and his disciples tore their garments, and they wept and cried and mourned.

IV:VI.2.   A. Scripture says, "Open your doors, O Lebanon, that the fire may devour your cedars" (Zech. 11:1).

B. That verse refers to the high priests who were in the sanctuary [on the day it was burned].

C. They took their keys in their hands and threw them upward, saying before the Holy One, blessed be he, "Lord of the world, here are your keys which you entrusted to us, for we have not been faithful custodians to carry out the work of the king and to receive support from the table of the king."

IV:VI.3.   A. Abraham, Isaac, and Jacob, and the twelve tribes were weeping, crying, and mourning.

IV:VI.4.   A. Scripture says, "Wail, O cypress tree, for the cedar is fallen, because the glorious ones are spoiled, wail, O you oaks of Bashan, for the strong forest is come down" (Zech. 11:2).

B. "Wail, O cypress tree, for the cedar is fallen" refers to the house of the sanctuary.

C. ". . . because the glorious ones are spoiled" refers to Abraham, Isaac, and Jacob, and the twelve tribes [who were weeping, crying, and mourning].

D. ". . . wail, O you oaks of Bashan" refers to Moses, Aaron, and Miriam.

E. ". . . for the strong forest is come down" refers to the house of the sanctuary.

F. "Hark the wailing of the shepherds, for their glory is spoiled" (Zech. 11:3) refers to David and Solomon his son.

G. "Hark the roaring of young lions, for the thickets of the Jordan are spoiled" (Zech. 11:3) speaks of Elijah and Elisha.

The story unfolds in a smooth way from beginning to end. It serves, overall, as an account of the power of the Torah to lead Israel through historical crises. The narrative traits of the story prove still more striking when, in chapter 6, we compare this account of the destruction to that in the Talmud of Babylonia, a very different story.

Specifically, the storyteller at three points places the sage in the scale against the emperor, Israel against Rome: (1) the comparison of Vespasian and the Jewish troops to Yohanan and the Jewish troops, (2) Vespasian and Yohanan in their direct encounter, and (3) the destruction itself. Then the Torah makes the difference, for in the end, Israel will outweigh Rome. The story's themes all form part of the larger theme of Torah learning. The centerpiece is Yohanan's knowledge that the Temple is going to be destroyed. This he acquired in two ways. First of all, his observation of the conduct of the Israelite army led him to that conclusion. Second, and more important, his knowledge of the Torah told him the deeper meaning of the event, which was in two parts. The one side had Rome get a new emperor; the other (counterpart) side had Israel get its program for the period beyond the destruction. The opening unit of the story, A–T, seems to me seamless. I can point to no element that could be omitted without seriously damaging the integrity of the story. I see no intrusions of any kind. If that is a correct judgment, then the climax must come only at S, confirmed by T and what follows. That is to say, it is the power of the sage to know the future because of his knowledge of the Torah. Establishing a place for the teaching of disciples and the performance of other holy duties forms a substrate of the same central theme. Deeper still lies the theme of the counterpart and opposite: Israel and Rome, sage and emperor. That motif occurs, to begin with at A and C, which have Vespasian and Yohanan say precisely the same thing, with one difference. Vespasian calls the Jewish army "idiots," and Yohanan calls the troops, "my sons." Otherwise the statements are the same. And the replies, B and D, are also the same. So the first episode sets the emperor and the sage up as opposites and counterparts.

The second episode has the people unwilling to listen to the sage—the emperor has no role here—leading the sage to conclude that it is time to "make an ark and go to sleep in it." If I had to choose a point of reference, it would be not the sleep of death—then Yohanan would have wanted a bier—but the ark of Noah. Yohanan then forms the counterpart, through the storyteller's choice of the word *ark,* to Noah, who will save the world beyond the coming deluge. I would then see F–G as a chapter in a complete story. E, on the one side, and H–J, on the other, link that cogent chapter to the larger context. E prepares us to understand why Vespasian recognizes Yohanan, an important detail, added precisely where it had to come, and H–J form the necessary bridge to what is coming.

The next component of the unitary story again places Vespasian in the balance against Yohanan. Now Yohanan tells Vespasian what is going to happen. Each party rises to power as a direct outcome of the destruction of the Temple: sage vs. emperor, one in the scale against the other. The colloquy with Vespasian at L–S forms the only part of the story that relies upon a narrative consisting of *he said to him . . . he said to him . . .* The point, of course, is clear as already stated. Then comes the necessary denouement, in two parts. First, the Temple actually was destroyed; we are told how at T–W. Second, Yohanan responded in mourning at X–Y. Here too we have that same counterpart and opposite: Rome, then Israel, with Israel represented by the sage and Rome by the emperor. What follows of course is not narrative, let alone story. Section IV:VI.2 provides an exegesis, A–B, followed by a colloquy. Section IV:VI.3 is a singleton, and IV:VI.4 joins the destruction of the Temple to the history of Israel and its heroes, all of whom wept as did Yohanan. But I do not see in the inclusion of IV:VI.4 an attempt to compare Yohanan to the named heroes. This is virtually certain, since the story itself at IV:VI.1.X invokes the figure of Eli, who is noteworthy for his omission in IV:VI.4.

What follows is another set of stories about the historical event of the destruction of the Temple. We deal with the victims in the aftermath of the war. These seem to me miscellaneous in character.

XVII:III.1.   A. One time Rabban Yohanan ben Zakkai was walking in the marketplace. He saw a young girl gathering barley from under the hooves of the cattle of Arabs. He said to her, "My daughter, who are you?"

B. She kept silent.

C. Again he said to her, "My daughter, who are you?"

D. She kept silent.

E. She said to him, "Hold it a minute." Then she covered herself with her hair and sat down before him. She said to him, "My lord, I am the daughter of Naqdimon b. Gurion."

F. He said to her, "My daughter, what ever became of the wealth of your father's house?"

G. She said to him, "My lord, is it not an apothegm in Jerusalem: '[Goldin:] Money will keep if you don't keep it,' and some say, ' . . . if you give charity.'"

H. He said to her, "What ever happened to your father-in-law's money?"

I. She said to him, "My lord, this came and took the other along with it."

J. At that moment said Rabban Yohanan ben Zakkai to his disciples, "For my entire life I have been reciting this verse of Scripture, 'If you do not know, O you fairest among women, go your way forth by the footsteps of the flock and feed your kids beside the shepherds' tents' (Song 1:8).

K. "But I never learned what it meant until I came to this day and I have now learned what it means.

L. "For the Israelites have fallen subject to the most despicable of all nations, and not only to that despicable nation alone, but even to the dung of their cattle."

M. The girl further said to him, "My lord, do you remember when you inscribed your seal on my marriage-contract?"

N. He said to her, "Yes I do," and he said to the disciples, "By the Temple service! I inscribed my seal on this girl's marriage-contract, and in it was written the sum of a thousand thousand golden *denars* in Tyrian coinage.

O. "In the time of this girl's father's household they never went from their houses to the house of the sanctuary before woolen rugs were spread out [for them to walk on]."

The appearance of the proof text accounts for the inclusion of this story, which does not intersect in any direct way with the base clause. This same theme continues in the sizable anthology on the theme of captive girls of rich families, and that makes it virtually certain that the anthological principle is pointed—the instability of money—and not merely topical—captive Israelite women.

VI:VI.1.   A. Why was he called *Sisit Hakkesset?*

B. Because he reclined on a silver couch at the head of all the great men of Israel.

We have nothing more than a gloss of the preceding story, about who was present when Eliezer's father came to disinherit him. What follows glosses the rest.

VI:VIII.1.   A. They tell concerning the daughter of Naqdimon b. Gurion that she had a bedspread worth twelve thousand golden *denars*.

B. She spent a Tyrian gold *denar* from Friday to Friday for [Goldin:] spice puddings.

C. She was awaiting levirate marriage [and the levir was yet a minor].

No one has mentioned the daughter, but that does not stop the compiler from intruding whatever he has in hand on that uninvited theme.

VI:IX.1.   A. Why was he called Naqdimon ben Gurion?

B. Because the sun's rays penetrated for his sake [a play on the root *NQD,* which occurs in both the name and in the verb for *penetrate through*].

C. [Explaining the reference to the sun's shining for his sake, the following story is told.] One time the Israelites went up to Jerusalem for a pilgrim festival, but they had no water to drink. [Naqdimon b. Gurion] went to an official and said to him, "Lend me twelve wells of water from now until such-and-such a day. If I do not pay you back twelve wells of water, I shall pay you twelve talents of silver," and they agreed on a due date.

D. When the time came, the official sent word to him, "Send me twelve wells of water or twelve talents of silver."

E. He said to him, "There is still time today."

F. The official ridiculed him, saying, "This whole year it has not rained, and now is it going to rain?"

G. The official went into the bath house, rejoicing.

H. Naqdimon went to the study house.

I. He wrapped himself in his cloak and arose to pray, saying before him, "Lord of the world, it is perfectly clear to you that I did not act in my own behalf or in behalf of the house of father. I acted only in your behalf, so that there would be water for the pilgrims."

J. Forthwith the skies got thick with clouds, and it rained until the twelve wells were filled with water and overflowing.

K. He sent word to the official, "Pay me the value that I have coming to me from you of the excess water [since I have now returned more water than I took]."

L. He said to him, "The sun has already set, and the excess water now has come into my possession."

M. [Naqdimon] went back into the study house, wrapped himself in his cloak and arose to pray, saying before him, "Lord of the world, do it again for me, just like before."

N. Forthwith the wind blew, the clouds scattered, and the sun shone.

O. He came out and the two met one another. He said, "I know perfectly well that the Holy One, blessed be he, has shaken his world only on your account."

The story in its own right is well composed and cogent, beginning to end. It makes its point through contrasts of details (e.g., G–H) and in general gives ample evidence of narrative care. No one has any interest in relating this story to the context of the earlier tales. The story is formed of the following elements. The beginning, C–G, introduces the point of tension—the risk taken by Naqdimon in behalf of the pilgrims. Then at the middle, H–L, the problem deepens. Naqdimon is able to provide the water, but there is more water than needed, and this the official claims for free. The climax and conclusion produces a second miracle, greater than the first, at M–O. So the story develops in sequences of ascending action, with each point leading to the next and drawing our interest toward what is to come. The net effect is powerful, because every detail contributes to the main point of tension and conflict, and because each component deepens our engagement. There are no easy solutions, and the miracle is truly miraculous.

VI:X.1.   A. Why was he called Ben Kalba Sabua [sated dog]?

B. Because whoever came into his house hungry as a dog went out of his house sated.

VI:X.2.   A. When Caesar Vespasian came to destroy Jerusalem, the zealots wanted to burn up all of [Ben Kalba Sabua's] goods.

B. Kalba Sabua said to them, "Why do you want to destroy this city and seek to burn up all those goods? Hold up for me until I can go into the house and see what I have in the house."

C. He went in and found he had enough food to feed everybody in Jerusalem for twenty-two years.

D. He immediately gave orders: "Heap it up, sort out the grain, sift and knead and bake and prepare food for twenty-two years for everybody in Jerusalem."

E. But they paid no mind to him.

F. What did the men of Jerusalem do? They brought the loaves of bread and bricked them into the walls and plastered them over with plaster.

VI:X.3.   A. [But ultimately] what did the men of Jerusalem have to do? They boiled straw and ate it.

B. And all the Israelites stationed near the walls of Jerusalem said, "Would that someone would give me five dates—I would go down and cut off five heads."

C. They would give him five dates, and he would go off and cut off five heads of Vespasian's troops.

D. Vespasian examined the excrement of the population and saw that there was not a trace of grain in it.

E. He said to his troops, "If these men, who are eating only straw can come out and kill off [our soldiers], if they had all the food that you are eating and drinking, how much the more so would they be wreaking havoc among you!"

The final gloss of the original story further enriches the materials on the third name on the list. The story, No. 2, is rather strange. It omits crucial details, for example, an explanation for F. To the storyteller, apparently, the contrast between the action at D–E and the fact at F makes the important point. The storyteller assumes that we know that the zealots burned the stores so as to encourage the resistance, a detail not in hand here. No. 3 presents a secondary development of the story, which yields a very positive picture of the zealots. It seems to me that No. 3 forms a cogent statement, beginning to end. It surely can stand by itself. Still, the two elements—burning the stores, the courage of the starving soldiers—do explain one another, with the former accounting for the conditions of starvation, the latter accounting for the daring of the Israelite army. Note that the entire appendix to the original story has no more bearing on the exposition of the saying of Avot than did the stories about Aqiba and Eliezer.

Since Israel's history took on shape and meaning in the conflict with Rome, the equal and opposite force on earth, and since in that conflict the sage weighed in against the emperor, events in the life of the sage formed the counterpart to happenings in the life of the emperor. When, therefore, we considered stories of the origins of sages, we took up the counterpart to tales of the origins and rise to power of emperors, and as we turn to stories of the death of sages, we take up the sages' counterpart to stories of the great deeds of emperors.

How the Sage Dies

Two moments in the life of the sage are of interest: origins (meaning the sage's beginning as a Torah disciple) and death. The death stories are told under the aspect of the Torah and serve to show the supernatural power of the Torah to transform even the moment of death into an occasion of Torah learning. The two points, start and finish, served to define and delineate the middle. How a sage coped with the death of a loved one had to align with how a sage studied the Torah; the Torah obviously provided the model of the correct confrontation. How a sage died—the death scene, with its quiet lessons—likewise presented a model for others. The encounter with death took narrative shape in the account of how the sage accepted comfort.

XIV:IV.1.   A. When the son of Rabban Yohanan ben Zakkai died, his disciples came in to bring him comfort.

B. R. Eliezer came in and took a seat before him and said to him, "My lord, with your permission, may I say something before you."

C. He said to him, "Speak."

D. He said to him, "The first Man had a son who died, and he accepted comfort in his regard. And how do we know that he accepted comfort in his regard?

E. "As it is said, 'And Adam knew his wife again' (Gen. 4:25). You, too, be comforted."

F. Said he to him, "Is it not enough for me that I am distressed on my own account, that you should mention to me the distress of the first Man?"

G. R. Joshua came in and said to him, "My lord, with your permission, may I say something before you."

H. He said to him, "Speak."

I. He said to him, "Job had sons and daughters who died, and he accepted comfort in their regard. And how do we know that he accepted comfort in their regard?

J. "As it is said, 'The Lord gave and the Lord has taken away, blessed be the name of the Lord' (Job 1:21). You too, be comforted."

K. Said he to him, "Is it not enough for me that I am distressed on my own account, that you should mention to me the distress of Job?"

L. R. Yosé came in and took a seat before him and said to him, "My lord, with your permission, may I say something before you."

M. He said to him, "Speak."

N. He said to him, "Aaron had two grown-up sons who died on the same day, and he accepted comfort in their regard.

O. "For it is said, 'And Aaron held his peace' (Lev. 10:3), and silence means only comfort. You too, be comforted."

P. Said he to him, "Is it not enough for me that I am distressed on my own account, that you should mention to me the distress of Aaron?"

Q. R. Simeon came in and said to him, "My lord, with your permission, may I say something before you."

R. He said to him, "Speak."

S. He said to him, "King David had a son who died, and he accepted comfort in his regard. You too, be comforted. And how do we know that he accepted comfort in his regard?

T. "As it is said, 'And David comforted Bath Sheba his wife and went in unto her and lay with her and she bore a son and called his name Solomon' (2 Sam. 12:24). You too, be comforted."

U. Said he to him, "Is it not enough for me that I am distressed on my own account, that you should mention to me the distress of King David?"

V. R. Eleazar b. Arakh came in. When he saw him, he said to his servant, "Take my clothes and follow me to the bathhouse [so that I can prepare to accept consolation], for he is a great man and I shall not be able to resist his arguments."

W. He came in and took a seat before him and said to him, "I shall draw a parable for you. To what may the matter be compared? To the case of a man with whom the king entrusted a treasure. Every day he would weep and cry saying, 'Woe is me, when shall I get complete and final relief from this treasure that has been entrusted to me.'

X. "You too, my lord, had a son, he recited from the Torah, Prophets and Writings, Mishnah, laws, lore, and has departed from this world without sin. You have reason, therefore, to accept consolation for yourself that you have returned your treasure, entrusted to you, whole and complete."

Y. He said to him, "R. Eleazar b. Arakh, my son, you have given comfort to me in the right way in which people console one another."

The structure of the story, focused on the superiority of Eleazar b. Arakh (counterpart to the constructions in The Fathers 2:2ff., built along the same lines), should not obscure its larger sense. The first four disciples, Eliezer, Joshua, Yosé, and Simeon, all invoke biblical models. Scripture is insufficient. Eleazar then presents an argument resting on the oral Torah: the son had studied the Torah, inclusive of the Mishnah, laws, and lore. He departed from this world without sin, so "you have returned the treasure entrusted to you." The written Torah presents a mere set of examples. The oral Torah, by contrast, provides not only the model but also the measure and the meaning. The sequence of names, to which our attention is first attracted, allows the message to be stated with great force, and the climactic statement underlines the power of the oral Torah to define the appropriate response to the death of the child. The polemic is clear and, we find, consistent with that of Hillel.

We come now to the stories about the death of a sage, with special reference to Yohanan ben Zakkai and his disciple, Eliezer, the only two death scenes (other than those of martyrs) presented in The Fathers According to Rabbi Nathan. Both death scenes respond to lists of omens pertinent to one's condition at death. In the first, Yohanan's, there is no correspondence at all, since Yohanan is not represented as dying with a serene mind.

XXV:I.1.   A. Ben Azzai says, "Whoever has a serene mind on account of his learning has a good omen for himself, and who does not have a serene mind on account of his learning has a bad omen for himself.

B. "Whoever has a serene mind on account of his impulse, has a good omen for himself, but [Goldin:] if his mind is distressed because of his impulse, it is a bad sign for him.

C. "For him with whom the sages are satisfied at the hour of death it is a good sign, and for him with whom sages are not satisfied at the hour of death it is a bad sign.

D. "For whoever has his face turned upward [at death] it is a good sign, and for whoever has his face turned toward the bed it is a bad sign.

E. "If one is looking at people, it is a good sign, at the wall, a bad sign.

F. "If one's face is glistening, it is a good sign, glowering, a bad one."

XXV:II.1.   A. At the time that Rabban Yohanan ben Zakkai was departing from this life, he raised up his voice and wept. His disciples said to him, "Lord, tall pillar, eternal light, mighty hammer, why are you weeping?"

B. He said to them, "Now am I going to appear before a mortal king, who, should he be angry with me, is angry only in this world, and if he should imprison me, imposes imprisonment only in this world, and if he should put me to death, imposes death only in this world, and not only so, but whom I can appease with words and bribe with money?

C. "Lo, I am going to appear before the King of kings of kings, the Holy One, blessed be he, who, should he be angry with me, is angry both in this world and in the world to come, whom I cannot appease with words or bribe with money.

D. "And furthermore, before me are two paths, one to the Garden of Eden, the other to Gehenna, and I do not know on which road, whether I shall be drawn down to Gehenna, or whether I shall be brought into the Garden of Eden."

E. And in this regard it is said, "Before him shall be sentenced all those who go down to the dust, even he who cannot keep his soul alive" (Ps. 22:30).

XXV:II.2. A. In regard to Moses Scripture says, "And I will take away my hand and you shall see my back, but my face shall not be seen" (Ex. 33:23).

B. And further, "And he spread it before me and it was written on its face and on its back" (Ez. 2:10).

C. "Its face" refers to this world, "its back," to the world to come.

D. Another interpretation: "its face" refers to the distress of the righteous in this world and the prosperity of the wicked in this world, "its back," to the reward given to the righteous in the world to come, and the punishment inflicted on the wicked in Gehenna.

XXV:II.3. A. "And there was written therein lamentations and jubilant sound and woe" (Ez. 2:10):

B. "Lamentations" refers to the penalty inflicted on the wicked in this world, as it is said, "This is the lamentation with which they shall lament, the daughters of the nations shall lament with it" (Ez. 32:16).

C. ". . . and jubilant sound and woe" refers to the reward of the righteous in the world to come, as it is said, "With an instrument of ten strings and with the psaltery, with a jubilant sound on the harp" (Ps. 92:4).

D. ". . . and woe": refers to the punishment that is coming to the wicked in the world to come, as it is said, "Calamity shall come upon calamity, and rumor upon rumor" (Ez. 7:26).

XXV:II.4. A. [Yohanan ben Zakkai] would say, "Clear the house on account of uncleanness and prepare a throne for King Hezekiah of Judah."

The narrative of XXV:II.1 hardly qualifies as a story, since we have little more than a tableau: the setting of the stage, the giving of a speech. Yohanan is dying and *he said to him . . . he said to him . . .* The message is very powerful. Yohanan reminds the disciples that the judgment at hand is inexorable and incorruptible, and he does not know which way he will now go. The colloquy hardly qualifies as a story, and when we come to Eliezer's, we see the possibilities for action as a vehicle for the unfolding of the narrative, characterization as a mode of making its point(s), and sustained sequences of exchange—whether word or deed—as the deep structure of the story. The essentially stationary character of the present death scene is shown at XXV:II.2–3, which form little more than exegeses of Scripture. At XV:II.4, then, we have a further *would say* for Yohanan. These snippets scarcely qualify as a story by any definition.

XXV:III.1.   A. [Ben Azzai] would say, "If one dies in a serene mind, it is a good omen for him, in derangement, it is a bad omen.

B. ". . . while speaking, it is a good omen, in silence, a bad omen.

C. ". . . in repeating words of the Torah, it is a good omen for him, in the midst of discussing business, it is a bad omen.

D. ". . . while doing a religious duty, it is a good omen, while involved with a trivial matter, it is a bad omen.

E. ". . . while happy, it is a good omen, while sad, a bad omen.

F. ". . . while laughing, a good omen, while weeping, a bad omen.

G. ". . . on the eve of the Sabbath, a good omen, at the end of the Sabbath, a bad omen.

H. ". . . on the eve of the Day of Atonement a bad omen, at the end of the Day of Atonement a good omen."

After the sizable interruption illustrating the first unit of the sayings, we revert to the completion of Ben Azzai's statement on this theme. A mark of the end of a systematic list is the change in the established pattern, as at H.

XXV:IV.1.   A. When R. Eliezer was dying—they say it was the eve of the Sabbath [toward dusk]—R. Aqiba and his colleagues came in to see him, and he was dozing in the room, sitting back [Goldin:] on a canopied couch. They took seats in the waiting room. Hyrcanus his son came in to remove his phylacteries [which are worn on weekdays but not on the Sabbath, about to begin]. But he did not let him do so, and he was weeping.

B. Hyrcanus went out and said to the sages, "My lords, it appears to me that my father is deranged."

C. [Eliezer] said to him, "My son, I am not the one who is deranged, but you are the one who is deranged. For you have neglected to light the lamp for the Sabbath, on which account you may become liable to a death penalty inflicted by heaven, but busied yourself with the matter of the phylacteries, on account of which liability is incurred, at worst, merely on the matter of violating the rules of Sabbath rest."

D. Since sages saw that he was in full command of his faculties, they came in and took up seats before him, but at a distance of four cubits [as was required, because Eliezer was in a state of ostracism on account of his rejection of the decision of the majority in a disputed case]. [Bringing up the case subject to dispute, so to determine whether he had finally receded to the decision of the majority,] they said to him, "My lord, as to a round cushion, a ball, [a shoe when placed on] a shoemaker's last, an amulet, and phylacteries that have been torn, what is the law as to their being susceptible to uncleanness? [Are they regarded as completed and useful objects, therefore susceptible, or as useless or incomplete and therefore not susceptible?]"

E. [Maintaining his earlier position,] he said to them, "They remain susceptible to uncleanness, and should they become unclean, immerse them as is [without undoing them, that is, exposing their contents to the water], and take great pains in these matters, for these represent important laws that were stated to Moses at Sinai."

F. They persisted in addressing to him questions concerning matters of insusceptibility and susceptibility to uncleanness as well as concerning immersion-pools, saying to him, "My lord, what is the rule on this matter?"

G. He would say to them, "Clean."

H. And so he went, giving the answer of susceptible to uncleanness to an object that could become unclean, and insusceptible to one that could not become unclean."

I. After a while R. Eliezer said to sages, "I am amazed at the disciples of the generation, perhaps they may be liable to the death penalty at the hand of Heaven."

J. They said to him, "My lord, on what account?"

K. He said to them, "Because you never came and performed the work of apprenticeship to me."

L. Then he said to Aqiba b. Joseph, "Aqiba, on what account did you not come before me and serve as apprentice to me?"

M. He said to him, "My lord, I had no time."

N. He said to him, "I shall be surprised for you if you die a natural death."

O. And some say, He said nothing to him, but when R. Eliezer spoke as he did to his disciples, forthwith [Aqiba's] [Goldin:] heart melted within him.

P. Said to him R. Aqiba, "My lord, how will I die?"

Q. He said to him, "Aqiba, yours will be the worst."

XXV:IV.2.   A. R. Aqiba entered and took a seat before him and said to him, "My lord, now repeat traditions for me."

B. He opened a subject and repeated for him three hundred rules concerning the bright spot [to which Lev. 13:1ff. refers in connection with the skin ailment translated as *leprosy*].

C. Then R. Eliezer raised his two arms and folded them on his breast and said, "Woe is me for these two arms, which are like two scrolls of Torahs, which now are departing from the world.

D. "For were all the oceans ink, all the reeds quills, all men scribes, they could not write down what I have learned in Scripture and repeated in Mishnah-traditions, and derived as lessons from my apprenticeship to sages in the session.

E. "Yet I have taken away from my masters only as much as does a person who dips his finger into the ocean, and I have taken away for my disciples only so much as a paintbrush takes from a paint tube.

F. "And furthermore, I can repeat three hundred laws on the rule: 'You shall not permit a sorceress to live.'"

G. Some say, "Three thousand."

XXV:IV.3.   A. "But no one ever asked me anything about it, except for Aqiba b. Joseph.

B. "For one time he said to me, 'My lord, teach me how people plant cucumbers and how they pull them up.'

C. "I said something, and the entire field was filled with cucumbers.

D. "He said to me, 'My lord, you have taught me how they are planted. Teach me how they are pulled up.'

E. "I said something, and all of the cucumbers assembled in a single place."

XXV:IV.4. A. Said R. Eleazar b. Azariah to him, "My lord, as to a shoe that is
on the shoemaker's list, what is the law? [Is it susceptible to uncleanness, as a
useful object, or insusceptible, since it is not fully manufactured and so finished as
a useful object?]"

B. He said to him, "It is susceptible to uncleanness."

C. And so he continued giving answers to questions, ruling of an object susceptible to uncleanness that it is susceptible, and of one insusceptible to uncleanness
that it is permanently clean, until his soul went forth as he said the word, "Clean."

D. Then R. Eleazar b. Azariah tore his clothes and wept, going forth and announcing to sages, "My lords, come and see R. Eliezer, for he is not in a state
of purity as to the world to come, since his soul went forth with the word pure on
his lips."

XXV:IV.5. A. After the Sabbath R. Aqiba came and found [Eliezer's corpse
being conveyed for burial] on the road from Caesarea to Lud. Then he tore his
clothes and ripped his hair, and his blood flowed, and he fell to the earth, crying out
and weeping, saying, "Woe is me for you, my Lord, woe is me, my master, for you
have left the entire generation orphaned."

B. At the row of mourners he commenced [the lament,] saying, " 'My father,
my father, chariot of Israel and its horsemen!' I have coins but no expert money-
changer to sort them out."

The snippets of death scenes of Eliezer are sewn together, but the distinct
components are fairly easy to recognize through the repetitions, on the one
side, and the shifts in setting and premise as to the location of authorities, on
the other. But the flow is smooth, beginning to end, a credit to the compiler.
The detail of No. 1 becomes a main point later on, that is, the ruling on objects Eliezer had held subject to uncleanness, sages taking the opposite view.
No. 1 moves along to the complaint of Eliezer that the disciples had kept their
distance from him. No. 2 picks up at this point, but by introducing Aqiba,
suggests that the tale is distinct from the foregoing, which already has him on
the scene. The same happens later with Eleazar b. Azariah's paragraph. No. 3
then goes back over the matter of No. 2—the distance of the disciples—and
goes over its own point. No. 4 does not appear to know anything about much
that has gone before, as I said, and No. 5 is independent as well, since up to
now we have had Aqiba at the death scene, while here Aqiba finds out about
the death only after the Sabbath and in a different setting.

The story serves as a good illustration for three of the positive omens Ben
Azzai has listed: "while speaking," "while repeating words of the Torah,"
and "on the eve of the Sabbath." But he clearly is not represented as happy or
cheerful or laughing, so, in the aggregate, I think that an illustration of the
omens of Ben Azzai formed a negligible consideration in the mind of the storyteller. The center of interest of the story is Eliezer's complaint against the
disciples, who did not study Torah through service to him. The interplay of
Eliezer and Aqiba then forms the centerpiece, with Nos. 1, 2, 3, and 5 placing
Aqiba at the heart of matters; Eleazar b. Azariah dominates at No. 4.

The materials form a nuanced and powerful story on their own. Each detail points toward the next; each sequence of action points toward the one to follow. The master, very much an individual and not a type, leaves a legacy of reproach, a distinctive and particular message. We have slight experience in dealing with sages as distinctive individuals, since stories generally represent them either as symbols on their own (e.g., the sage as against the emperor) or as models of virtues for the many to emulate (e.g., Hillel's patience, Yohanan b. Zakkai's resort to the Torah to cope with the destruction of the Temple). The following is a brief reprise of the same materials.

> XIX:II.1.   A. When R. Eliezer fell ill, his disciples came in to see him and took seats before him. They said to him, "Our lord, teach us something."
>
> B. He said to them, "This is what I shall teach you: go forth and let each take responsibility for the honor owing to his fellow.
>
> C. "And when you say your prayers, know before whom you are standing up to pray.
>
> D. "And on account of this teaching, you will gain the merit to enter the world to come."
>
> XIX:III.1.   A. Said R. Eleazar b. Azariah, "There are five things that we learned from R. Eliezer [on that occasion], and we got more pleasure from them than we got from them when he was alive.
>
> B. "And these are the topics: the rule, as to uncleanness, covering a round cushion, ball, shoe last, amulet, and phylactery that was torn.
>
> C. "[We said to him,] 'In these matters concerning which you gave rules for us, what is the law?'
>
> D. "He said to us, 'They are subject to uncleanness, and [should they contract uncleanness] be careful in their regard to immerse them just as is, for these are absolutely firm rulings that were stated to Moses at Mount Sinai.'"

This seems to me a mere reprise of the foregoing. A different sort of death scene describes the martyrdom of sages. We have already encountered the following story.

> XXXVIII:V.1.   A. **A sword comes into the world because of the delaying of justice and perversion of justice, and because of those who teach the Torah not in accord with the law.**
>
> XXXVIII:V.2.   A. When they seized Rabban Simeon b. Gamaliel and R. Ishmael on the count of death, Rabban Simeon b. Gamaliel was in session and was perplexed, saying, "Woe is us! For we are put to death like those who profane the Sabbath and worship idols and practice fornication and kill."
>
> C. Said to him R. Ishmael b. Elisha, "Would it please you if I said something before you?"
>
> D. He said to him, "Go ahead."
>
> E. He said to him, "Is it possible that when you were sitting at a banquet, poor folk came and stood at your door, and you did not let them come in and eat?"
>
> F. He said to him, "By heaven [may I be cursed] if I ever did such a thing! Rather, I set up guards at the gate. When poor folk came along, they would bring them in to me and eat and drink with me and say a blessing for the sake of Heaven."

G. He said to him, "Is it possible that when you were in session and expounding [the Torah] on the Temple mount and the vast populations of Israelites were in session before you, you took pride in yourself?"

H. He said to him, "Ishmael my brother, one has to be ready to accept his failing. [That is why I am being put to death, the pride that I felt on such an occasion.]"

I. They went on appealing to the executioner for grace. This one [Ishmael] said to him, "I am a priest, son of a high priest, kill me first, so that I do not have to witness the death of my companion."

J. And the other [Simeon] said, "I am the patriarch, son of the patriarch, kill me first, so that I do not have to witness the death of my companion."

K. He said to him, "Cast lots." They cast lots, and the lot fell on Rabban Simeon b. Gamaliel.

L. The executioner took the sword and cut off his head.

M. R. Ishmael b. Elisha took it and held it in his breast and wept and cried out: "O holy mouth, O faithful mouth, O mouth that brought forth beautiful gems, precious stones and pearls! Who has laid you in the dust, who has filled your mouth with dirt and dust?

N. "Concerning you Scripture says, 'Awake, O sword, against my shepherd and against the man who is near to me'" (Zech. 13:7).

O. He had not finished speaking before the executioner took the sword and cut off his head.

P. Concerning them Scripture says, "My wrath shall wax hot, and I will kill you with the sword, and your wives shall be widows, and your children fatherless" (Ex. 22:23).

The story establishes the tension at the outset: why do we die as do sinners? This question is resolved in the colloquy at C–H, at which Act I concludes. The second act has the sages appeal to the executioner to spare the one the sight of the martyrdom of the other (I–L). The third and final component has Ishmael's lament: the mouth that taught the Torah will be avenged. The sage who dies in peace addresses his lessons to the Torah community: the decline of the great tradition because of the failure of the sages and their disciples. The sage who dies as a martyr teaches a lesson of hope to Israel at large: God will ultimately exact justice of those who sin by persecuting Israel, just as God exacts strict justice even for pride.

The materials we have reviewed, with their beginnings, middles, and endings; their actions, whether described or merely implied within verbal exchanges; and their tensions and resolutions, follow the pattern familiar within the earlier categories. That positive trait is joined to a negative one: just as before, the story about a sage never serves to prove a proposition concerning the meaning of a verse of Scripture. The subject-matter—the story about the sage, hero of the oral Torah, as distinct from the hero of the written Torah— does generate its own narrative literary conventions, which differ from those of stories about scriptural figures, and a few remarkably cogent propositions do emerge from stories on sages. To these we now turn.

The Propositions of Sage-Stories

We want to know what, if any, points emerge from stories about sages and how these propositions relate to those of stories about scriptural heroes.

The following propositions emerge in the stories about the sage's origin:

1. VI:V.1. Great Torah authorities began their study of the Torah in their mature years.

2. VI:V.1. Patience and persistence in the study of the Torah will guarantee progress in learning.

3. VI:V.1. Words of the Torah will wear down the heart and produce repentance. It follows that the purpose of studying the Torah is to purify the heart and produce repentance.

4. VI:V.1. Study of the Torah requires systematic analytical inquiry, explanation of detail in terms of a whole, not merely repetition of what is written down. Aqiba is the model of the analytical mode.

5. VI:V.2. This is not a story, and its point is already made by the story at hand: patience and persistence wear down the rock.

6. VI:V.3. This is not a story, and it contains no point.

7. VI:V.4–5 plus 6. People should study even though they are poor. Wives who make it possible for their husbands to study the Torah will be richly rewarded.

8. VI:VI.1–3. One may begin study of the Torah in mature years.

9. VI:VI.1–3. A person who gains a bad odor because of devotion to study of the Torah will become famous in the study of the Torah.

10. VI:VI.4. One who cuts his ties to his family because of devotion to study of the Torah wins out in the end over his siblings and inherits his family's property; more generally: Sacrifice in the study of the Torah produces a reward.

Stories on a common theme yield a single message: People may begin study of the Torah at any point in life, and if they work hard, they will achieve success, riches, and fame. If they cut off their ties from their family, they will end up inheriting their family's estate, and wives who tolerate their long absences and support them and their families will share in their success, riches, and fame. It follows that the stories on the common theme of the origins of great masters, as preserved in The Fathers According to Rabbi Nathan, respond to the problem of the breakup of the families of mature men who choose to study the Torah by promising success, riches, and fame. The lesson of the origins of the great masters is to give up home and family in favor of the Torah.

The stories about patience yield the following propositions on how the knowledge of the Torah affects the personality and character of the sage, and so make their own cogent point.

1. XV:IV.1. One should be patient even when put to the test. Extraordinary patience is the mark of the great sage.

2.   XV:V.1. The oral Torah comes down from the ancestors and has to
be accepted in good faith, since it is only by tradition that the Torah, written
or oral, is to be received and understood.

3.   XV:V.2. The great sage is patient, and through patience and reason
wins people to the Torah. The sage who is impatient drives people away from
the Torah and deprives them of eternal life.

4.   XII:XIII.1. One who reads the Torah but does not serve as a disciple
of the sages does not understand the requirements of the Torah and makes
errors that will cost him his life.

5.   XLI:II.1. If one does not spend his time studying the Torah, he is
punished by sickness.

6.   XLI:III.1. A sage must treat other people with unfailing respect: One
should always be as soft as a reed and not as tough as a cedar.

We may state the point of these stories in a simple sentence: The sage
learns through study of the Torah—which is accomplished solely by service
to the master—to be patient, affable, and forebearing. The stories follow diverse patterns, but overall the literary conventions we outlined earlier apply
here as well: these stories have a beginning, middle, and end; they rest not
only on verbal exchanges but on described or implicit action; they unfold from
a point of tension and conflict to a clear resolution; and they rarely invoke a
verse of Scripture. Thus, where a distinct subject comes into view, the narrator of sage-stories nonetheless follows a fixed set of narrative conventions.
The point of differentiation among stories derives from the contrast of their
topics; stories about sages are told in one way, and those about Scripture and
its heroes in another.

The stories we have reviewed under "Sagacity and History" establish the
following propositions.

1.   IV:VI.1. The sage had the foresight that would have prevented the
destruction of the Temple. All that was required was to give the gentile monarch a sign of submission.

2.   IV:VI.1. The sage had the foresight to know that Vespasian would
be made emperor. This he learned through his deep knowledge of the Torah.

3.   VI:IV.1. The sage had the foresight to plan even before the destruction of Jerusalem for the life of Israel afterward. That life would involve study
of the Torah by master and disciples, the saying of prayer, and the fulfilment
of religious duties.

4.   VI:IV.1. Israel and Rome weigh in the balance against one another,
the emperor and the sage.

5.   XVII:III.1. The destruction of the Temple placed Israel under the
rule of despicable nations.

6.   VI:IX.1. Divine grace will produce a miracle for someone who takes
risks in behalf of the community at large. This is not a Torah-study story, and
it is not told about a sage.

7.   VI:X.2–3. This story is not told about a sage, but its point is like

those of sage-stories: the rich man had foresight and showed generosity, but the zealots ruined things.

These propositions yield a simple point: Through knowledge of the Torah, the sage leads Israel to the age to come, when Israel will supplant Rome. The leadership of zealots on the battlefield led to the destruction of the Temple, the senseless destruction of the food supply of Jerusalem, and the calamity that overtook Israel. The leadership of the sages, armed with foresight and backed by God, will show the right way. The fresh topic—the sages and history—does not require the invention of modes of narrative different from those that served to deal with the sages' origins and their correct personality. We find the same narrative conventions as before.

The lessons imparted by the stories of the sage's death follow.

1. XIV:IV.1. The oral Torah is the true source of comfort.

2. XXV:II.1. When a sage dies, he appears before an incorruptible judge; moreover, he does not know for sure what his fate will be.

3. XXV:III.1–XXV:IV.1–5. The sage dies in full command of his faculties, giving rulings on questions of the Torah, teaching disciples, assured of knowledge of the future by reason of his mastery of the Torah. The sage at death underlines his place in a chain of tradition, having learned from his teachers and handed on to his students knowledge of the Torah. But the tradition progressively diminishes, as the failure of each generation to acquire mastery of the Torah equivalent to that of its predecessor exacts a cost through neglect and forgetfulness of the Torah. The disciples have therefore to bear a heavy burden of guilt for neglect of the Torah that they should acquire from their master, just as he bears that same burden of guilt for not learning what he should have learned.

4. XXXVIII:V.2. Sages suffer the death penalty for the sin of pride.

5. XXXVIII:V.2. Sages are martyred but know that, in due course, God will punish those who have sinned against them.

The death scenes yield a variety of lessons, since they present nuanced not merely conventional portraits, and they include a measure of action; they are not merely set-piece speeches. I take the main point of these scenes to be God's perfect justice. This emerges at Nos. 2, 4, and 5, but cannot be excluded even from the story of Eliezer's death, No. 3. The historical events represented by sages' deaths, therefore, are so portrayed as to bring the comfort of the conviction of divine vengeance for injustice and divine faithfulness in exacting justice on sinners and evildoers—Israelites and gentiles alike. For if the sage is punished for mere pride, there can be no limit to the matter—just as Yohanan b. Zakkai says.

Thus the subject-matter of these stories—sages—does indeed generate its own narrative conventions, which differ from those that guide writers of Scripture-stories, and these conventions apply to all types of stories about sages. Do we find cogent propositions emerging from sage-stories? Yes, and these propositions intersect, whether the story concerns the origin of the sage, his particular sagacity, his role in the history of Israel, or his death. The propositions that emerge from the stories presented under the heading "Sagacity and History" are of special importance, and the following section examines them in greater depth.

Names Not Celebrated, Stories Not Told

Our comparison of The Fathers and The Fathers According to Rabbi Nathan requires that we take up one final question: Do we detect differences in the repertoire of names, as much as in types of writing and modes of cogent discourse? Indeed we do. The Fathers lists authorities ignored or treated as inconsequential in the later work, just as The Fathers According to Rabbi Nathan covers themes and tells stories without counterpart in the earlier work. The Fathers pays equal attention to names of authorities associated with the patriarchate: Gamaliel and Judah the Patriarch, for instance. The Fathers According to Rabbi Nathan, in contrast, invests little energy in portraying authorities of the patriarchate. Within the repertoire of names of The Fathers and The Fathers According to Rabbi Nathan, considerable selectivity has dictated the choices: Hillel (with Shammai), then Yohanan ben Zakkai and his disciples, Aqiba, Eleazar b. Azariah, Ishmael b. Elisha, and Simeon b. Gamaliel. Among the names on the list of chapter 1, only Hillel provides the occasion for storytelling. Of the names associated with the patriarchate—The Fathers 2:1–7—not one finds a place in our stories. Among names we identify as patriarchal—Gamaliel, Judah, and Judah's sons—only one, Simeon b. Gamaliel, makes an appearance, and then with the confession of guilt for the sin of pride. We may therefore state that when choosing names for celebration, the authorship of the stories gave preference to heroic figures of the sages' estate and neglected their counterparts in the patriarchal administration.

    That observation takes on still greater import when we recall the systematic neglect of Rabbi's comments on sages. The authorship of the Fathers According to Rabbi Nathan not only does not comment on The Fathers 2A:1, it also ignores everything that follows, up to the appearance of Yohanan b. Zakkai at The Fathers 2:8, except for sayings of a Hillel, imputed to The Hillel. The movement from one document to the next bears a polemic conveyed in the selection of authorities whose statements merit sustained attention. The Fathers According to Rabbi Nathan takes slight interest in the patriarchate and treats as authoritative the sayings of figures to whom the later sages traced their intellectual (and supernatural) origins. The proposition that I find implicit is that the sage and not the patriarch takes precedence in the life of the Torah. Of still greater interest, the authorship of The Fathers According to Rabbi Nathan has presented a set of propositions that would have surprised the authorship of The Fathers. The stories *not* told by the earlier authorship but told by the later one present evidence of a considerable shift in viewpoint and perspective. That fact constitutes a principal result of the comparisons and analyses I have now worked out.

We earlier identified topics covered in The Fathers According to Rabbi Nathan. We now ask which of these topics and propositions identified as particular to The Fathers According to Rabbi Nathan receive amplification through stories, and which do not. To review: topics in The Fathers According to Rabbi Nathan that lack all counterpart in restatement and development in the Fathers make the following points:

1. One should study the Torah, and other things will take care of themselves—a claim of a more supernatural character than the one in The Fathers.

2. Sages seem to be portrayed as supernatural figures rather than mainly as political leaders, eager to conciliate and reconcile the other.

3. The later document provides to the teleological question an eschatological answer altogether lacking in the earlier one.

This third point requires a brief reprise. The definitive category is social and therefore national, raising the issue not of the private person but of holy Israel, not of private life and destiny but national history and the future of Israel. The concern then is what will happen to the nation in time to come, meaning the coming age, not the coming life of the resurrection. The Fathers According to Rabbi Nathan is consistent and one-sided when it focuses not so much on the individual as on the nation, and promises not the life of the world to come so much as the coming age, the Messianic time. The framers of the Fathers According to Rabbi Nathan redefine the teleology at hand and focus it upon historical and social categories, rather than those that emerge from the life and death of the individual.

The following points strike me as critical:

1. The sage is now—in the Fathers According to Rabbi Nathan—not judge and teacher alone but also a supernatural figure.

2. Study of the Torah in preference to making a living promises freedom from the conditions of natural life; that is, it creates a new family, new father and brothers, in the place of the old.

3. Israel, the holy people seen as a supernatural social entity, takes center stage, with the sage as leading actor in behalf of Israel.

Now, the stories we have reviewed turn out to fit these propositions quite symmetrically. Specifically, stories about sages represent the study of the Torah as the source for success, riches, and fame. The sage stands at the center of the national life and fate; his knowledge of the Torah gives him foresight. The sage marks the transition of Israel from this age to the coming age, weighing in the balance against the emperor just as Israel and Rome take opposite sides of the scale. To state the matter simply: the stories about the sage make in detail the very points that, in general, mark the message and propositions that are specific to The Fathers According to Rabbi Nathan.

In particular, the stories cited under "Sagacity and History" exhibit truly original statements, which lie utterly beyond the imagination of the framers of The Fathers. The sage had the foresight that would have prevented the destruction of the Temple. All that was required was to give the gentile monarch a sign of submission. The sage had the foresight to know that Vespasian would be made emperor. This he learned through his deep knowledge of the Torah. The sage had the foresight to plan even before the destruction of Jerusalem for the life of Israel afterward. That life would involve study of the Torah by master and disciples, the saying of prayer, and the fulfillment of religious duties. Israel and Rome weigh in the balance against one another, the emperor and the sage. The destruction of the Temple placed Israel under the rule of despicable nations. Divine grace will produce a miracle for someone who takes risks in behalf of the community at large.

In these propositions of The Fathers According to Rabbi Nathan, we move far from the range of topics treated in The Fathers, for sayings in that document do not allude to the destruction of the Temple and say nothing about Rome. The stories in our document that are not told in The Fathers begin in that simple fact. Were we to rely upon The Fathers for knowledge of the world in which Israel lived, the circumstances in which the sayings before us were to be carried out, we should know nothing whatsoever. The burden and message of the stories are twofold: (1) the centrality of the sage and his Torah in the supernatural life of Israel, and (2) the critical role of the sage in the movement of the age from this world, with Rome in command, to the coming age, the time of Israel and sages. Where the story tells us something that sayings have not told us—and cannot have told us—it concerns history. The medium fits the message: story carries the burden of history. The question is, Do these stories in particular bear the distinctive messages I have identified? We turn now to broader questions of comparison and contrast.

Part Three

Comparisons and Contrasts:
The Story in The Fathers According to Rabbi Nathan in Canonical Context

6

These Stories in Particular: The Stories in The Fathers According to Rabbi Nathan in Comparison to Their Use in Other Compositions

The Canonical Context

We cannot assume that the authorship of The Fathers According to Rabbi Nathan has a unique claim to have used stories in particular or narratives in general to set forth its propositions. For if others told stories about these topics in these ways, then the allegation that our authorship has made a distinctive choice to deliver a message particular to itself comes under doubt. We may well take the position that these writers did more or less what everybody was doing in their time and place (whenever, wherever, that may have been). Then the movement from The Fathers to The Fathers According to Rabbi Nathan, taking place upon the royal road of narrative and through the vehicle of the sage-story, would turn out to be merely adventitious and not of weighty consequence. So the meaning of all things depends, as it should, upon context, which imparts consequence to mere fact.

We must therefore first compare (in this chapter) the discrete *stories* before us to their counterparts (if they have parallels) in other compilations and then compare the *document* before us to other documents in the canon of the Judaism of the Dual Torah (chapter 7). For only through comparing stories, on the one side, and documents, on the other, will we find out what we do not yet know: whether these stories in particular serve, as others do not, and whether our document serves, as others do not, to impart to The Fathers According to Rabbi Nathan the importance that I claim for it. That is to say, do stories enter the Judaism of the Dual Torah in particular through the stories told in our document? And, further, are the messages carried by this medium, which is new to our document in its canonical context, unique to that document? These questions frame what is logically the next (and final) stage in our inquiry.

The first possibility among the two at issue here gives rise to the following question: Do these stories appear only here? If so, the shift from the earlier to the later document takes on one set of meanings; if not, then different conclusions must be drawn. Specifically, if the stories added by the authorship of the later document prove unique (within the canon) to that document, we learn that the shift in the contents from The Fathers to The Fathers According to Rabbi Nathan took place specifically through the composition of stories to make distinctive points that could best be made in the form of those stories. Then, using The Fathers According to Rabbi Nathan as the case, we learn that stories entered canonical Judaism because the medium of the story was found most suitable for delivering a message of a particular sort.

The question that signals the second possibility is this: Are the stories shared with other documents? If the bulk of the stories prove commonplaces, to my mind it would follow that the resort to the story and its message that characterizes the movement from the earlier to the later writing forms part of a larger shift in canonical writings overall. In that case our document would testify to something beyond itself. Within its own framework, the movement from The Fathers to The Fathers According to Rabbi Nathan would exemplify the development of the story as a medium for discourse, but the document by itself would bear no particular weight.

Accordingly, what we want to know is whether, and how, the particular stories before us make a difference. Clearly, the use of stories as a general policy of the formation of a document did matter to the later authorship, which resorted to literary genres earlier neglected. While the authorship of The Fathers was content to name an authority and say what he said, assuming that the saying by itself bore the full burden of meaning, the compilers and editors of The Fathers According to Rabbi Nathan made two complementary decisions: first, to tell stories about the names in hand, and second, to deliver messages not alone through the received media—the well-framed apothegm, the parable, or the exegetical exercise—but also through the story.

Stories That Matter

How shall we identify those stories that mattered a great deal to the authorship of The Fathers According to Rabbi Nathan? They must be the ones that bear the principal burden of the later document. Let us review what is fresh and important in The Fathers According to Rabbi Nathan:

1. One should study the Torah, and other things will take care of themselves—a claim in behalf of Torah study of a more supernatural character than the one in The Fathers.

2. Sages seem to be portrayed more as supernatural figures than as the political leaders, eager to conciliate and reconcile the other, that The Fathers supposes them to be.

3. The later document, through its stories and sayings, imparts to the teleological question an eschatological answer altogether lacking in the earlier one.

Among the stories reviewed in the preceding chapter, therefore, the following carry the message that is original and paramount in The Fathers According to Rabbi Nathan:

1. VI:IV–VI. Origins of Aqiba and Eliezer. These stories bear the message that Torah study imposes new, supernatural relationships on existing, natural ones.

2. XV:IV–V. The patience of Hillel; the Dual Torah. These stories contribute the important points that the sage is characterized by patience and that people have to rely on tradition mediated by sages as to the validity of the oral Torah.

3. XII:XIII. Not studying the Torah as a disciple leads to misinformation, which can produce the death penalty. The stress on discipleship in Torah study is characteristic.

4. XLI:III. Simeon b. Eleazar improperly treated an ugly man. He apologized and gave a public address on the importance of being as soft as a reed and not as tough as a cedar, that is, malleable. The trait of the sage is amiability.

5. IV:V–X. The sage and the destruction of the Temple; the sage as counterpart of the emperor; the destruction and deeds of loving-kindness as surrogate. The sage plays the critical role in principal historical events.

6. XVII:III. Yohanan ben Zakkai and the daughter of Naqdimon b. Gurion. Song 1:8. The sage interprets verses of Scripture in light of current historical events.

7. XIV:IV. Death of Yohanan b. Zakkai's son. Comfort comes not from scriptural counterparts but from teaching of the oral Torah.

8. XXV:II–IV (and XIX:II–III). Deaths of Yohanan ben Zakkai and Eliezer. Attitude of masters at death.

9. XXXVIII:V. Martyrdom of Simeon b. Gamaliel and Ishmael. Simeon admitted to sin of pride. Sage should not be proud and is punished if he is. God takes seriously the most minor failing of a sage.

Three questions define the next step in our inquiry. First, are these stories unique to The Fathers According to Rabbi Nathan, or do they occur in prior documents? Second, if the stories do not appear earlier, are there parallel or counterpart stories about the same authorities, or are these essentially new stories without precedent as to type? If we know that a story in the later document is fresh and without parallel or precedent, we may credit its use to the authorship of The Fathers According to Rabbi Nathan. Their selection of the story (whether or not they made it up, and that we cannot know) then forms part of a deliberate statement that is unique to their document, not a routine reversion to conventional materials and themes. Third, if the stories do appear earlier, then what is the relationship of earlier versions to the ones before us? In asking this question, we move from assessing the statement of The Fathers According to Rabbi Nathan to placing that document in its broader canonical context. If a story appears in documents generally thought to precede the one before us, we may assess what the present authorship has done to that story— added, deleted, revised—in making it suitable for use in their document.

Old or New?

We begin with a brief survey of the available parallel versions of the stories before us. We turn for guidance to the parallels to the apparatus supplied by Schechter in his edition of The Fathers According to Rabbi Nathan. In addition, for materials on Hillel, Yohanan ben Zakkai, and Eliezer, I refer to my *The Rabbinic Traditions about the Pharisees before 70* (Leiden: E. J. Brill, 1971), chaps. 1–3; *Development of a Legend. Studies on the Traditions Concerning Yohanan ben Zakkai* (Leiden: E. J. Brill, 1970); and *Eliezer ben Hyrcanus. The Tradition and the Man,* Vol. 1 (Leiden: E. J. Brill, 1973), chaps. 1–2. These studies cover all of the figures before us except for Aqiba and the second-century figures: Simeon b. Gamaliel, Ishmael, and Simeon b. Eleazar.

1.   *VI:IV–VI. Origins of Aqiba and Eliezer*

Aqiba. Schechter cites a number of pertinent passages, which we shall briefly review. What they demonstrate is that in fact our story has no parallels. B. Ket. 62b (with parallel at b. Ned. 50a–b, b. Shab. 59b) has a quite distinct story about Aqiba's beginnings; a paraphrase follows.

> Aqiba was the shepherd of Ben Kalba Sabua. The master's daughter fell in love with him. She became betrothed to him in secret and sent him off to study the Torah. He went and studied for twelve years, coming back with twelve thousand disciples. He heard someone say to his betrothed wife, "How long will you live like a widow?" She replied that, so far as she was concerned, he should study another twelve years, which he went and did. When he came back at the end of that period, she kissed his feet. His disciples were going to push her away, when Aqiba said to them, "Leave her alone, mine and yours are hers." Her father heard a great man had come to town and went to him and asked him to invalidate his vow that had forbidden his daughter from benefitting from his property, because she had become betrothed to the absent scholar. Aqiba said, "Would you have taken the vow if you had known that he would become a great man?" The father replied, "Had he known even a small amount of the Torah, I would not have made the vow." Aqiba said, "I am the man." Ben Kalba Sabua fell and kissed his feet and gave him half his estate.

The points of contact with our story are few and far between. Despite the interjection of details important in Eliezer's story—Ben Kalba Sabua, and his vow and retraction—we have to regard as essentially independent the story of Aqiba's origins in The Fathers According to Rabbi Nathan.

B. Ned. 50a–b includes the detail about the golden tiara. The couple lived together in poverty, and Aqiba told her, "If only I could afford it, I would present you with a golden tiara of Jerusalem." The sequence of stories provides an account of six incidents out of which Aqiba became rich, of which the estate of his father-in-law was only one. Y. Shab. 6:1:X.D, the same as B. Shab. 59b, refers to the golden tiara that Aqiba gave his wife. Sifré Dt. 357 refers to Aqiba's studying the Torah for forty years. The upshot is that there is no parallel to the story told in our document.

Eliezer. The story of Eliezer's beginnings, in contrast to that of Aqiba's, does have a close counterpart. The available version covers the main points of the story we have in The Fathers According to Rabbi Nathan, although it contributes a considerable component that fits the interests of the framers of the document in which the story occurs. Specifically, it identifies the theme of Eliezer's famous address.

Genesis Rabbah 42:1

1. A. "It came to pass in the days of Amraphel, [king of Shinar, Arioch, king of Ellasar, Chedorlaomer, king of Elam, and Tidal, king of Goiim]" (Gen. 14:1):

B. R. Joshua in the name of R. Levi opened discourse [by citing the following verse]: "The wicked have drawn out the sword" (Ps. 37:15).

C. The illustrative case concerns R. Eliezer. His brothers were ploughing on level ground, and he was ploughing on hilly ground. His cow fell and broke its leg. But it was to his advantage that his cow had broken its leg. [For] he fled and went to R. Yohanan b. Zakkai.

D. He was eating clods of dirt [having no money to buy food] until his mouth produced a bad odor. They went and told Rabban Yohanan b. Zakkai, "R. Eliezer's breath stinks."

E. He said to him, "Just as the odor of your mouth stank on account of your studying the Torah, so may the fragrance of your learning pervade the world from one end to the other."

The Fathers According to Rabbi Nathan

VI:VI.1. A. How did R. Eliezer ben Hyrcanus begin [his Torah study]?

B. He had reached the age of twenty-two years and had not yet studied the Torah. One time he said, "I shall go and study the Torah before Rabban Yohanan ben Zakkai."

C. His father Hyrcanus said to him, "You are not going to taste a bit of food until you have ploughed the entire furrow."

D. He got up in the morning and ploughed the entire furrow.

E. They say that that day was Friday. He went and took a meal with his father-in-law.

F. And some say that he tasted nothing from the sixth hour on Friday until the sixth hour on Sunday.

VI:VI.2. A. On the way he saw a rock. He picked it up and took it and put it into his mouth.

B. And some say that what he picked up was cattle dung.

C. He went and spent the night at his hostel.

VI:VI.3. A. He went and entered study session before Rabban Yohanan ben Zakkai in Jerusalem.

B. Since a bad odor came out of his mouth, Rabban Yohanan ben Zakkai said to him, "Eliezer my son, have you taken a meal today?"

C. He shut up.

D. He asked him again, and he shut up again.

E. He sent word and inquired at his hostel, and asked, "Has Eliezer eaten anything with you?"

F. They sent word to him, "We thought that he might be eating with my lord."

G. He said, "For my part, I thought that he might be eating with you. Between me and you, we should have lost R. Eliezer in the middle."

H. He said to him, "Just as the odor of your mouth has gone forth, so will a good name in the Torah go forth for you."

F. After some days his father came up to disinherit him from his property, and he found him sitting and expounding a lesson with the great figures of the realm in session before him, namely, Ben Sisit Hakkesset, Nicodemus son of Gurion, and Ben Kalba Sabua.

G. He was giving an exposition of this verse, as follows: " 'The wicked have drawn out the sword and have bent the bow' (Ps. 37:14) refers to Amraphael and his allies.

H. " 'To cast down the poor and needy' (Ps. 37:14) refers to Lot.

I. " 'To slay such as are upright in the way' (Ps. 37:14) refers to Abraham.

J. " 'Their sword shall enter into their own heart' (Ps. 37:15) in line with this verse: 'And he divided his forces against them by night, he and his servants, and routed them' " (Gen. 14:15).

K. His father said to him, "My son, I came up here only to disinherit

VI:VI.4.   A. Hyrcanus, his father, heard that he was studying the Torah with Rabban Yohanan ben Zakkai. He decided, "I shall go and impose on Eliezer my son a vow not to derive benefit from my property."

B. They say that that day Rabban Yohanan ben Zakkai was in session and expounding [the Torah] in Jerusalem, and all the great men of Israel were in session before him. He heard that he was coming. He set up guards, saying to them, "If he comes to take a seat, do not let him."

C. He came to take a seat and they did not let him.

D. He kept stepping over people and moving forward until he came to Ben Sisit Hakkesset and Naqdimon b. Gurion and Ben Kalba Sabua. He sat among them, trembling.

E. They say on that day Rabban Yohanan ben Zakkai looked at R. Eliezer, indicating to him, "Cite an appropriate passage and give an exposition."

you from my property. Now, lo, all of my property is handed over to you as a gift [and not by the law of inheritance, which would not allow me to give you everything]."

L. He said to him, "So far as I am concerned, the property falls into the category of *herem* [and is forbidden to me]. Rather, divide it equally among my brothers."

F. He said to him, "I cannot cite an appropriate passage."

G. He urged him, and the other disciples urged him.

H. He went and cited an opening passage and expounded matters the like of which no ear had ever heard.

I. And at every word that he said, Rabban Yohanan ben Zakkai arose and kissed him on his head and said, "My lord, Eliezer, my lord, you have taught us truth."

J. As the time came to break up, Hyrcanus his father stood up and said, "My lords, I came here only to impose a vow on my son, Eliezer, not to derive benefit from my possessions. Now all of my possessions are given over to Eliezer my son, and all my other sons are disinherited and will have no share in them."

The differences between the two versions do not seem to bear any obvious message. The one significant variation is that Genesis Rabbah's story knows the verse on which Eliezer gave his exposition, while that item is not important in our document; but of course the reason that the story occurs in Genesis Rabbah is that one item. Genesis Rabbah covers the preliminaries somewhat more rapidly, makes more sense about Eliezer's leaving than do the father's instructions about finishing the furrow, and makes less ado about the stinking breath. The Fathers According to Rabbi Nathan Nos. 1–3 work on that one item, while it is rapidly passed over in Genesis Rabbah's version: an apothegm that is part of the conventional repertoire, but not the main event. Genesis Rabbah Gff. then are not known in the version of The Fathers According to Rabbi Nathan. The disinheritance story runs pretty much the same way, serving as climax in both, but the elegant conclusion at Genesis Rabbah L is lacking in our document.

The two documents have used essentially the same outline, but emphasize different sets of details. I prefer the version of our document, because of its ample account of the colloquy surrounding the public address, and because of its entirely appropriate disinterest in precisely what Eliezer said, which distracts from the main point. If I had to make a choice as to which is the later and better worked out version, it would surely be ours. If we knew for certain that a better-developed statement is later than an abbreviated one, we could conclude that our document in this matter comes later than Genesis Rabbah, hence beyond ca. 400–450. Later revisions, however, can yield an abbreviated, streamlined version of a story, and I cannot explain why the framers of an allegedly later version would omit what they did, unless, in their judgment, that detail detracted from what they wished to stress. So, in all, the matter seems to me indeterminate, with only one firm conclusion possible: a common outline has served the two authorships. In any event the version in our document goes over familiar themes, and we cannot claim that the genre of stories about the origins of sages by itself is the contribution of our authorship.

2.   *XV:IV–V. The Patience of Hillel; the Dual Torah.*

The Bavli has the same story as our document, with no discernible shifts in message. Differences between our version of the story of Hillel's patience and Shammai's impatience and that at B. Shab. 30b–31a are difficult to find. The following composite shows how the two documents overlap. The changes in the version in the Bavli (Talmud of Babylonia) are indicated in boldface type; materials in The Fathers According to Rabbi Nathan but not in the Bavli are in italics.

XV:IV.1.   A. What characterized the patience of Hillel the Elder?

B. They tell the following case, concerning two people, who went and made a bet with one another for four hunded *zuz.*

C. They stipulated, "Whoever can go and infuriate Hillel will get the four hundred *zuz.*"

D. One of them went [to try]. That day was a Friday, toward nightfall, and Hillel was washing his hair. The man came and knocked on the door, saying, "Where is Hillel, where is Hillel?"

E. Hillel wrapped himself up in his cloak and came to meet him. He said to him, "Speak."

F. **[In B. Shab. the first item is: why are the heads of the Babylonians round?]**

He said to him, "Why are the eyes of the people of Palmyra [Tadmor] bleary?"

G. He said to him, "Because they live in the sands of the desert [B. Shab. lacks:] *and the winds blow and scatter the sands into their eyes. Therefore their eyes are bleary.*"

H. He went and waited a while and came back and knocked on the door.

I. He said, "Where is Hillel, where is Hillel?"

J. He wrapped himself up in his cloak and came out.

K. He said to him, "My son, what do you need?"

L. He said to him, "I need to ask a matter of law."

M. He said to him, "Go ahead."

N. He said to him, "Why are the feet of the Africans flat?"

O. He said to him, "Because they live by swamps, [B. Shab. lacks:] *and every day walk in water, therefore their feet are flat.*"

[B. Shab.:] "I have many questions to ask, but fear that you may become angry.

Thereupon he robed, sat before him, and said, "Ask all the questions you have to ask."

"Are you the Hillel whom they call the patriarch of Israel?"

"Yes."

"If that is you, may there not be many like you in Israel . . ."

P. The man went his way, waited a while, came back, and knocked on the door.

Q. He said, "Where is Hillel, where is Hillel?"

R. He wrapped himself in his cloak and went out.

S. He said to him, "What do you need to ask?"

T. He said to him, "I have to ask a matter of law."

U. He said to him, "Ask." He then wrapped himself in his garment and sat down before him.

V. He said to him, "What do you need to ask?"

W. He said to him, "Is this the way princes reply? May people like you not become many in Israel."

X. He said to him, "God forbid! Watch yourself. What do you want?"

Y. [B. Shab. 30b–31a places this at the beginning, with slightly different wording:] He said to him, "On what account are the heads of the Babylonians long?"

Z. He said to him, "My son, you have asked an important 'law.' It is because over there they do not have smart midwives. [B. Shab. lacks:] *When the baby is born, the ones who deal with it are slave-boys and slave-girls. Therefore their heads are long. But here, where we have smart midwives; when a baby is born, they raise it in a cradle and rub its head. Therefore their heads are round."*

AA. He said to him, "You have cost me four hundred *zuz.*"

BB. He said to him, "Hillel is worth your losing four hundred *zuz* without Hillel's losing his temper."

XV:V.1. A. [B. Shab. 31a lacks:] *What characterized the impatience of Shammai the Elder?*

B. They say there was the case of a man who stood before Shammai. He said to him, "My lord, how many Torahs do you have?"

C. He said to him, "Two, one in writing, one memorized."

D. He said to him, "As to the one in writing, I believe you. As to the memorized one, I do not believe you."

E. He rebuked him and threw him out.

F. He came before Hillel. He said to him, "My lord, how many Torahs were given?"

G. He said to him, "Two, one in writing, one memorized."

H. He said to him, "As to the one in writing, I believe you. As to the memorized one, I do not believe you."

I. He said to him, "My son, sit."

J. He wrote for him, *Alef, bet.*

K. He said to him, "What is this?"

L. He said to him, "An *alef.*"

M. He said to him, "This is not an *alef* but a *bet.*"

N. He said to him, "What is this?

O. He said to him, "*Bet.*"

P. He said to him, "This is not a *bet* but a *gimmel.*"

Q. He said to him, "How do you know that this is an *alef* and this is a *bet* and this a *gimmel?* But that is what our ancestors have handed over to us—the tradition that this is an *alef,* this a *bet,* this a *gimmel.* Just as you have accepted this teaching in good faith, so accept the other in good faith."

[B. Shab. 31a adds:] **It further happened that a certain pagan came to Shammai and said to him, "Convert me on condition that you teach me the whole Torah while I am standing on one foot."**

He threw him up with the builder's cubit in his hand.

He went to Hillel, who converted him, saying to him, "What is hateful to you, do not do to your neighbor. That is the whole Torah, all the rest is commentary. Go and learn."

XV:V.2.   A. There was the case of a gentile who was passing behind a synagogue and heard a child reciting in Scripture: "This is the clothing which they shall make: a breast plate, ephod, and robe" (Ex. 28:4).

B. He came before Shammai and said to him, "My lord, all this honor—for whom is it designated?"

C. He said to him, "It is for the high priest who stands and carries out the service at the altar."

D. He said to him, "Convert me on the stipulation that you make me high priest so that I may carry out the service at the altar."

E. He said to him, "Is there no priesthood in Israel, and do we not have high priests to stand and carry out the acts of service at the altar assigned to the high priest, so that a mere convert who has come only with his staff and wallet may come and take up the service of the high priest?"

F. He threw him out.

G. He came before Hillel and said to him, "My lord, convert me, on the stipulation that you make me high priest so that I may carry out the service at the altar."

H. He said to him, "Sit, and I shall tell you something [of the rules of the office you propose to enter]. For if someone proposes to greet a mortal king, is it not logical that he should learn the rules of going in and coming out?"

I. He said to him, "Yes."

J. [B. Shab. 31a lacks:] *"You, who wish to greet the King of kings of kings, the Holy One, blessed be he, surely should learn how to enter the house of the Holy of Holies, how to set up the lamps, how to offer an offering on the altar, how to arrange the table, how to set out the wood."*

K. He said to him, *"Do what you think appropriate."*

L. He first wrote for him, Alef, bet, *and the man learned the letters.*

M. Then he presented the *Torah of the Priests* [the books of Leviticus and Numbers], and the man went on learning the words until he came to the verse, "The non-priest who draws near [the altar] shall die" (Num. 1:51).

[B. Shab., 31a adds:] **He said to him, "To whom does this verse apply?"**

He said to him, "Even to King David of Israel."

N. The proselyte constructed an argument a fortiori concerning himself: if an Israelite, who is called a son of the Omnipresent, and concerning whom the Presence of God has said, "And you shall be mine as a kingdom of priests and a holy people" (Ex. 19:6), nonetheless is subject to Scripture's admonition, "The non-priest who draws near [the altar] shall die" (Num. 1:51), I, who am a mere proselyte, who has come only with my wallet, all the more so!"

[B. Shab. adds:] **Then he went before Shammai and said to him, "Am I then eligible to be a high priest? Is it not written in the Torah, 'And the stranger who comes near shall be put to death'?"**

O. The proselyte was reconciled on his own.

P. He came before Hillel the Elder and said to him, "May all the blessings that are in the Torah rest on your head, for if you had been like Shammai the Elder, you would have wiped me out of this world and of the world to come. Your humility has brought me into this world and the coming one."

Q. [B. Shab. 31a lacks:] *They say that to that proselyte two sons were born. One he called Hillel, and one he called Gamaliel, and they called them Hillel's converts.*

The differences seem to me negligible, although the Bavli has one entire sequence lacking in The Fathers According to Rabbi Nathan. Overall, however, we can have no doubt that before us is a single story, used with slight and minor variations both in the Bavli and in The Fathers According to Rabbi Nathan. I see no clear pattern in the relationships between the two versions. Our version is somewhat more fully spelled out, yet the Bavli's version is somewhat richer in the famous "Do not unto your neighbor" saying. If I had in hand only the materials shared by both documents, I would guess that the framers of the story in our document have tended in some small measure to amplify and expand details in the other. But the same thing can be said, at a number of points, of the Bavli's version's authorship. So we cannot conclude that our version is later than that of the Bavli, nor is it copied verbatim from the Bavli (for if it were, why omit the famous saying about love of neighbor?).

3. *XII:XIII*

Yohanan ben Zakkai: Not studying the Torah as a disciple leads to misinformation, which can produce the death penalty. This story has no parallel.

4. *XLI:III*

Simeon b. Eleazar improperly treated an ugly man. He apologized and gave a public address on the importance of being as soft as a reed and not as tough as a cedar, that is, malleable. This story occurs at B. Ta. 20a–b, as part of a sequence of exegesis of 1 Kgs. 14:15: "For the Lord will smite Israel as a reed is shaken in the water." This yields the notion that a reed is better than a cedar. Then comes our story, with minor changes, which are indicated as before.

XLI:III.1.   A. [B. Ta. 20a–b adds:] **A man should always be soft as a reed and not hard as a cedar.]** There is the case of R. Simeon b. Eleazar, who was coming from the house of his master in Migdal Eder [B. Ta.:] **Migdal Gedor**, riding on an ass and making his way along the sea shore **feeling happy because he had studied a great deal of Torah**. He saw an unusually ugly man, **who said to him, "Peace be to you."** He said to him, "Empty head! What a beast you are! Is it possible that everyone in your town is as ugly as you are?"

B. He said to him, "And what can I do about it? Go to the craftsman who made me and tell him, 'How ugly is that utensil that you have made!'"

C. When R. Simeon b. Eleazar realized that he had sinned, he got off his ass and prostrated himself before the man, saying to him, "I beg you to forgive me."

D. He said to him, "I shall not forgive you until you go to the craftsman who made me and tell him, 'How ugly is that utensil that you have made!'"

E. [B. Ta. lacks:] *He ran after the man for three miles.* The people of the town came out to meet him. They said toward him, "Peace be to you, my lord."

F. He said to them, "Whom do you call, 'my lord'?"

G. They said to him, "The one who is going along after you."

H. He said to them, "If this is a 'my lord,' may there not be many more like him in Israel."

I. They said to him, "God forbid! And what has he done to you?"

J. He said to them, "Thus and so did he do to me."

K. They said to him, "Nonetheless, forgive him [B. Ta.:] **for he is a man much learned in the Torah**."

L. He said to them, "Lo, [B. Ta.:] **for your sakes** I forgive him, on the condition that he not make a habit of acting in that way."

M. On that same day R. Simeon entered the great study-house that was his and gave an exposition: "'One should always be as soft as a reed and not as tough as a cedar.'

N. [B. Ta. lacks:] *"In the case of a reed, all the winds in the world can go on blowing against it, but it sways with them, so that when the winds grow silent, it reverts and stands in its place.* And what is the destiny of a reed? In the end a pen is cut from it with which to write a scroll of the Torah.

O. [B. Ta. lacks:] *"But in the case of a cedar it will not stand in place, but when the south wind blows against it, it uproots the cedar and turns it over. And what is the destiny of a cedar? Foresters come and cut it down and use it to roof houses, and the rest they toss into the fire.*

P. *"On the basis of this fact they have said, 'One should always be as soft as a reed and not as tough as a cedar.'"*

The differences do not seem to me substantial, though there is a slight tendency to introduce the consideration that the sage should be forgiven because he is a Torah master. But our version knows that theme. As in the preceding case, we cannot treat our version as a close copy of that of the Bavli or vice versa.

5. *IV:V–X*

Yohanan ben Zakkai: The sage and the destruction of the Temple; the sage as counterpart of the emperor; the destruction and deeds of loving-kindness as surrogate. On the escape from Jerusalem, we have a sizable story at B. Git. 56a. It comprises a pastiche of materials, intersecting at only a few points with our document's version. For the present purpose a paraphrase of the elements suffices; in the next chapter, we return to the component of the story that deals with Yohanan ben Zakkai in particular. Where the text is cited, it is in the translation of M. Simon, *Gittin,* pp. 254–60. I insert the pertinent parallels of our document's story.

1. Superscription: R. Yohanan said, "What is illustrative of the verse, 'Happy is the man who fears always, but he who hardens his heart shall fall into mischief' (Prov, 28:14)? The destruction of Jerusalem came through Qamsa and Bar Qamsa; the destruction of Tur Malka through a cock and a hen; the destruction of Betar through the shaft of a feather.''

2. Because of the contention between Qamsa and Bar Qamsa the one gave a party and did not invite the other, who came anyhow and got thrown out. The sages present did not object. The injured party informed against them, saying, "The Jews are rebelling against you." This led to the destruction of the Temple.

3. The emperor sent Nero, who produced an omen to indicate the city would fall. He had a boy repeat the verse of Scripture he had just learned, which was Ez. 25:14, predicting that Edom-Rome would destroy the Temple. He became a proselyte, from whom Meir was descended.

4. He sent against them Vespasian. Three wealthy men in the city, Naqdimon, Ben Kalba Sabua, and Ben Sisit Hakkesset were there. Each had enough to keep the city in food, drink, and fuel. The sages in the city wanted to make peace with the Romans. The zealots would not agree, but burned the stores of wheat and barley, so producing a famine.

5. Martha daughter of Boethus, rich woman, could not get food. She ultimately went without her shoes to find food, some dung stuck to her foot, and Yohanan b. Zakkai invoked the verse, "The tender and delicate woman, which would not adventure to set the sole of her foot upon the ground" (Deut. 28:5).

6. Sadoq fasted for forty years so that Jerusalem would not be destroyed.

7. Abba Sikra, head of the zealots, was son of the sister of Yohanan b. Zakkai. Yohanan asked him how long he was going to starve the people to death. The nephew said he could do nothing about it. Yohanan said, "Devise some plan for me to escape; perhaps I shall be able to save a little." Abba Sikra advised him to pretend to be sick, then to die: "Let then your disciples get under your bed, but no others, so that they will not notice that you are still light, since they know that a living being is lighter than a corpse." He did so, and R. Eliezer went under the bier from one side, Joshua from the other. When they reached the door, some men wanted to put a lance through the bier. He said to them, "Shall they say, 'They have pierced their master'?" They wanted to give it a push, and so on. He escaped.

The focus of this story is not on Yohanan b. Zakkai, who takes a subordinate part. It provides a cause for the catastrophe, explaining who brought the Romans down on the Jews. Our document does not answer the question. The story further stresses the zealots' destruction of the stores of food, drink, and fuel; it proceeds to the further story of Martha, yielding the homily on Deut. 28:5, and then turns to Sadoq. Yohanan is introduced only by making him an uncle of the head of the zealots, the principal actors in this version. The initiatives all belong to Abba Sikra, who tells Yohanan what to do. The disciples or Abba Sikra ("he") have the wit to get Yohanan out safely. Yohanan does nothing to impress Vespasian and gets little enough from him. In a word, the

Bavli's version of events does not accomplish what our document's story does, which is to place the sage into the balance as the opposite and equal of the emperor and Israel's principal actor and active intellect. I refer the reader to the text given above and review here only the most important component of the version of B. Git.:

> 8. When he reached the Romans, he said, "Peace to you O king . . ." Vespasian: "Your life is forfeit on two counts, first, I am not a king, and you call me one, and, second, if I am a king, why did you not come until now?" Yohanan: You are a king [plus Is. 11:34]. But Yohanan had no answer to the other question.
>
> 9. A messenger from Rome brought word that he had been made king. Vespasian could not put on his boot, or take off the one already on his foot, because his foot had swelled with pride. Yohanan explained why and solved the problem.
>
> 10. "You can make a request of me." "Give me Yavneh and its sages, the chain of Gamaliel, and physicians to heal Sadoq."

The counterpart in The Fathers According to Rabbi Nathan is as follows.

> K. They opened the ark and he stood before him.
>
> L. He said to him, "Are you Rabban Yohanan ben Zakkai? Indicate what I should give you."
>
> M. He said to him, "I ask from you only Yavneh, to which I shall go, and where I shall teach my disciples, establish prayer [Goldin: a prayer house], and carry out all of the religious duties."
>
> N. He said to him, "Go and do whatever you want."
>
> O. He said to him, "Would you mind if I said something to you."
>
> P. He said to him, "Go ahead."
>
> Q. He said to him, "Lo, you are going to be made sovereign."
>
> R. He said to him, "How do you know?"
>
> S. He said to him, "It is a tradition of ours that the house of the sanctuary will be given over not into the power of a commoner but of a king, for it is said, 'And he shall cut down the thickets of the forest with iron, and Lebanon [which refers to the Temple] shall fall by a mighty one'" (Is. 10:34).
>
> T. People say that not a day, two, or three passed before a delegation came to him from his city indicating that the [former] Caesar had died, and they had voted for him to ascend the throne.

The differences between the two versions of the event are self-evident. The main point of difference from our perspective is that the version of The Fathers According to Rabbi Nathan serves the larger polemic of the document in favor of the supernatural standing and perception of the sage.

It remains to note that two components of our document's story make no appearance in the counterpart at B. Git. 56a–b; these are The Fathers According to Rabbi Nathan IV:V.1–2, given above.

6. *XVII:III*

The story of Yohanan ben Zakkai and the daughter of Naqdimon b. Gurion has a variety of parallels. In the present instance, referring back to

XVII:III.1, given above as our base version, we review the ways in which the other versions lay out the elements of the story, in sequence of redaction of the documents: first, Tosefta to Yerushalmi, then the less certain sequence of Sifré Deut. and Mekhilta, and finally, Bavli. We proceed in paraphrase.

Tos. Ketubot 5:9–10. The daughter of Naqdimon had a large dowry. Eleazar b. Sadoq says he saw her gathering barley from the dung of horses in Acre and cited Song 1:8.

Y. Ketubot 5:11. Martha daughter of Boethus had a large dowry. Eleazar reported seeing her in Acre, and cited Deut. 28:56 and also Song 1:8. This set of course knows nothing of Yohanan.

Sifré Dt. 305. Yohanan was riding on an ass, with disciples following, and saw a girl picking barley from the dung of Arab cattle. When she saw him, she wrapped herself in her hair and asked for food. She reminded him that she was the daughter of Naqdimon and that he had signed her marriage contract. He remembers that, and also that her family would walk to the temple on carpets. Then he cites Song 1:8: "For when Israel does God's will, no one can rule them, but when not, the lowest nation rules them, even their cattle." This seems to me a rearrangement of essentially the same components as occur in our version.

Mekhilta Bahodesh 1:1 (Lauterbach vol. 2, 293–95). Citation of Ez. 40:1, Hag. 1:15, Song 1:8, Deut 28:47–48. Then Yohanan going to Emmaus saw a girl picking. . . . Asked disciples who she was. They: She is Jewish, and the horse belongs to an Arab. Yohanan: Now I know the meaning of Song 1:8. You were unwilling to be subject to God, now are subject to Arabs, to pay the head-tax to the temple, now pay fifteen *sheqels,* repair roads for pilgrims, now do so for the enemy, thus Deut. 28:47–48. The point is stated with great force: You would not do for God what you now do for your enemy. Our document does not make that proposition explicit.

B. Ket. 66b. Yohanan riding ass, going out of Jerusalem. Saw girl as above. When she saw him, she covered herself in her hair and asked for food. He: Whose daughter are you? She: Naqdimon's. What happened to your father's wealth? She cites proverbs, asks why he does not remember her marriage contract. He: I remember. He: "Happy are you O Israel, when you do God's will, no nation can rule you, but when not, even the meanest people, even their cattle."

Clearly there are two versions of the same story: (1) that of T. Ket. and Y. Ket., involving Eleazar b. Sadoq, and (2) the other set, Mekhilta, Sifré Dt., B. Ket. 66b, and our document's, all involving Yohanan.

The closest pair is formed of the Bavli and The Fathers According to Rabbi Nathan. The version of the Mekhilta introduces both Song 1:8 and Deut. 28:47–48; It omits the marriage contract. Sifré Dt. has the marriage contract and then Song 1:8, which is a superior sequence of components. B. Ket. 66b omits the proof texts entirely. Regarding the differences among the four pertinent accounts, it seems to me that the issue is whether the focus of narrative is the exegesis of Scripture or the figure of the sage. The Bavli's version is extreme in focus on the latter, and equally extreme is Sifré Dt.'s and Mekhilta's emphasis on the former. This mishmash of materials leaves no question about the availability of the theme worked out in our document, and clearly the authorship of The Fathers According to Rabbi Nathan has told the story in a way that is not original to them, since the Bavli's version is quite close. The differences should not be missed. The climax at B. Ket. 66b, "Happy are you O Israel," is merely a way-station en route to the story about the wealth of the family and the rich marriage contract of the girl. Shifting the order—Song 1:8, then the marriage contract, as against the Bavli's omission of Song 1:8 altogether—seems to me to mark the Bavli's version as smoother. Its climax does come at the end and make the point most effectively. To generalize, the exegetical compilations focus tales on exegetical problems, and the narrative of the Bavli, on the sage. Our document takes a middle position, siding with the Bavli's preference to focus on the authority, on the one side, but with the exegetical compilations' interest in the proof text, on the other. The joining of Song 1:8 and Deut. 28:47–48 is lost for our document, yet it is the key for the exegetical versions of the narrative. Our document omits the disciples, who have no role. The conversation is dramatic, with the girl identifying herself; she cites the apothegm, and then Yohanan introduces Song 1:8.

7.   *XIV:IV*

The story of the death of Yohanan b. Zakkai's son has no parallel.

8.   *XXV:II–IV (plus XIX:II–III)*

The deaths of Yohanan ben Zakkai and Eliezer occur together, but a separate and different version of Eliezer's also circulated.

Death Scene of Yohanan b. Zakkai and Eliezer b. Hyrcanus. Once more we refer to our document's version, XXV:II.1, and compare it to the ones that appear in other canonical writings. Our document treats Yohanan's death by itself, because it has a quite separate and original picture of Eliezer's. But Yerushalmi Sot. 9:16 (the same as A.Z. 3:1) presents as a single pattern the death scenes of Yohanan and Eliezer, as follows.

> A. R. Jacob b. Idi in the name of R. Joshua b. Levi: "When he was dying, Rabban Yohanan b. Zakkai gave orders, saying, 'Clear out the courtyard on account of the coming corpse-uncleanness and set up a throne for Hezekiah, King of Judah.'"
>
> B. R. Eliezer, his disciple, when dying, gave orders, saying, "Clear out the courtyard on account of coming corpse-uncleanness and prepare a throne for Rabban Yohanan b. Zakkai."

The Yerushalmi's picture of Yohanan's death misses the powerful speech given to him by the authorship of our document, focusing only upon a detail that, in The Fathers According to Rabbi Nathan, appears tacked on. We cannot regard as totally fresh our document's picture of Yohanan's death, but we must view the principal component of that picture—the "two-ways" saying—as original, and that is the important point. The Bavli, however (as usual) provides the one important counterpart to our document's tale. The Bavli's version ignores what is important in the Yerushalmi's picture of Eliezer's death, which is his repetition of Yohanan's statement followed by his provision of a throne for Yohanan. The version at B. Berakhot 28b further places Eliezer before Yohanan and includes material for Eliezer that is completely different both from what Yohanan says here and from that covered in our document's picture of Eliezer's death scene.

B. Ber. 28b/4 : 2 : II
A. *Teno rabbanan:*
B. When R. Eliezer fell ill, his disciples came in to pay a call on him. They said to him, "Our master, teach us the ways of life, so that through them we may merit the world to come."
C. He said to them, "Be attentive to the honor owing to your fellows, keep your children from excessive reflection and set them among the knees of disciples of sages, and, when you pray, know before whom you stand, and on that account you will merit the life of the world to come."
D. And when R. Yohanan b. Zakkai fell ill, his disciples came in to pay a call on him. When he saw them, he began to cry. His disciples said to him, "Light of Israel, pillar at the right hand, mighty hammer, on what account are you crying?"
E. He said to them, "If I were going to be brought before a mortal king, who is here today and gone tomorrow to the grave, who, should he be angry with me, will not be angry forever, and if he should imprison me, will not imprison me forever, and if he should put me to death, whose sentence of death is not for eternity, and whom I can appease with the right words or bribe with money, even so I should weep.
F. "And now that I am being brought before the King of kings of kings, the Holy One, blessed be he, who endures forever and ever, who, should he be angry with me, will be angry forever, and if he should imprison me, will imprison me forever, and if he should put me to death, whose sentence of death is for eternity, and whom I cannot appease with the right words or bribe with money, and not only so, but before me are two paths, one to the Garden of Eden, and the other to Gehenna, and I do not know by which path I shall be brought, and should I not weep?"
G. They said to him, "Our lord, bless us."
H. He said to them, "May it be God's will that the fear of Heaven be upon you as much as the fear of mortal man."
I. His disciples said, "Just so much?"
J. He said to them, "Would that it were that much. You should know that when a person commits a transgression, one says, 'I hope no person sees me.'"
K. When he was dying, he said to them, "Clear out utensils from the house, because of the uncleanness [of the corpse, which I shall convey when I die], and prepare a throne for Hezekiah, king of Judah, who is coming."

The death-saying of Yohanan has its counterpart, as we see, and so does Eliezer's death scene as compared to Yohanan's.

Eliezer Alone. The details of Eliezer's death scene have counterparts elsewhere. The allusion to teaching how to gather cucumbers by sorcery in our story has a quite distinct parallel involving Aqiba at T. San. 11:5 and Joshua at Y. San. 7:13. There are death scenes at Y. Shab. 2:7 and B. Sanh. 68a, as follows.

Y. Shab. 2:7. R. Eliezer was dying on the eve of the Sabbath, and Hyrcanus came to remove his phylacteries. Eliezer rebuked him, as in our version. When his disciples saw that he answered them sagaciously, they came and asked him questions and he ruled on the unclean, "unclean," and on the clean, "clean," and when he said *clean,* his soul expired. R. Joshua removed his phylacteries and embraced and kissed him, saying, "My master, my master, the vow has been released." This is the same version as in our document, but vastly briefer; the entire middle section, involving Aqiba, is absent.

B. Sanh. 68a. The Bavli then fills in all the details. The passage is generally similar to the one in our document, component by component: for example, when Hyrcanus comes to remove the phylacteries, in The Fathers According to Rabbi Nathan, Eliezer rebukes him; in the Bavli's version Aqiba rebukes him. Then we have the exchange, "Why did you come?" "To study Torah." "Why not before now?" "We had no time." "I'll be surprised if you die a natural death, and Aqiba's will be the most cruel of all." He then bewails his two arms, like scrolls of the Torah; then comes the saying on the cucumbers, then the sequence on the ball, shoemaker's last, amulet, leather bag with pearls, and small weight, and he dies in pronouncing the word *clean.* Joshua announces that the vow is annulled. Aqiba meets the bier, Aqiba delivers the funeral oration. A redactional subscript ties the story to its setting at B. Sanh. 68a: "Thus from this story we see that he learned this from Eliezer, not from Joshua." In all, therefore, Eliezer's death scene as we have it in The Fathers According to Rabbi Nathan is almost the same as the version in the Bavli.

9. XXXVIII:V

Martyrdom of Simeon b. Gamaliel and Ishmael. In The Fathers According to Rabbi Nathan, Simeon admitted to sin of pride before he was put to death. The version at Mekhilta Neziqin (Lauterbach 3:141–43, Is. 53–73) contains only the first part of the story (in Lauterbach's translation), and that version is entirely different from ours.

"You shall not afflict any widow or fatherless child . . . if you afflict in any way": this tells that one becomes guilty of oppression only after he has repeated the act. At the time when R. Simeon and R. Ishmael were led out to be killed, R. Simeon said to R. Ishmael, "Master, my heart fails me, for I do not know why I am to be killed."

XXXVIII:V.1. A. **A sword comes into the world because of the delaying of justice and perversion of justice, and because of those who teach the Torah not in accord with the law.**

XXXVIII:V.2. A. When they seized Rabban Simeon b. Gamaliel and R. Ishmael on the count of death, Rab-

R. Ishmael said to him, "Did it never happen in your life that a man came to you for a judgment or with a question and you let him wait until you had sipped your cup or had tied your sandals or had put on your cloak? And the Torah has said, "If you afflict in any way"—whether it be a severe affliction or a light affliction. Whereupon R. Simeon said to him, "You have comforted me, master." [The passage proceeds: "When R. Simeon and R. Ishmael were killed, R. Aqiba said to his disciples, 'Be prepared for trouble. For if something good had been destined to come upon our generation, R. Simeon and R. Ishmael . . . would have been the first ones to receive it . . ."].

ban Simeon b. Gamaliel was in session and was perplexed, saying, "Woe is us! For we are put to death like those who profane the Sabbath and worship idols and practice fornication and kill."

C. Said to him R. Ishmael b. Elisha, "Would it please you if I said something before you?"

D. He said to him, "Go ahead."

E. He said to him, "Is it possible that when you were sitting at a banquet, poor folk came and stood at your door, and you did not let them come in and eat?"

F. He said to him, "By heaven [may I be cursed] if I ever did such a thing! Rather, I set up guards at the gate. When poor folk came along, they would bring them in to me and eat and drink with me and say a blessing for the sake of Heaven."

G. He said to him, "Is it possible that when you were in session and expounding [the Torah] on the Temple mount and the vast populations of Israelites were in session before you, you took pride in yourself?"

H. He said to him, "Ishmael my brother, one has to be ready to accept his failing. [That is why I am being put to death, the pride that I felt on such an occasion.]"

I. They went on appealing to the executioner for grace. This one [Ishmael] said to him, "I am a priest, son of a high priest; kill me first, so that I do not have to witness the death of my companion. . . ." [No counterpart in the Mekhilta's version.]

The details at The Fathers According to Rabbi Nathan D–F directly contradict the premise of the version of the Mekhilta, which accuses the sage of doing precisely what he here denies doing. The Mekhilta's version works well in its redactional context, for the purpose there is to illustrate the result of not treating in a just and respectful manner the least among plaintiffs.

How the one version relates in sequence to the other is difficult to say. On the one side, one could argue that the redactors of the version used in the

Mekhilta have taken the shell of the story but not its kernel and have imparted their own substance. On the other, one could argue that our version is equally appropriate to its redactional context, serving as it does as an explanation of why the sword does its work, and is hence a deliberate revision of the other, removing the truly damaging admission of guilt and introducing the (more forgiveable?) sin of pride. A third reading might treat the two stories as essentially independent, each set of authors drawing upon the same setting for its own distinctive purpose. If we had a clearer notion of the time in which the two documents reached closure, we might come to a more trustworthy assessment of the probabilities.

If New, Then What Changes?

What, then, is new in the stories that have no counterparts in other documents? Do we discern a consistent pattern of introducing into stories that first appear in our document the propositions that mark what is fresh and important in The Fathers According to Rabbi Nathan? The facts are as follows; the numbers are those assigned above under the heading "Old or New?"

1. VI:IV–VI. Origins of Aqiba. The version before us has no parallel. The various stories of how Aqiba got rich do not invoke the details of our story; instead they make Aqiba the son-in-law of Ben Kalba Sabua, who behaved toward Aqiba and his wife the way Eliezer's father had acted toward him, first of all rejecting, then embracing, his decision to study the Torah. We have already noted that the story of the origins of Eliezer does have an important parallel.

3. XII:XIII. Not studying the Torah as a disciple (cf. appendix 7) leads to misinformation, which can produce the death penalty.

5. IV:V–X. The sage and the destruction of the Temple; the sage as counterpart of the emperor; the destruction, and deeds of loving-kindness as surrogate. There is no counterpart at all to Yohanan's colloquy with Joshua that deeds of loving-kindness constitute the counterpart to sacrifices of atonement. While the Bavli's version of the destruction of Jerusalem goes over a few of the same motifs as does the story in The Fathers According to Rabbi Nathan, nonetheless the two stories are essentially autonomous. What is new in The Fathers According to Rabbi Nathan is every major point of emphasis of the story of Yohanan's escape. The sage takes the central part; he undertakes all initiatives. He does more than merely react to the decisions and errors of others. Moreover, he forms the bridge from Temple to Torah: rising from his bier, he points toward a center of Torah study as the next step, out of Jerusalem. He further identifies a surrogate for the offerings, so long as the Temple lies in ruins, in acts of loving-kindness, a doctrine that, in concrete deed, forms the counterpart to the sages' stress on the tamed emotions, conciliatory

attitude, and ethic of self-abnegation that characterizes both The Fathers and The Fathers According to Rabbi Nathan.

7. XIV:IV. The story of the death of Yohanan b. Zakkai's son occurs only in our document. Its point, as we have noted, is that the true source of comfort derives from mastery of the oral Torah.

9. XXXVIII:V. Martyrdom of Simeon b. Gamaliel and Ishmael; Simeon admits to the sin of pride. The parallel as to its framework—the execution of the authorities—yields no intersections of the principle propositions. Hence we have to regard our document's story as unique.

Viewed in the aggregate, the stories that occur in particular in our document contain some new points, but they do not show conclusively that what is new in The Fathers According to Rabbi Nathan occurs mainly in stories told for the first time in that document.

If Old, Then How Different?

The catalogue presented here serves the same purpose as the foregoing. We want to know whether stories from our document that appear in other canonical writings overall tend *not* to contain those fresh and important points that mark the movement from The Fathers to The Fathers According to Rabbi Nathan.

1. VI:IV–VI. Origins of Eliezer. We have already compared the two versions of the story about Eliezer. The principal points of difference derive from the redactional context of the story in Genesis Rabbah. Otherwise all of the principal elements of the story occur in both versions, with some changes in wording and in minor detail.

2. XV:IV–V. The patience of Hillel; the Dual Torah. As we have seen, the version of these materials at B. Shab. 30b–31a is almost the same as the one in The Fathers According to Rabbi Nathan.

4. XLI:III. Simeon b. Eleazar improperly treated an ugly man. The version of this story at B. Ta. 20a–b is not much different from that in our document. There are variations in wording, but each component in the one version has its counterpart in the other.

6. XVII:III. Yohanan ben Zakkai and the daughter of Naqdimon b. Gurion. This is given numerous parallels, surveyed in the third section of this chapter.

8. XXV:II–IV (+ XIX:II–III). Deaths of Yohanan ben Zakkai and Eliezer. The death scene of Yohanan has a forerunner at Y. Sot. 9:16, (same as Y. A.Z. 3:1) and a solid counterpart at B. Ber. 28b. The former introduces only one element, the concern for corpse-uncleanness and for the coming of Hezekiah, but the latter version runs over the same ground as ours, nearly verbatim. Eliezer's death scene has an approximate counterpart at Y. Shab.

2:7 and an exact counterpart at B. Sanh. 68b. Neither of these death stories, then inaugurates new themes or provides fresh material.

Not studying the Torah as a disciple is hardly a fresh proposition; study through discipleship, after all, is a motif of The Fathers itself. The story of the comfort of Yohanan after his son's death bears an implicit stress on the oral Torah, but that is not the centerpiece of the story. That a sage admits to the sin of pride and suffers a penalty for it is no surprise to the storyteller who recorded the patience of Hillel, let alone the authors of those many apothegms about the importance of humility. The only story that strikes me as substantial and fresh is the version of the destruction of the Temple that lays its stress on the centrality of Yohanan ben Zakkai; yet we cannot draw important conclusions on the strength of that one genuinely interesting contribution, in which the medium serves with remarkable aptness for the particular message of the story.

Obviously, the closest friend of our document is the Bavli. Its versions of stories shared with The Fathers According to Rabbi Nathan as well as other compilations always fall closest to those in our document. Nonetheless, these stories, in whole or in part, do occur both in The Fathers According to Rabbi Nathan and in diverse other compilations, not only in the Bavli. The random pattern—some stories in The Fathers According to Rabbi Nathan prove original; others occur in a variety of compilations—leads to one significant negative result: We cannot look to the character of the stories contributed by the authorship of The Fathers According to Rabbi Nathan for guidance on the shift from the Fathers to that work.

The Contribution of the Story: Why Was This Medium Chosen for This Particular Message?

The approach of this chapter does not tell us why the medium of the sage-story was selected to deliver the particular messages that such stories carry in The Fathers According to Rabbi Nathan (or, therefore, in any other document). Let me explain why the question has to be reframed.

The present experiment has yielded negative results. I perceive no important differences in doctrine or proposition among the stories that are unique to our document and that also appear elsewhere. One story of a sage's origins is new; the other is not. One story of the destruction of the Temple in Jerusalem occurs in the Bavli; the other here, so the theme is shared. The proposition made by one story answers its question, the one made by the other responds to a quite different question. That is to say, one set of stories in the Bavli answers its question, and the other, equally cogent story in The Fathers According to Rabbi Nathan responds to a different issue altogether. True, the medium carries the distinctive messages we have outlined, but not in a way that makes the medium special *as used in our document in particular.*

Quite to the contrary, while the story bears messages in The Fathers According to Rabbi Nathan that are not found in The Fathers, there are three probative facts to consider. First, other documents use some of these same stories to bear identical propositions. Second, other documents use some of these same stories to deliver different messages. Third, of far greater probative weight, other modes of framing the same messages besides the sage-story serve other authorships entirely well.

Indeed, the authorship of The Fathers According to Rabbi Nathan stands within the same circle of values and convictions as the authorship of the Yerushalmi and especially of the Bavli. We must therefore reframe our question. We wish to know two things. First, where, when, and why did people resort to the story as a medium for a distinctive message? Second, what is special about The Fathers According to Rabbi Nathan? The essentially negative—that is, inconsistent—results of our analysis in this chapter require us to broaden our inquiry beyond the document at hand. Comparison with other documents will reveal what makes our document unusual. As promised at the outset, I will present ample proof that the authorship of The Fathers According to Rabbi Nathan indeed followed a rhetorical and topical program that marks the document as out of the ordinary—even while sharing a logical and propositional program with a variety of other authorships and their documents.

The Documentary Perspective on the Advent of the Story

The stories taken individually do not permit us to distinguish one document from the next. Some are particular to our document; some are not, and we may assume that the same is true of other documents. Since some stories float from document to document, our understanding of the advent of the story as a medium must emerge not from the contents of the several stories—that has led us to a dead end. Rather, the correct approach is documentary, requiring that we *characterize the use of stories by a given document. We must compare the role of the story in other documents to the role of the story in The Fathers According to Rabbi Nathan.*

Through these comparisons we will discover how the medium of the story has proved particularly suitable for the message that it served to deliver. Let me conclude precisely where I began. The point of differentiation locates itself not in the content of the stories but in the character of the document, and perspective on that large question requires the comparison not of the stories of one document with those of the next. As we compare the preferences of diverse authorships as to narratives and their use in particular *documents,* we confirm our new perspective: *the issue of the entry of the story into the canonical writings of Judaism proves to have not a literary but a documentary character.*

7

The Story in General:
Its Function in The Fathers According to
Rabbi Nathan and in Other Compositions

Contradiction and Conundrum

Since we cannot show that the repertoire of stories in The Fathers According to Rabbi Nathan stands by itself in the larger canon of the Judaism of the Dual Torah, we confront sets of incompatible facts. First the contradiction, then the conundrum.

One fact is that these stories as a group do form a distinct unit in The Fathers According to Rabbi Nathan when that document is compared to The Fathers. Furthermore, the same stories convey propositions and other messages in the later document that the authorship of the earlier writing does not present. Not only so, but the stories as a set also utilize rhetorical forms with no counterparts in The Fathers. So the first set of facts points to the stories as a distinct component in the unfolding of the documents, from The Fathers to The Fathers According to Rabbi Nathan.

But another set of facts contradicts the first, for while standing together in the later document, the same stories exhibit striking divisions when compared with one another. Specifically, we find that some of them are unique to The Fathers According to Rabbi Nathan, and others are shared, in whole or in part, with other compositions. That simple fact requires close attention. This means that we cannot treat the story in The Fathers According to Rabbi Nathan as itself undifferentiated, for a clear point of distinction requires us to separate unique stories from those held in common. On the face of it, we cannot state that the story as such, or even the sage-story, with its rich specificities, first made an appearance within the canon of the Dual Torah in the pages of our document. That is not the fact. But what are we to learn from what *is* the fact: that the sage-story serves the compositors of The Fathers According to Rabbi Nathan as the medium for the expression of its particular messages in its distinctive rhetorical, logical, and topical manner? The conundrum now has been laid out: the sage-story is unique *in* its document but not *to* its document. What does that mean?

To answer that question, we require more facts, which derive from the further differentiation of the sage-stories in our compilation, We have come to a point of distinction: shared versus unique. Do the unique stories differ as a group from the shared ones? Are there traits that are peculiar to one group? In asking whether stories that are unique to The Fathers According to Rabbi Nathan and stories that are shared constitute two distinct groups, I simply invoke the superficial and obvious point of differentiation now fully established. The criteria for comparison, of course, are precisely those that have permitted us to distinguish The Fathers from The Fathers According to Rabbi Nathan: rhetoric, topic, logic.

As we have moved away from the details of our two writings and brought the later one into relationship with other documents, a further angle of vision has shaped our perceptions, which we cannot now neglect. Once we see The Fathers According to Rabbi Nathan and its complement of stories in relationship to other documents, we find it necessary to ask about the use of stories in other documents of the canon of the Judaism of the Dual Torah. When we view a number of documents from a single perspective, the comparisons prove to be illuminating.

What Is at Stake?

The questions just set forth appear deceptively simple, but at stake are facts that lead to considerable progress in characterizing the formative history of the Judaism of the Dual Torah. Let me explain by laying out the alternative conclusions and describing the contradictory directions in which each leads.

1. We can readily distinguish the stories that are unique to The Fathers According to Rabbi Nathan from those shared with other writings. The former exhibit traits of rhetoric, logic, and even topic or proposition that set them apart from the latter.

2. We cannot differentiate among the stories before us. Whether unique to The Fathers According to Rabbi Nathan or shared among other documents, the stories are a uniform set, sharing common indicative traits of rhetoric, logic, and topic or proposition (as, on the surface, they seem to do within The Fathers According to Rabbi Nathan.

If the first alternative is valid, then the advent of one kind of story in the development of The Fathers into The Fathers According to Rabbi Nathan is not adventitious but the result of a considered decision to choose distinctive medium of discourse, the sage-story, to convey a well-crafted message. It follows that the stories unique to The Fathers According to Rabbi Nathan mark a distinctive step in the unfolding of that document. Including the shared stories involved a separate set of decisions of considerably less consequence. The unique stories testify to the formation of a consensus by an authorship and tell us many of the traits of that consensus. Furthermore, the first alternative points to the limits of a document as indeed decisive, since the authorship has been shown to have made its own choices concerning the system it wished to set forth. That authorship proves to have stood apart from other authorships, if not in every detail, at least in the important aspects of its exercise of a particular taste and judgment.

If the second alternative is valid, then the story as such forms the center of inquiry, and differentiating stories of one document from those of another rests upon false premises. Stories as a group (e.g., the sage-story) form the definitive category, not narrative, or stories, or the sage-story as evidenced in a particular document. The authorship of a given document then has been limited to selecting, from a common and available range of materials, items of particular interest, for one reason or another, to the document they proposed to compile; the authorship has had no important role in shaping the stories.

That result further calls into question the conception that the authorships of documents materially participated in framing the narratives they used (or, at least, the particular classification of narratives discussed here). That negative results carries in its wake a positive one as well. Another authorship *did* produce the sage-stories (or, stories in general, or even narratives of all kinds—at this stage in the argument it makes no difference). That authorship implemented its choices on matters of taste and judgment in the telling of stories on a broad variety of subjects—it followed its conventions and did its work. Perhaps it created documents of its own, exhibiting those uniformities in topic, logic, and rhetoric that have so impressed us in the Fathers and The Fathers According to Rabbi Nathan (not to mention the Mishnah, Leviticus Rabbah, Genesis Rabbah, and a variety of other rabbinic canonical writings). But we no longer have those documents.

We know, as a matter of fact, that we may divide into three distinct classifications, based solely on topic, all sizable units of discourse (completed arguments) in the entire canon of the Judaism of the Dual Torah. These are (1) amplifications of the Mishnah, in documents roughly deemed exegetical, in that they are organized around and held together by the structure of the Mishnah; (2) amplifications of Scripture, conforming to the same description but framed around Scripture; and (3) stories, in which the principle of cogency derives not from a prior text, whether Scripture or Mishnah, but from a narrative tension and its resolution (e.g., in the life of a hero of Scripture or of the oral Torah). The first of the three classifications includes the Tosefta, the Yerushalmi, and the Bavli. The second includes Genesis Rabbah, Leviticus Rabbah, Sifra, Sifré to Numbers, Sifré to Deuteronomy, and other compilations of materials that hold together by reference to the premise of Scripture. But not a single document in the entire canon has an organizing principle that derives from the sustained biography of a hero, whether of the written or the oral Torah: no life of Moses (such as Philo wrote), no life of Aqiba.

My initial observation about how some Christians found important the telling of stories that other Christians did not trouble to preserve allows us to see some of the consequences of these two contradictory results. We know that there were stories. Were they once connected and even continuous, or can they have been connected by the way in which authorships put things together? In that case, the canon at one point contained gospels of sages but later rejected that mode of conglomeration and composition. Or were the stories essentially creations or selections out of random materials? In that case, the Judaism of the Dual Torah never resorted to gospels of heroes. Rather, the person was subordinated to the purposes of the system.

These turn out to be very high stakes indeed, since substantial questions of a literary and a religious character find more than preliminary answers in the humble exercise we now undertake. I will show two definitive facts. First, The Fathers According to Rabbi Nathan really does differ from other documents in a way that settles the questions set forth above. Second, the unique set of sage-stories does differ from the other sort, the stories shared with other documents.

I differentiate among the stories within The Fathers According to Rabbi Nathan by showing that in two important dimensions, rhetoric and topic, the sage-stories that occur (in the extant canon) solely in our document form a singular statement. First, their narrative program in its rhetoric (narrative plan and technique) tends to set them apart from the stories (even in the same document) that have counterparts elsewhere. Second, stories about sages form a far larger proportion of the narratives in our document than they do in any other compilation in the canon of Judaism in late antiquity that we survey. So in two of the three definitive traits of any cogent writing—rhetoric, topic, and logic or proposition—The Fathers According to Rabbi Nathan is a unique entity. We may say that within the terms of rhetoric and topic, the story enters Judaism through this document in particular. In logic and proposition, the story does not stand by itself but bears messages shared among other modes of syllogistic discourse. In that dimension, then, The Fathers According to Rabbi Nathan does not serve as the entry-point of the story into the Judaic canon of the Dual Torah. But within the choices laid out just now, that conclusion is of merely limited interest.

As to the comparison of The Fathers According to Rabbi Nathan to other documents, our document will be seen to stand by itself in important ways. Let me describe the method of arriving at this second result. Our inquiry is in two stages. First, we want to classify the canonical writings according to their traits and preferences with respect to narratives in general: Do they resort to narratives in the way in which our document does, in some other way, or not at all? Second, we identify those documents to which The Fathers According to Rabbi Nathan is similar in terms of both its use of stories about sages and its mode of telling those stories. The results show that stories unique to our document do set it apart from other writings and therefore testify to the distinctive mind-set of the authorship before us. Thus we settle—I think in rather an encompassing way, even though through a very particular case—the questions spelled out in part 2 of this book. The implications of the findings for the history of Judaism are not negligible, and the use of the same methods for the history of Christianity is promising as well.

Differentiating the Varied Uses of the Story in Diverse Documents of the Dual Torah

Comparing document to document requires establishing a common plane of comparison. For that purpose, we revert to our original classification of narratives. We want to know how the authorships of diverse documents utilized narratives, with special reference to the proportions of narratives by *types*. We realize that our authorship in particular has employed stories about sages for a distinctive and important purpose within their larger composition, and we ask whether their preferences find a counterpart among the authorships of other documents. When we have identified those compositions that share a preference for sage-stories, we may then compare the use of such stories and the mode of telling them.

We sample the canonical documents,[1] following a single set of tractates through the Mishnah, Tosefta, Yerushalmi, and Bavli, as well as an equivalent sample through Sifra, Sifré to Numbers, Genesis Rabbah, Leviticus Rabbah, The Fathers, and The Fathers According to Rabbi Nathan. These are the writings I have translated and for which I have already provided an easy system of analytical notation. The system is uniform throughout. No other rabbinic documents in any language have a notation system that permits specific reference to completed units of thought, hence the canonical sample I have selected. For the legal compilations I take as sample tractates Sukkah, Sotah, and Sanhedrin, covering the three divisions of the Mishnah common to both the Yerushalmi and the Bavli (the second, third, and fourth) and treating a mainly legal tractate, a mostly nonlegal one, and a mixed one, as well as a short, medium, and long one. I believe these categories encompass the range of possibilities.

Proportions of Narrative Types in The Fathers According to Rabbi Nathan

Our earlier survey yielded the following types of narratives in The Fathers According to Rabbi Nathan: (1) parable, (2) setting for, or formal precipitant of, a saying, (3) precedent, and (4) story. The story is further divided into two subspecies: Scripture-story and sage-story. Table 1 shows the proportions of each of the narrative types in The Fathers According to Rabbi Nathan.

1. The method worked out here for the distribution of stories is followed for the distribution of ideas, symbols, and myths in my *The Canonical History of Ideas. The Place of the So-Called Tannaite Midrashim, Mekhilta, Attributed to R. Ishmael, Sifra, Sifré to Numbers, and Sifré to Deuteronomy* (Atlanta: Scholars Press for South Florida Studies in the History of Judaism, 1990).

TABLE 1
Proportions of Narrative Types in The Fathers According to Rabbi Nathan

Narrative Type	No. Examples	Percentage
Parable	16	24.6
Setting for a saying	6	9.2
Precedent or illustration	10	15.3
Scripture-story	9	13.8
Sage-story	24	36.9
Totals	65	99.8 (rounding yields <100%)

TABLE 2
Proportions of Narrative Types in The Fathers According to Rabbi Nathan and Other Canonical Documents (%)

Document	Parable	Setting for a Saying	Precedent or Illustration	Scripture-Story	Sage-Story
Fathers	24.6	9.2	15.3	13.8	36.9
Mishnah			100.0		
Tosefta		6.0	62.5	15.6	15.6
Sifra			100.0		
Sifré to Numbers					100.0
Yerushalmi	2.8	8.6	21.7	39.1	27.5
Genesis Rabbah	30.7	11.5	9.0	46.1	11.5
Leviticus Rabba	26.3	10.5	21.0	21.0	21.0
Pesiqta	28.5	8.5		31.4	31.4
Bavli	14.1	11.0	14.1	40.4	20.8

Narrative Types in the Mishnah and the Tosefta

For the Mishnah, we have nine narratives, all of them precedents. For the Tosefta, I count thirty-two. The breakdown is shown in table 2. The inclusion in T. Sot. of a number of sage-stories is noteworthy. Their character, however, should be noted. T. 13:3–4 is not much of a narrative, in that the weight of the story is carried by *he said to him . . . he said to him. . . .* In fact, the story forms a narrative setting for a saying, although the elaborate character of the setting requires us to classify the item as a story. In T. 13:4 an echo says something. There is no real plot to the story of the priest at T. 13:8. The colloquy of Joshua and the mourners consists of *he said to him . . . he said to him. . . .* Simeon the Righteous is the subject not merely of a narrative but a real story with a plot line of sorts. Comparison to some of the ambitious stories we have seen (e.g., Yohanan ben Zakkai and Vespasian, the execution of the two great sages) shows that Tosefta's stories leave considerable room for future development, but they also tell us that the framers of that document, in the case of Sotah, could and did utilize stories to good effect. Precedents and illustrations of a narrative character form the paramount representation of the narrative in both the Mishnah and the Tosefta; I found no parables, few efforts to use a narrative to set the stage for a saying, few scriptural stories (none in the Mishnah), and few sage-stories (none in the Mishnah).

Narrative Types in Sifra and Sifré to Numbers

The sample of narratives is negligible for both Sifra and Sifré to Numbers. Neither one makes much use of narratives for establishing its propositions. (I surveyed a very large sample of the second of the two.) While some narratives in both exegeses are attributed to Mishnah authorities, a random sample turns up a remarkably small number, and we must conclude that, overall, neither authorship found much use for narratives of any kind. (See table 2.)

Narrative Types in the Yerushalmi, Genesis Rabbah, and Leviticus Rabbah

The narratives in Genesis Rabbah are mainly parables. The so-called Scripture-stories are nearly always invented conversations rather than stories in the sense of plot and action, with beginning, middle, and end. Percentages for all three documents appear in table 2.

Narrative Types in Pesiqta deRab Kahana and the Bavli

Many of the stories about sages in Sanhedrin have to do with minim in controversy with sages. The survey of B. Sanhedrin yields an enormous number of Scripture-stories. The number of sage-stories we find in that same tractate is exaggerated by their character; the larger number of them deal with disputes between sages and heretics, emperors, or Roman matrons, all of them cast in a narrative form that requires their classification as stories. None of them, however, parallel in narrative character and focus the stories we find in The Fathers According to Rabbi Nathan.

The Narrative Program of The Fathers According to Rabbi Nathan Compared to That of Other Canonical Documents

The samples I have taken permit speculation on probabilities. Since our focus is on the characteristics of The Fathers According to Rabbi Nathan, we proceed to address a set of comparisons that permit us to classify that document in relationship to others of the canon of late antiquity. Table 2 summarizes the percentages of narrative types in the documents sampled. Starting with the foundation document, the Mishnah, we make a single stunning observation: The Fathers According to Rabbi Nathan differs in *every* aspect of the narrative. The Mishnah makes use of narratives solely as precedents or illustration, whereas our authorship follows a more varied program.

Comparison with Sifra and Sifré to Numbers yields nothing consequential, because the sample of narratives in the exegesis of legal materials attributed to Tannaite authorities (I deliberately took a very sizable sample) contains almost no narratives at all. The other authorships' interest in narrative as a mode of presenting ideas proves negligible. Once more, The Fathers According to Rabbi Nathan differs in *every* aspect of the narrative.

The next three documents, all assigned to the period ca. 400–450, present interesting contrasts. Our authorship finds substantially more interest in the parable than does the authorship behind our sample of the Yerushalmi. In this regard, the exegetical compilations on Genesis and Leviticus, with their enormous representation of narratives for purposes other than precedent or illustration, are quite similar to The Fathers According to Rabbi Nathan. A noteworthy point of differentiation is evident in the substantially greater interest in Genesis Rabbah and the Yerushalmi in Scripture-stories than in sage-stories. For Genesis Rabbah, that is predictable; for the Yerushalmi, it is not. But there is another, more important point of difference, and this is predictable also. *The proportion in The Fathers According to Rabbi Nathan of sage-stories to the total representation of narratives is 50 percent greater than in the Yerushalmi, three times greater than in Genesis Rabbah, and somewhat more than 50 percent greater than in Leviticus Rabbah.*

Indeed, there is a rough reversal in the proportions of scriptural to sage-stories between The Fathers According to Rabbi Nathan and Genesis Rabbah: somewhat under three times more sage-stories than Scripture-stories in The Fathers According to Rabbi Nathan as against four times more Scripture-stories than sage-stories in Genesis Rabbah. The consistently strong interest in parables characteristic of Genesis Rabbah, Leviticus Rabbah, and The Fathers According to Rabbi Nathan is important. To me it means that when exegetes of Scripture and of other-than-legal conceptions undertook to explain their ideas, they resorted equally to diverse kinds of stories: parables, Scripture-stories, and sage-stories. The point of differentiation among the documents is thus the proportions of the latter two narrative forms.

This same result emerges with the last two documents of the canon, Pesiqta deR. Kahana and the Bavli. Interestingly, the former follows the pattern of Leviticus Rabbah in its equal preference for the two types of stories. The Bavli falls into line with the Yerushalmi in its strong interest in Scripture-stories over sage-stories, in a proportion of two to one, a reversal of the nearly three-to-one proportion of sage-stories to Scripture-stories in the Fathers According to Rabbi Nathan.

The result of this rather considerable work of sampling may be stated very simply: Within the canon of Judaism in late antiquity, the authorship of The Fathers According to Rabbi Nathan stands by itself in its choice of sage-stories over all other narrative types. It presents the highest proportion of sage-stories to the total representation of narratives among the documents we have reviewed and a strikingly small proportion of Scripture-stories in comparison to the other documents. Its use of precedents or illustrations is limited and certainly lower, in proportion to all its narratives, than in the legal-exegetical writings—Mishnah, Tosefta, and Yerushalmi. That is not surprising, since the legal-exegetical writings as a matter of conventional necessity make use of precedents, on the one side, and narrative settings for sayings, on the other. Had I listed as a narrative every example of a legal saying beginning, "When Rabbi X came, he said . . . ," or "They met in the market, and he said . . . ," and similar pseudo-narrative conventions, the disproportions would be still more substantial.

As a matter of probability, therefore, I lay down the following rules:

1. Scripture-stories, sage-stories, and parables tend to run together. The authorship of a document that makes substantial use of the one ordinarily makes substantial use of the other two.

2. Exegeses of Scripture (represented by Genesis Rabbah, Leviticus Rabbah, and Pesiqta deR. Kahana) employ a far higher proportion of parables than exegeses of the Mishnah (Tosefta, Yerushalmi, and Bavli).

3. Legal texts—Mishnah, Tosefta, Sifra, Sifré to Numbers—make modest use of scriptural stories; limited use of such stories also marks The Fathers According to Rabbi Nathan.

4. Scriptural exegetical texts—Genesis Rabbah, Leviticus Rabbah, Pesiqta—and Mishnah-exegetical texts of the later period—the Yerushalmi and Bavli—make very substantial use of Scripture-stories in proportions of from two to four times more than their use of sage-stories.

Thus The Fathers According to Rabbi Nathan is an essentially anomalous text in the following aspects:

1. It uses in proportion far more sage-stories than does any other document in the canon.

2. It stands by itself among other than scriptural-exegetical compilations in its modest use of Scripture-stories.

The second statement, we now realize, in fact constitutes little more than a repetition, in different terms, of the first (and assuredly justifies my insistence on distinguishing Scripture-stories from sage-stories). Clearly, the type of narrative selected for bearing the message has changed. That need not require us to suppose that people first did one thing and then did something else; different contemporary authorships can have exhibited distinctive preferences. But it is the fact that sage-stories, as distinct from scriptural stories, precedents, parables, and other types of narratives, predominate in our document and no other.

The Singular Stories Revisited: The New and the Old

Once we realize what sets The Fathers According to Rabbi Nathan apart from the other components of the canon we have surveyed, we also define in a new light what we wish to analyze in the stories in that document. Specifically, our attention is directed to those sage-stories *without parallel* in the prior compositions and compilations of rabbinic writings. These stories, we now know, represent what is new in the new type of document represented by The Fathers According to Rabbi Nathan: sage-stories lacking precedent. If anything is going to tell us how to correlate medium and message and therefore how to frame the question of the story in the Judaism under study, it will be that set of stories.

For the framing of a thesis, indeed, we find ourselves in an enviable situation. We have stories that go over the same ground: two with prior parallels and two without. Aqiba's origins are narrated for the first time in The Fathers According to Rabbi Nathan; Eliezer's story goes over entirely familiar ground; Yohanan b. Zakkai's part in the story of the destruction of Jerusalem in our document has no parallel, but the theme is familiar. We can therefore compare these treatments of the same topic and identify what is original in our composition's presentation of them.

Origins of Aqiba vs. Origins of Eliezer

The story of Aqiba's beginning of Torah study (VI: V.1) is in three parts B–F, G–H, and I–J. In the first part, Aqiba's motivation is explained: "Now if something soft can wear down something hard, words of Torah—how much the more so should they wear down my heart." In the middle part Aqiba's action is worked out: he studied with his son—that is the point of dramatic paradox—"until he had learned the entire Torah." In the climactic conclusion, he silences the greatest masters of the day by his powerful capacity to ask the right question—the very point with which the story began. The whole is a unity, with a conclusion that reverts to the prologue and shows how the original gift—asking the right and logical question to produce the desired action—yields the desired result. There is a second narrative that seems to me not fully worked out: the story of the bundle of twigs and its use for various purposes (VI: V.4). This story forms a more conventional restatement, in Aqiba's terms, of the motif of the poor disciple who becomes a rich scholar; we noted that the same motif is worked out in a story about Hillel. The same judgment can be made about the story of the wife who stands by her husband in his poor years of Torah study but then enjoys a rich reward (VI: V.6). Thus the main story comes first and exhibits strikingly effective narrative cogency. Everything else is unrealized or conventional.

As to Eliezer's counterpart (with its parallels in prior or contemporary canonical documents), VI: VI.1 forms one unit. We look for motivation and do not find it: "He had reached the age of twenty-two years and had not yet studied the Torah. One time he said, 'I shall go and study the Torah before Rabban Yohanan ben Zakkai.'" Why he made that decision we do not know. His father's statement (C) has no relationship to Eliezer's. Eliezer has announced his plan. His father says he will not have any food until he has ploughed the entire furrow. He gets up and does so. The entire narrative is disconnected, and VI: VI.2 does not help matters. What follows (VI: VI.3) is connected to the foregoing, in that it has the theme of Eliezer's not eating properly, but it is really a setting for an apothegm: "Just as the odor of your mouth has gone forth, so will a good name in the Torah go forth for you."

We have to regard VI: VI.4 as an autonomous and more successful item, one with an important counterpart at Genesis Rabbah, as we have seen. The dramatic action begins with the father's plan to disinherit Eliezer. There is no motivation for the decision, although, in context, one is surely implied by the earlier component of the sequence. Apart from the absence of motivation, however, the rest flows. Hyrcanus is forced to the front. As part of his plan, Yohanan assigns Eliezer a front position as well. Eliezer speaks, Yohanan praises him, and Hyrcanus reverses his decision. The action again is a triad: the plan, the address under dramatic circumstances, and the conclusion with its reversal of the plan. The storyteller does not have to tell us the topic of Eliezer's speech, let alone what he says. Why Genesis Rabbah's storytellers have included those details we know; whether or not they have given us the original story and the authorship of The Fathers According to Rabbi Nathan has provided a more cogent adaptation we shall never know. If I had to choose the more fully developed version, it would be that of Genesis Rabbah, because there we have an attempt to provide motivation for Eliezer's action. He was ploughing, the cow broke its leg, Eliezer fled to Yohanan. But that motivation raises more questions than it settles: Why to Yohanan b. Zakkai? What is the role of Torah-study in all this? The statement of the bad-breath saying is more succinct; by contrast, there are several false starts in the version of The Fathers According to Rabbi Nathan. The subject-matter of the public address at Genesis Rabbah bears no relationship to the dramatic event of the father's disinheriting the son. Then the response of the son, so admirable, has no counterpart in our document. In all, Genesis Rabbah has given us a smooth and superior version of the matter, including details that vastly improve on the rather primitive and unsuccessful conglomeration of details in our document. On that basis I should be inclined to see our document's version as not only the more primitive, but also the earlier of the two, but there is no way of settling the matter—and not much is at stake.

One thing does make a difference, however, and that is the contrast between the two stories about sages' origins presented in our document, the first without prior parallel, the second with. What seems to me to characterize the unique story in contrast to the one with parallels in prior or contemporary compilations is the success of the former. Let me attempt to state matters in terms of a general theory. It is now a matter of fact that even if we did not know that a sage-story occurs only in The Fathers According to Rabbi Nathan, we should be able to suggest so on the basis of indicative traits. A sage-story that occurs only in The Fathers According to Rabbi Nathan will exhibit the following traits:

1. Narrative cogency, with a beginning, middle, and climactic conclusion. Each component of the whole will fit tightly to its neighbors, fore and aft, and all will form a single whole.

2. Attention to motivation, worked out early.

3. The climactic conclusion refers back to the beginning and ties the whole together.

Let us now test the formal rules of narrative just proposed by comparing the two stories of the destruction of the Temple.

The Sage and the Destruction of the Temple: The Two Narratives

The story of Yohanan b. Zakkai and the destruction of the Temple comes to us in two completely unrelated tales: The Fathers According to Rabbi Nathan IV:VI.1 and B. Git. 56a–b. The redactor's excuse for including the former—the story of Yohanan and Joshua—need not detain us. That narrative, though unique, is hardly comparable to a story such as the one that follows; it merely sets the stage for a saying: "We have another mode of atonement" plus Hos. 6:6. The enormous and powerful story of Yohanan and Vespasian accomplishes a variety of tasks. Its main point—the comparison and contrast of the sage and the emperor—is introduced at the outset and worked through the whole. I need not rehearse the observations we have already considered on that point. As to the story's narrative traits, we find close attention to the motivation of both parties—Yohanan and Vespasian. Yohanan does what he does because he is disappointed when the fighters reject his counsel that they accept Roman rule. Vespasian does what he does because he knows that Yohanan is a loyalist. So the action commences with a full picture of what is at stake and why the two contenders do what they do. And the point registers that the loyalist rabbi loves Israel, while the enemy emperor does not. So the motivation of the rabbi is represented in the most positive light. The main body of action forms a bridge, just as in the story about Aqiba's origins. It looks like the center, but in fact it merely forms a connection between two distinct chapters. Yohanan gets out of the town with the assistance of his disciples: he pretends to be a corpse. Why he has to do so—the fighters will not let anyone out—is not spelled out, but it is assumed. "Do you not know that a corpse is not kept overnight in Jerusalem" explains why the fighters let the corpse out. The second and climactic encounter of sage and emperor then commences without preparation or explanation. Vespasian gives Yohanan what he wants, and Yohanan tells Vespasian what he cannot object to hearing. The sage's power consists in his mastery of the meaning of Scripture and application of Scripture to events. The concluding section (W–Y) is a necessary epilogue, but not part of the dramatic sequence in three acts. We certainly find narrative cogency in three parts, all of them tightly fitting to the others. Motivation for the principal actors is introduced with great power. The conclusion brings us back to the beginning. The contrast of the sage going to Yavneh, mourning the destruction of Jerusalem, yet pointing toward a long future, and the emperor returning to Rome completes the tableau—an active tableau indeed.

My earlier reprise of the counterpart story, at B. Git. 56a–b, has already shown us the alternative treatment of the same topic. We have a sequence of stories, formed into a thematic pastiche. The story of Qamsa and Bar Qamsa (No. 2) supplies a theory of motivation for the Romans' attack on Jerusalem, which our account has omitted, but it does not explain the actions of the principals. No. 3 is a totally distinct component, with no bearing on events. The advent of Vespasian is not central; he is a chapter. The important point is now the destruction of the stores of wheat and barley, with its complement, the story of Martha, daughter of Boethus. Then comes Sadoq, the conclusion of the sequence. The Jews are starving because of their own foolish deeds; Sadoq has fasted because of his piety. The contrast drawn, the tale ends abruptly. Then comes the sequence involving Yohanan (No. 7 in my earlier précis). Let us review the story, in Maurice Simon's translation:

I. A. Abba Sikra, the head of the *biryoni* in Jerusalem, was the son of the sister of Rabban Yohanan b. Zakkai. He sent to him, saying, "Come to visit me privately."

B. When he came, he said to him, "How long are you going to carry on in this way and kill all the people with starvation?"

C. He replied, "What can I do? If I say a word to them, they will kill me."

D. He said, "Devise some plan for me to escape. Perhaps I shall be able to save a little."

E. He said to him, "Pretend to be ill, and let everyone come to inquire about you. Bring something evil-smelling and put it by you so that they will say you are dead. Let then your disciples get under your bed, but no others, so that they shall not notice that you are still light, since they know that a living being is lighter than a corpse."

F. He did so, and R. Eliezer went under the bier from one side and R. Joshua from the other.

II. G. When they reached the door, some men wanted to put a lance through the bier.

H. He said to them, "Shall they say, 'They have pierced their master'?"

I. They wanted to give it a push.

J. He said to them, "Shall they say that they pushed their master?"

III. L. They opened a town gate for him and he got out.

M. When he reached the Romans, he said, "Peace to you, O King, peace to you, O king."

N. He said, "Your life is forfeit on two counts, one because I am not a king and you call me king, and again, if I am a king, why did you not come to me before now?"

O. He replied, "As for your saying that you are not a king, in truth you are a king, since if you were not a king, Jerusalem would not be delivered into your hand, as it is written, 'And Lebanon shall fall by a mighty one.' 'Mighty one' applies only to a king, as it is written, 'And their mighty one shall be of themselves,' and Lebanon refers to the sanctuary, as it says, 'This goodly mountain and Lebanon' (Deut. 3:25). As for your question, why if you are king did I not come to you until now, the answer is that the *biryoni* among us did not let me."

P. He said, "If there is a jar of honey around which a serpent is wound, would they not break the jar to get rid of the serpent?"

Q. He could give no answer. . . .

IV.   R. At this point a messenger came to him from Rome saying, "Up, for the emperor is dead, and the notables of Rome have decided to make you head."

S. He had just finished putting on one boot. When he tried to put on the other, he could not. He tried to take off the first, but it would not come off. He said, "What is the meaning of this?"

T. R. Yohanan said to him, "Do not worry: the good news has done it, as it says, 'Good tidings make the bone fat' (Prov. 15:30). What is the remedy? Let someone whom you dislike come and pass before you, as it is written, 'A broken spirit drieth up the bones'" (Prov. 17:22).

U. He did so and the boot went on.

V. He said to him, "Seeing that you are so wise, why did you not come to me til now?"

W. He said, "Have I not told you?"

X. He said, "I too have told you."

V.   Y. He said, "I am now going and will send someone to take my place. You can, however, make request of me, and I will grant it."

Z. He said to him, "Give me Yavneh and its sages, and the chain of Rabban Gamaliel, and physicians to heal R. Sadoq."

I see five parts to the whole, with threads joining one part to the next. I and II are closely tied, and then III–V. But if we had one set without the other, there would be slight loss to narrative cogency. The first two parts deal with why and how Yohanan left Jerusalem, the second group with the colloquy with the emperor. The opening part supplies motivation for Yohanan's leaving Jerusalem, but the hero is Abba Sikra, not Yohanan. In the second part Yohanan plays no role. In the third part Yohanan resorts to the Torah to appease the emperor (not named), amply quoting proof texts to the emperor. But the sage proves unequal to the occasion. In the fourth part the sage interprets for the emperor his problem in putting on his boots. Then the emperor goes over the ground of the third part, once more leaving the sage in the defensive position. Finally (V) the sage makes his request, the climax and conclusion of the story, at Z. The complex is not a story about the sage and the emperor. It is a story about *an event,* in which the sage plays an important, but subordinated role. The motivation of the players is not clarified. Why the emperor grants anything at all—if he does—we do not know. We know why he ought not to have done anything for the sage. Why Abba Sikra concurs with Yohanan's view and helps him we are not told; at best family loyalty is implied. Yohanan's motivation is clear; he thinks the fighters' policy unwise and hopeless. But the account of his program and motivation hardly answers the important questions.

The version of events concerning Yohanan b. Zakkai in B. Git. exhibits a measure of narrative cogency within its two large units, but the break between parts I–II and III–V is jarring and leaves the latter set without motivation. We have no reason to account for the emperor's favor to the sage. The motivation of Yohanan is clear, but that of the emperor is not, so the components of the story do not cohere. The climactic conclusion in no way brings us back to the beginning, and the two sets of components are left essentially autonomous.

Furthermore, the larger setting in no way coheres with this particular story. In that larger setting, Yohanan's story plays only a minor part. In fact, the string of stories conforms to the one about Yohanan in only one respect: what we have overall is not a story about the emperor and the sage, and what we have in respect to Yohanan also is not a story about the emperor and the sage. The criteria I outlined earlier permit us to distinguish this version of events from that of The Fathers According to Rabbi Nathan. Knowing those criteria but not the documentary locus or origin of either story, we could readily have assigned one version of events to our document and the other to some other compilation.

Two More Narratives: The Death of the Sage, and the Starving Girl

To test the unfolding thesis that the sage-story that is unique to our document conforms to a set of pronounced narrative traits, while a sage-story that appears also in other documents need not exhibit those traits, we turn to two more thematic sets, the sage's death and the story of the starving girl, which occur in our document and others.

The Death of Yohanan b. Zakkai and Eliezer. The version of Yohanan's death scene contains no action; no beginning, middle, or end; no clear statement of motivation; and no climax and resolution of tension. The add-on involving Eliezer simply goes over the same tale twice with a new name; at no point does it explain why Eliezer said just what Yohanan had said.

The Death of Eliezer. The story at The Fathers According to Rabbi Nathan XXV: IV, with its counterparts in the Talmuds, begins with the account of how the master is in full command of his senses, so that sages can consult him. The focus of the story is the ostracism of Eliezer, the great mastery of Eliezer, and the penalty for disciples who did not study with him. The first part, XXV: IV.1, has a persuasive beginning that establishes Eliezer's mental alertness, and a solid middle, with the discourse on what is clean and unclean. But there is no cogency, because the story trails off into the complaint against the disciples and has no real end at all. In fact, it cannot have an end because the redactor wishes to join XXV: IV.2 with XXV: IV.1, so Eliezer cannot be permitted to die before Aqiba takes center stage on his own. But when Aqiba does come in, Eliezer ignores him, teaches whatever he teaches, and then IV.2F–G form the bridge to XXV: IV.3. Section XXV: IV.4 then introduces a colloquy with Eleazar b. Azariah. If this passage had been joined to XXV: IV.1, it would provide a fine conclusion, but as things now stand, we do not have a cogent story, with a beginning, middle, and end; we do not have a clear picture of the motivation of the various parties. We do not have a conclusion that resolves the tension of the story. We have a set of stories on a theme, none of them conforming to the pattern we have discerned among the stories unique to our document.

The Starving Girl. The story about the starving girl exists in several versions. All of them, whether or not Yohanan b. Zakkai is the principal, conform to a single pattern—and it is not the one we seek. In each instance the story serves only to set the stage for a sermon. There is some pretense at action (e.g., "when she saw Yohanan, she said," and so on), but we look in vain for a beginning, middle, and end, motivation, and a conclusion that resolves the tension that generated the action. Rather than action, the story mainly portrays an appropriate tableau for the message that is to be delivered.

The tale about the patience of Hillel and the Dual Torah (The Fathers According to Rabbi Nathan XV:IV–V) and the improper behavior of Simeon b. Eleazar await attention. Is there no story occurring in both The Fathers According to Rabbi Nathan and other documents that conforms to the simple traits I have isolated? On the one side, there is a well-wrought narrative. It has a beginning, which creates the tension of whether or not Hillel can be made to lose his temper. A sequence of matched episodes—the bleary eyes, the flat feet, the elongated heads of the Babylonians—forms the middle. The end comes with "Hillel is worth your losing four hundred *zuz* without Hillel's losing his temper." What is lacking are two components of the stories that are unique to our document: first, a clear statement of motivation, and second, action. Without these, we have no tension, only a set-piece tableau. All we have by way of storytelling is description of the circumstances in which an exchange of statements takes place. We have no description of what people did, only of what they said or the context in which they said it. What we have at XV:V.1 is still more a narrative setting for a saying: "Just as you have accepted this teaching in good faith, so accept the other in good faith." What characterizes our stories, by contrast, is that they do not end with a stunning saying, the presentation of which the story has accomplished. If I had to select one story in the set that most closely adheres to the narrative patterns I have identified, it is XV:V.2, the gentile who wanted to become high priest. Here we have not only exchanges of statements but concrete action; we also are told the motivation of the gentile, who draws his own conclusions based on reasoning about what is said. The story has a strong beginning, the encounter with Shammai; the middle, Hillel's instruction; and then the conclusion and climax: the convert's reasoning out of matters on his own. Drawing the moral at the end (P) hardly constitutes an exploitation of the narrative for the purpose of providing a setting for a famous saying. So here is a satisfactory conclusion—an exception to the rule. Here then is the rule that permits us to predict which stories will be shared between The Fathers According to Rabbi Nathan and some other rabbinic composition, and which will be particular to The Fathers According to Rabbi Nathan:

1. Stories in canonical writings of the Judaism of the Dual Torah that exhibit the narrative qualities previously defined will prove particular to The Fathers According to Rabbi Nathan, while stories that follow other narrative conventions will be shared between that document and some other.

That is not to suggest that all stories that conform to the specified narrative conventions occur in The Fathers According to Rabbi Nathan—far from it. But there is a rule that does hold firm within the sample at hand:

2. Stories exhibiting the narrative character that distinguishes items unique to The Fathers According to Rabbi Nathan do occur elsewhere; but in other documents they will not form nearly so sizable a component of the narrative repertoire as they do in The Fathers According to Rabbi Nathan.

The upshot is that the story—the sage-story—with a beginning, middle, end, movement from start to finish, tension, and narrative resolution—enters the canon of the Judaism of the Dual Torah through The Fathers According to Rabbi Nathan. The important propositions contributed by the authorship of that document found in the medium of the sage-story the suitable mode of delivering the message they wished to state. And, as we realize, the message was not distinctive to that authorship, any more than the messages of any of the canonical documents of the Judaism of the Dual Torah were unique to their authorships.

The Story in General

Let me now review the result of the completed inquiry:

1. Sage-stories that exhibit the traits I have specified do occur in other documents, but in The Fathers According to Rabbi Nathan, they form the largest proportion of the types of narratives employed in the document.

2. The traits that characterize sage-stories that occur only in The Fathers According to Rabbi Nathan permit us to differentiate those stories from stories that are shared with other compilations and so to identify what is distinctive about them.

We can, in fact, predict the location of a sage-story on the basis of its narrative traits. Stories characterized by action, with a beginning, middle, and end, in which behavior is given motivation and the climax clearly marked at the conclusion, will prove unique to The Fathers According to Rabbi Nathan. These may be differentiated from other stories in two ways. First, stories about scriptural topics or heroes do not follow the same pattern as do stories about sages. Second, stories about sages contain described action, implicit or fully exposed, and not merely sequences of *he said to him . . . he said to him*. Nor do stories about sages serve merely as elaborate settings for (famous) sayings. In two ways—first, rhetoric; second, topic—these two propositions permit us to distinguish stories in The Fathers According to Rabbi Nathan from stories in other documents, as well as from the broader narrative repertoire of the literature as a whole.

But what about logic, inclusive of proposition? I cannot imagine distinguishing by proposition or inner logical cogency as part of a broader system our stories from other stories, our document from other documents. Quite to the contrary. The surface of our document is covered with the detritus of the doctrines that come to systematic expression in other documents. If we ask the authorship of The Fathers According to Rabbi Nathan to direct us to its points of emphasis, they will certainly want us to attend to their doctrine of the supernatural character of the study of the Torah, and to the eschatological teleology, focused upon the nation as a whole, they have framed for the system, as distinct from the ahistorical teleology centered upon the individual in this life and the life to come that is so paramount in The Fathers. Neither of these critical propositions originates here. Both are commonplaces in the two Talmuds. That brief observation brings us to the logical conclusion of this inquiry. Once we notice that rhetorically and topically The Fathers According to Rabbi Nathan establishes an independent statement for itself, we realize that logically and propositionally it forms a chapter in a very large statement indeed. The full dimensions and the entirety of the details of that large statement come to systematic expression in no one piece of writing in the rabbinic canon of late antiquity; all of them appeal to a system that, individually and systematically, none of them exposes whole or in large part. So the next problem is the doctrinal cogency of diverse documents: the Judaism that infuses all of the documents and relies for complete and sufficient statement on none of them.

The result may be stated very simply. While in rhetoric and topic, but not in logic and proposition, the story enters Judaism through The Fathers According to Rabbi Nathan, the propositions of the Judaism of the Dual Torah constitute the premises of a variety of documents, and the rhetorical and topical expression of those premises in concrete terms emerges in diverse ways among the canonical writings. We therefore know the limits of documents and can define what will form their particular statement and what will constitute a shared and general message. In so stating, I have reached the outer bounds of the documentary inquiry into the formation of Judaism: rhetoric and topic are distinctive to the document; logic and proposition are shared among documents. How to investigate the unfolding of logic and proposition in the formative history of the Judaism of the Dual Torah defines the next question.

8

Judaism and Story

A particular kind of story in The Fathers According to Rabbi Nathan served a particular purpose, conveying a message that that authorship found best expressed in that medium. Not all narratives, or even all stories, in our document come under that generalization. But all sage-stories that are unique to The Fathers According to Rabbi Nathan in rhetoric and logic, but not in proposition, turn out to have a very clear-cut purpose. A particular mode of cogent and intelligible discourse, one variety of the sage-story, serves as a distinctive medium to convey a well-crafted message. In this way the limits of the document do delineate boundaries between one kind of sage-story and another kind, and that result tells us that the documentary statement represents choices concerning the system that the authorship wished to set forth. The authorship of The Fathers According to Rabbi Nathan stood apart from other authorships, certainly not in every detail—they did, after all, adopt for themselves the structure and contents of The Fathers!—but in important aspects of their work, seen all at once. It follows that our authorship has materially participated in the framing of narratives of a particular species and subspecies. If there was a preexisting corpus of stories from which our authorship chose some but not others, then one of two conclusions must follow. Either that preexisting corpus did not encompass the sage-stories unique to The Fathers According to Rabbi Nathan (and that makes us wonder how sizable that preexisting corpus can have been), or the other (not necessarily prior) authorships had access to that common corpus but did not choose these particular stories. There is no way of knowing which of these two conclusions is correct, but it hardly matters, for the upshot, either way, is the same. That is, these particular stories, with their distinctive narrative conventions, represent the taste and judgment of a singular authorship, even though they do not necessarily originate with that authorship.

What then does it mean to know that a given authorship has made particular choices about how to tell stories of a distinctive narrative character in order to convey a well-crafted message? To answer that question we come, at the end, to the matter with which we began, namely, Paul's choices about telling, or not telling, stories about Jesus. The facts are as stated by Günther Bornkamm, in his *Paul* (p. 110):

> Never does he make the slightest effort to expound the teaching of the historical Jesus. Nowhere does he speak of the rabbi from Nazareth, the prophet and miracle-worker who ate with tax collectors and sinners.

That is not to suggest that sayings of Jesus did not circulate in Paul's time or that they were not of interest to him. But if Paul knew stories, he did not think it important to (re)tell them. A decade later, Mark, then Matthew, Luke, and John (and for a long time thereafter the apocryphal authors) told such stories and turned them into biographies of a distinctly Christian character: gospels. David L. Dungan (*The Sayings of Jesus in the Churches of Paul* [Philadelphia: Fortress, 1971], pp. 139ff.) has shown that Paul applies received sayings within "a general pattern of similar interpretation and application of the same sayings in the Church of his day." Paul did not "republish" the teachings of Jesus in story form (Dungan, p. 145). Yet Dungan has shown that Paul "actually used—*cited*—a considerable number of Jesus' teachings." Whether the reason is that Paul had a direct encounter with Christ in revelation (Gal. 1: 11ff.) or that he was not interested in the "historical Jesus" (2 Cor. 5:16) has no bearing upon our problem. However Paul wished to present and represent the teachings of Jesus Christ, it was not through the mode of cogent discourse accomplished by narrative, and it was not through the medium of storytelling. And yet—and here Dungan's results accord with considerable scholarship on the history of Christianity—Paul certainly did stand well within the unfolding Christian religious system that his letters and the four Evangelists together composed and stated. Dungan's concluding remarks set the stage for the conclusion I wish to present here:

> The alleged contrast between Pauline Christianity and that branch of the early Church which preserved the Palestinian-Jesus-tradition that finally ended up in the Synoptic gospels is a figment of the imagination. In fact they were one and the same branch—for precisely in Paul's careful preservation of, and yet selective and discriminating obedience to, the Lord's commands, do we see prefigured the characteristic traits of the Hellenistic Christian gospel editors. (P. 150)

In differentiating sage-stories as uniquely told in the Fathers According to Rabbi Nathan from sage-stories (and, all the more so, other narratives) as composed in other documents, I have placed at the fore the question of the relationship of a religious system as a whole to the principal parts of which it is composed, which I take to be a problem parallel to that of the interplay of Paul and the Gospels—each distinctive, yet all received by the Church as a coherent canon of inspired truth.

Let me first make a negative point. We cannot differentiate the messages of the unique stories from the messages of the shared ones in The Fathers According to Rabbi Nathan. The stories unique to our document bear distinctive traits of intellect and narrative convention, but I see no message in them that would have amazed those storytellers whose work occurs both in The Fathers According to Rabbi Nathan and a variety of other documents. So what is special to our authorship and what is shared among various authorships? The answer yields the positive point. Setting The Fathers According to Rabbi Nathan side by side with The Fathers, we find that our authorship makes a number of important points that the authorship of The Fathers does not make—or even accommodate. And those very same points, fresh to our documents, play an important role in those other documents with which (as I showed in chapter 7) our authorship shares striking affinities in its interest in narrative in general and the story in particular: the Yerushalmi and the Bavli and their closest friends. So, over all, there is a correlation between extensive use of narrative and an interest in history, biography, eschatology, the holy society, and related matters. What we should have to demonstrate, beyond that simple fact, is that our authorship's particular conceptions concerning these shared interests, worked out in common genres of writing, differed from those of the others in the closely parallel writings. I cannot do so, and I doubt that it can be done.

If that is the fact, then there is a dimension in which a number of distinct documents, seen whole as well as examined for differences in their large-scale constituents, do intersect. The measure of that dimension is taken in a simple way. I state it as a question: do we perceive commonalities of topic and proposition that link diverse documents and distinguish one set of writings from others that lack those features? If we do, then we may point to those shared propositions and topics as a system of thought that encompasses several documents and draws them together into a single common statement. Certainly we may point to premises common to Yerushalmi, Bavli, The Fathers According to Rabbi Nathan, and related writings, but not explicitly affirmed or implicitly stated in The Mishnah, The Fathers, Tosefta, and associated writings. And the contrary, of course, is also the case. Both sets of premises can be systematically described, and each (I state as a matter of hypothesis) requires its distinctive medium of expression, and perhaps a particularly appropriate mode of cogent discourse as well.

The upshot is that documents form components of encompassing religious systems, *Judaisms* (in the terminology I have used to cope with data such as those under discussion here). Stories make their entry into a Judaism because they serve an important purpose, one that, in the view of authorships of important writings, could not have been accomplished so well in any other way. The advent of stories therefore attests, in its own way, to the character of the (complete) system to which the stories give (partial) expression. It is no accident that the authorship of The Fathers did not include narratives in general and sage-stories in particular, even while that authorship was composing its picture of the formation and transmission of the Torah revealed to Moses at

Sinai. Neither is it adventitious that the authorship of The Fathers According to Rabbi Nathan reached a different view of narrative and its power to present in detail the larger statement that that authorship wished to make.

In so stating, we move across the frontier that separates one document from another and toward that common ground that is shared by two or more authorships. And that is the difference that our improved understanding of the place of the story in the document(s) before us makes. In seeing a document as in some ways different from and in other ways congruent to other documents, we have seen as much as the documentary focus allows us to see within the limits of one piece of writing. We also learn, moving outward from a single document and reaching an appropriate neighbor, how to know related from utterly unrelated authorships. And that seems to me the logical next step in the study of history of the formation of Judaism. The approach worked out in the five volumes that conclude here draws us onward from documentary description to the analysis and (ultimately) the interpretation of a Judaic religious system. We have reached the end of what books read on their own can tell us about the formation of the Judaism of the Dual Torah. Once we demonstrate that, in some important ways, a given piece of writing rests upon premises shared with other documents, the identification of those shared premises takes priority.

But how are we to identify the sources that tell us about those premises, and once the category of the document has been exhausted, what other category takes its place? The answer to these questions derives from our understanding of a religious system: a Judaism and its principal parts. So let me point to the road ahead by saying what I understand by a religious system. A Judaism encompasses three things that are one:

1. A world-view which, by reference to the intersection of the supernatural and the natural worlds, accounts for how things are and puts them together into a cogent and harmonious picture

2. A way of life which expresses in concrete actions the world-view and which is explained by that world view

3. A social group for which the world view accounts, which is defined in concrete terms by the way of life, and which therefore gives expression to the world view and is defined as an entity by that way of life.

As we realize, a book is not the same as a system, though a book may well presuppose a world view, refer to a way of life, and (through its authorship) address a distinct social group. A religious system, further, is one that appeals to God as the principal power, and a Judaic system is a religious system that identifies the Hebrew Scriptures (Old Testament) as a principal component of its canon. A Judaism, then, comprises not merely a theory—a book—distinct from social reality, but an explanation for the group ("Israel") that gives social form to the system and an account of the distinctive way of life of that group. A Judaism is not a book, even though various books testify to the characteristics of a (single) Judaism. Let me state with emphasis: *a Judaic system derives from and focuses upon a social entity, a group of Jews who (in their minds at least) constitute not* an *Israel but* Israel. The conception of an *authorship* therefore forms the bridge from book to system, the notion of a shared and consensual statement forming the centerpiece and keystone.

The history of religion, or of a religion, is not a problem of historical and linear narrative—first came this, then came that. Quite to the contrary, within a given family of similar religions (e.g., the family of Judaisms or of Christianities), a number of religious systems may compete. Each will write for itself a history that exhibits three traits: (1) it will claim unitary status, that is, to represent the whole—to be *Judaism,* not just *a Judaism;* (2) it will place itself in a linear relationship to all that has gone before and that is to come; and (3) it will allege that it forms the increment, the accumulation of all truth, in the historical tradition in which it stands. These three modes of self-understanding, the unitary, linear, and incremental views, ordinarily characterize the inner-looking view of religious systems. But these claims testify to their opposite: diversity within the religious family, plurality of lines of development out of the past, and (it follows) not a single development or increment, but multiple possibilities, all of them realized somewhere and somehow. The historian of religion must make sense of the claims of unity and of linear and incremental development, but need not entertain their validity in the face of the contrary facts of plurality, diversity, and multiplicity. There have been many Judaisms, many Christianities, and many Islams. True, there also is one Judaism, orthodox ("right doctrine") and normative; one Christianity ("The Church's one foundation is Jesus Christ the Lord"); and, most assuredly, one nation of Islam, and it is the theological task of Judaism, Christianity, and Islam to tell us precisely what that singular Judaism, Christianity, and Islam are.

We have begun not from the whole (all Judaisms seen as one Judaism) but from the smallest principal parts of one part, a single book, that leads us to another book, and these together require us to investigate premises common to two or more books—premises not framed as generalities but, in the pages now closing, as very specific and indicative facts: modes of thought, media of discourse, as much as the shared message. The reason we began where we did is simply stated: We cannot make choices among the evidence and declare one system to be orthodox and normative unless we also pretend that other evidence does not exist. That is why instead of announcing that all books (of a certain canonical sort) are in, and no other books exist, I began with one book that all parties concur is critical to one system (that was the Mishnah, then Scripture) and worked my way outward from there. A Judaism (or other religious system) speaks of the whole. But if we wish to know how a Judaism works, what holds it together, we begin not from the whole but the parts and move outward from the detail to the whole. Thus, in the nature of things, we reach the farthest limits of one whole—from one book at a time to one system at a time.

The Sayings of The Fathers

Chapter One

1:1. Moses received the Torah at Sinai and handed it on to Joshua, Joshua to elders, and elders to prophets. And prophets handed it on to the men of the great assembly. They said three things, "Be prudent in judgment. Raise up many disciples. Make a fence for the Torah."

1:2. Simeon the Righteous was one of the last survivors of the great assembly. He would say, "On three things does the world stand: On the Torah, and on the Temple service, and on deeds of loving-kindness."

1:3. Antigonus of Sokho received [the Torah] from Simeon the Righteous. He would say, "Do not be like servants who serve the master on condition of receiving a reward, but [be] like servants who serve the master not on condition of receiving a reward. And let the fear of Heaven be upon you."

1:4. Yosé ben Yoezer of Zeredah and Yosé ben Yohanan of Jerusalem received [the Torah] from them. Yosé ben Yoezer says, "Let your house be a gathering place for sages. And wallow in the dust of their feet, and drink in their words with gusto."

1:5. Yosé ben Yohanan of Jerusalem says, "Let your house be open wide. And seat the poor at your table ["make the poor members of your household"]. And don't talk too much with women. (He referred to a man's wife; all the more so is the rule to be applied to the wife of one's fellow. In this regard did sages say, "So long as a man talks too much with a woman, he brings trouble on himself, wastes time better spent on studying the Torah, and ends up an heir of Gehenna.")

1:6. Joshua ben Perahyah and Nittai the Arbelite received [the Torah] from them. Joshua ben Perahyah says, "Set up a master for yourself. And get yourself a companion-disciple. And give everybody the benefit of the doubt."

1:7. Nittai the Arbelite says, "Keep away from a bad neighbor. And don't get involved with a bad person. And don't give up hope of retribution."

1:8A. Judah ben Tabbai and Simeon ben Shetah received [the Torah] from them.

1:8B. Judah ben Tabbai says, "Don't make yourself like one of those who advocate before judges [while you yourself are judging a case]. And when the litigants stand before you, regard them as guilty. But when they leave you, regard them as acquitted (when they have accepted your judgment)."

1:9. Simeon ben Shetah says, "Examine the witnesses with great care. And watch what you say, lest they learn from what you say how to lie."

1:10. Shemaiah and Avtalyon received [the Torah] from them. Shemaiah says: "Love work. Hate authority. Don't get friendly with the government."

1:11. Avtalyon says, "Sages, watch what you say, lest you become liable to the punishment of exile, and go into exile to a place of bad water, and disciples who follow you drink bad water and die, and the name of Heaven be thereby profaned."

1:12. Hillel and Shammai received [the Torah] from them. Hillel says: "Be disciples of Aaron, loving peace and pursuing grace, loving people and drawing them near to the Torah."

1:13A. He would say [in Aramaic], "A name made great is a name destroyed, and one who does not add, subtracts.

1:13B. "And who does not learn is liable to death. And the one who uses the crown, passes away."

1:14. He would say, "If I am not for myself, who is for me? And when I am for myself, what am I? And if not now, when?"

1:15. Shammai says, "Make your learning of the Torah a fixed obligation. Say little and do much. Greet everybody cheerfully."

1:16. Rabban Gamaliel says, "Set up a master for yourself. Avoid doubt. Don't tithe by too much guesswork."

1:17. Simeon his son says, "All my life I grew up among the sages, and I found nothing better for a person [the body] than silence. And not the learning is the thing, but the doing. And whoever talks too much causes sin."

1:18. Rabban Simeon ben Gamaliel says, "On three things does the world stand: on justice, on truth, and on peace." As it is said, "Execute the judgment of truth and peace in your gates" (Zech. 8:16).

Chapter Two

2:1. Rabbi says, "What is the straight path which a person should choose for himself? Whatever is an ornament to the one who follows it, and an ornament in the view of others. Be meticulous in a small religious duty as in a large one, for you do not know what sort of reward is coming for any of the various religious duties. And reckon with the loss [required] in carrying out a religious duty against the reward for doing it; and the reward for committing a transgression against the loss for doing it. And keep your eye on three things, so you will not come into the clutches of transgression. Know what is above you. An eye which sees, and an ear which hears, and all your actions are written down in a book."

2:2. Rabban Gamaliel, a son of Rabbi Judah the Patriarch says, "Fitting is learning in the Torah along with a craft, for the labor put into the two of them makes one forget sin. And all learning of the Torah which is not joined with labor is destined to be null and causes sin. And all who work with the community—let them work with them [the community] for the sake of Heaven. For the merit of the fathers strengthens them, and the righteousness which they do stands forever. And, as for you, I credit you with a great reward, as if you had done [all the work required by the community].

2:3. "Be wary of the government, for they get friendly with a person only for their own convenience. They look like friends when it is to their benefit, but they do not stand by a person when he is in need."

2:4. He would say, "Make His wishes into your own wishes, so that He will make your wishes into His wishes. Put aside your wishes on account of His wishes, so that He will put aside the wishes of other people in favor of your wishes. Hillel says: Do not walk out on the community. And do not have confidence in yourself until the day you die. And do not judge your companion until you are in his place. And do not say anything which cannot be heard, for in the end it will be heard. And do not say, 'When I have time, I shall study,' for you may never have time."

2:5. He would say, "A coarse person will never fear sin, nor will an *am-ha-Aretz* ever be pious, nor will a shy person learn, nor will an ignorant person teach, nor will anyone too occupied in business get wise. In a place where there are no individuals, try to be an individual."

2:6. Also, he saw a skull floating on the water and said to it [in Aramaic], "Because you drowned others, they drowned you, and in the end those who drowned you will be drowned."

2:7. He would say, "Lots of meat, lots of worms; lots of property, lots of worries; lots of women, lots of witchcraft; lots of slave girls, lots of lust; lots of slave boys, lots of robbery. Lots of the Torah, lots of life; lots of discipleship, lots of wisdom; lots of counsel, lots of understanding; lots of righteousness, lots of peace. [If] one has gotten a good name, he has gotten it for himself. [If] he has gotten teachings of the Torah, he has gotten himself life eternal."

2:8A. Rabban Yohanan ben Zakkai received [the Torah] from Hillel and Shammai. He would say, "If you have learned much Torah, do not puff yourself up on that account, for it was for that purpose that you were created." He had five disciples, and these are they: Rabbi Eliezer ben Hyrcanus, Rabbi Joshua ben Hananiah, Rabbi Yosé the Priest, Rabbi Simeon ben Nethanel, and Rabbi Eleazar ben Arakh.

2:8B. He would list their good qualities, "Rabbi Eliezer ben Hyrcanus—a plastered well, which does not lose a drop of water. Rabbi Joshua—happy is the one who gave birth to him. Rabbi Yosé—a pious man. Rabbi Simeon ben Nethanel—a man who fears sin, and Rabbi Eleazar ben Arakh—a surging spring."

2:8C. He would say, "If all the sages of Israel were on one side of the scale, and Rabbi Eliezer ben Hyrcanus were on the other, he would outweigh all of them."

2:8D. Abba Saul says in his name, "If all of the sages of Israel were on one side of the scale, and Rabbi Eliezer ben Hyrcanus was also with them, and Rabbi Eleazar [ben Arakh] were on the other side, he would outweigh all of them."

2:9A. He said to them, "Go and see what is the straight path to which someone should stick."

2:9B. Rabbi Eliezer says, "A generous spirit." Rabbi Joshua says, "A good friend." Rabbi Yosé says, "A good neighbor." Rabbi Simeon says, "Foresight." Rabbi Eleazar says, "Good will."

2:9C. He said to them, "I prefer the opinion of Rabbi Eleazar ben Arakh, because in what he says is included everything you say."

2:9D. He said to them, "Go out and see what is the bad road, which someone should avoid." Rabbi Eliezer says, "Envy." Rabbi Joshua says, "A bad friend." Rabbi Yosé says, "A bad neighbor." Rabbi Simeon says, "A loan." (All the same is a loan owed to a human being and a loan owed to the Omnipresent, the blessed, as it is said, "The wicked borrows and does not pay back, but the righteous person deals graciously and hands over [what is owed]" (Ps. 37:21).

2:9E. Rabbi Eleazar says, "Ill will."

2:9F. He said to them, "I prefer the opinion of Rabbi Eleazar ben Arakh, because in what he says is included everything you say."

2:10A. They [each] said three things.

2:10B. Rabbi Eliezer says, "Let the respect owing to your companion be as precious to you as the respect owing to yourself. And don't be easy to anger. And repent one day before you die. And warm yourself by the fire of the sages, but be careful of their coals, so you don't get burned—for their bite is the bite of a fox, and their sting is the sting of a scorpion, and their hiss is like the hiss of a snake, and everything they say is like fiery coals."

2:11. Rabbi Joshua says, "Envy, desire of bad things, and hatred for people push a person out of the world."

2:12. Rabbi Yosé says, "Let your companion's money be as precious to you as your own. And get yourself ready to learn the Torah, for it does not come as an inheritance to you. And may everything you do be for the sake of Heaven."

2:13. Rabbi Simeon says, "Be meticulous about the recitation of the Shema and the Prayer. And when you pray, don't treat your praying as a matter of routine; but let it be a [plea for] mercy and supplication before the Omnipresent, the blessed, as it is said, 'For He is gracious and full of compassion, slow to anger and full of mercy, and repents of the evil' (Joel 2:13). And never be evil in your own eyes."

2:14. Rabbi Eleazar says, "Be constant in learning of the Torah; and know what to reply to an Epicurean; and know before whom you work, for your employer can be depended upon to pay your wages for what you do."

2:15. Rabbi Tarfon says, "The day is short, the work formidable, the workers lazy, the wages high, the employer impatient."

2:16. He would say, "It's not your job to finish the work, but you are not free to walk away from it. If you have learned much Torah, they will give you a good reward. And your employer can be depended upon to pay your wages for what you do. And know what sort of reward is going to be given to the righteous in the coming time."

Chapter Three

3:1A. Aqabiah b. Mehallalel says, "Reflect upon three things and you will not fall into the clutches of transgression: Know (1) from whence you come, (2) whither you are going, and (3) before whom you are going to have to give a full account of yourself.

3:1B. "From whence do you come? From a putrid drop. Whither are you going? To a place of dust, worms, and maggots.

3:1C. "And before whom are you going to give a full account of yourself? Before the King of kings of kings, the Holy One, blessed be he."

3:2A. R. Hananiah, Prefect of the Priests, say, "Pray for the welfare of the government. For if it were not for fear of it, one man would swallow his fellow alive."

3:2B. R. Hananiah b. Teradion says, "[If] two sit together and between them do not pass teachings of the Torah, lo, this is a seat of the scornful, as it is said, 'Nor sits in the seat of the scornful' (Ps. 1:1). But two who are sitting, and words of the Torah do pass between them—the Presence is with them, as it is said, 'Then they that feared the Lord spoke with one another, and the Lord hearkened and heard, and a book of remembrance was written before him, for them that feared the Lord and gave thought to his name' (Mal 3:16). I know that this applies to two. How do I know that even if a single person sits and works on the Torah, the Holy One, blessed be He, sets aside a reward for him? As it is said, 'Let him sit alone and keep silent, because he has laid it upon him'" (Lam. 3:28).

3:3. R. Simeon says, "Three who ate at a single table and did not talk about teachings of the Torah while at that table are as though they ate from dead sacrifices (Ps. 106:28), as it is said, 'For all tables are full of vomit and filthiness [if they are] without God' (Ps. 106:28). But three who ate at a single table and did talk about teachings of the Torah while at that table are as if they ate at the table of the Omnipresent, blessed is he, as it is said, 'And he said to me, "This is the table that is before the Lord"'" (Ez. 41:22).

3:4. R. Hananiah b. Hakhinai says, "(1) He who gets up at night, and (2) he who walks around by himself, and (3) he who turns his desire to emptiness—lo, this person is liable for his life."

3:5. R. Nehunia b. Haqqaneh says, "From whoever accepts upon himself the yoke of the Torah do they remove the yoke of the state and the yoke of hard labor. And upon whoever removes from himself the yoke of the Torah do they lay the yoke of the state and the yoke of hard labor."

3:6. R. Halafta of Kefar Hananiah says, "Among ten who sit and work hard on the Torah the Presence comes to rest, as it is said, 'God stands in the congregation of God' (Ps. 82:1). And how do we know that the same is so even of five? For it is said, 'And he has founded his group upon the earth' (Am. 9:6). And how do we know that this is so even of three? Since it is said, 'And he judges among the judges' (Ps. 82:1). And how do we know that this is so even of two? Because it is said, 'Then they that feared the Lord spoke with one another, and the Lord hearkened and heard' (Mal. 3:16). And how do we know that this is so even of one? Since it is said, 'In every place where I record my name I will come to you and I will bless you'" (Ex. 20:24).

3:7A. R. Eleazar of Bartota says, "Give him what is his, for you and yours are his. For so does it say about David, 'For all things come of you, and of your own have we given you'" (I Chron. 29:14).

3:7B. R. Simeon says, "He who is going along the way and repeating [his Torah tradition] but interrupts his repetition and says, 'How beautiful is that tree! How beautiful is that ploughed field!'—Scripture reckons it to him as if he has become liable for his life."

3:8. R. Dosetai b. R. Yannai in the name of R. Meir says, "Whoever forgets a single thing of what he has learned—Scripture reckons it to him as if he has become liable for his life, as it is said, 'Only take heed to yourself and keep your soul diligently, lest you forget the words which your eyes saw' (Deut. 4:9). Is it possible that this is so even if his learning became too much for him? Scripture says, 'Lest they depart from your heart all the days of your life' (Deut. 4:9). Thus he becomes liable for his life only when he will sit down and actually remove [his learning] from his own heart."

3:9A. R. Haninah b. Dosa says, "For anyone whose fear of sin takes precedence over his wisdom, his wisdom will endure. And for anyone whose wisdom takes precedence over his fear of sin, wisdom will not endure."

3:9B. He would say, "Anyone whose deeds are more than his wisdom—his wisdom will endure. And anyone whose wisdom is more than his deeds—his wisdom will not endure."

3:10A. He would say, "Anyone from whom people take pleasure—the Omnipresent takes pleasure from him. And anyone from whom people do not take pleasure, the Omnipresent does not take pleasure from him."

3:10B. R. Dosa b. Harkinas says, "(1) Sleeping late in the morning, (2) drinking wine at noon, (3) chatting with children, and (4) attending the synagogues of the ignorant drive a man out of the world."

3:11. R. Eleazar the Modite says, "(1) He who treats Holy Things as secular, and (2) he who despises the appointed times, (3) he who humiliates his fellow in public, (4) he who removes the signs of the covenant of Abraham, our father (may he rest in peace), and (5) he who exposes aspects of Torah not in accord with the law, even though he has in hand learning in the Torah and good deeds, will have no share in the world to come."

3:12. R. Ishmael says, "(1) Be quick [in service] to a superior, (2) efficient in service [to the state], and (3) receive everybody with joy."

3:13. R. Aqiba says, "(1) Laughter and lightheadedness turn lewdness into a habit. (2) Tradition is a fence for the Torah. (3) Tithes are a fence for wealth. (4) Vows are a fence for abstinence. (5) A fence for wisdom is silence."

3:14A. He would say, "Precious is the human being, who was created in the image [of God]. It was an act of still greater love that it was made known to him that he was created in the image [of God], as it is said, 'For in the image of God he made man' (Gen. 9:6).

3:14B. "Precious are Israelites, who are called children to the Omnipresent. It was an act of still greater love that it was made known to them that they were called children to the Omnipresent, as it is said, 'You are the children of the Lord your God' (Deut. 14:1).

3:14C. "Precious are Israelites, to whom was given the precious thing. It was an act of still greater love that it was made known to them that to them was given that precious thing with which the world was made, as it is said, 'For I give you a good doctrine. Do not forsake my Torah' (Prov. 4:2).

3:15. "Everything is foreseen, and free choice is given. In goodness the world is judged. And all is in accord with the abundance of deed[s]."

3:16A. He would say, "(1) All is handed over as a pledge, (2) and a net is cast over all the living. (3) The store is open, (4) the storekeeper gives credit, (5) the account-book is open, and (6) the hand is writing.

3:16B. "(1) Whoever wants to borrow may come and borrow. (2) The charity-collectors go around every day and collect from man whether he knows it or not. (3) And they have grounds for what they do. (4) And the judgment is a true judgment. (5) And everything is ready for the meal."

3:17A. R. Eleazar b. Azariah says, "If there is no learning of the Torah, there is no proper conduct. If there is no proper conduct, there is no learning in the Torah. If there is no wisdom, there is no reverence. If there is no reverence, there is no wisdom. If there is no understanding, there is no knowledge. If there is no knowledge, there is no understanding. If there is no sustenance, there is no Torah-learning. If there is no Torah-learning, there is no sustenance."

3:17B. He would say, "Anyone whose wisdom is greater than his deeds—to what is he to be likened? To a tree with abundant foliage, but few roots. When the winds come, they will uproot it and blow it down, as it is said, 'He shall be like a tamarisk in the desert and shall not see when good comes, but shall inhabit the parched places in the wilderness' (Jer. 17:6). But anyone whose deeds are greater than his wisdom—to what is he to be likened? To a tree with little foliage, but abundant roots. For even if all the winds in the world were to come and blast at it, they will not move it from its place, as it is said, 'He shall be as a tree planted by the waters, and that spreads out its roots by the river, and shall not fear when heat comes, and his leaf shall be green, and shall not be careful in the year of drought, neither shall cease from yielding fruit'" (Jer. 17:8).

3:18. R. Eleazar Hisma says, "The laws of bird-offerings and of the beginning of the menstrual period—they are indeed the essentials of the Torah. Calculation of the equinoxes and reckoning the numerical value of letters are the savories of wisdom."

Chapter Four

4:1. Ben Zoma says, "Who is a sage? He who learns from everybody, as it is said, 'From all my teachers I have gotten understanding' (Ps. 119:99). Who is strong? He who overcomes his desire, as it is said, 'He who is slow to anger is better than the mighty, and he who rules his spirit than he who takes a city' (Prov. 16:32). Who is rich? He who is happy in what he has, as it is said, 'When you eat the labor of your hands, happy will you be, and it will go well with you' (Ps. 128:2). ["Happy will you be—in this world, and it will go well with you—in the world to come."] Who is honored? He who honors everybody, as it is said, 'For those who honor me I shall honor, and they who despise me will be treated as of no account'" (I Sam. 2:30).

4:2. Ben Azzai says, "Run after the most minor religious duty as after the most important, and flee from transgression. For doing one religious duty draws in its wake doing yet another, and doing one transgression draws in its wake doing yet another. For the reward of doing a religious duty is a religious duty, and the reward of doing a transgression is a transgression."

4:3. He would say, "Do not despise anybody and do not treat anything as unlikely. For you have no one who does not have his time, and you have nothing which does not have its place."

4:4A. R. Levitas of Yavneh says, "Be exceedingly humble, for the future of humanity is the worm."

4:4B. R. Yohanan b. Beroqa says, "Whoever secretly treats the Name of Heaven as profane publicly pays the price. All the same are the one who does so inadvertently and the one who does so deliberately, when it comes to treating the Name of Heaven as profane."

4:5A. R. Ishmael, his son, says, "He who learns so as to teach—they give him a chance to learn and to teach. He who learns so as to carry out his teachings—they give him a chance to learn, to teach, to keep, and to do."

4:5B. R. Sadoq says, "Do not make [Torah teachings] a crown in which to glorify yourself or a spade with which to dig." So did Hillel say, "He who uses the crown perishes. Thus have you learned: Whoever derives wordly benefit from teachings of the Torah takes his life out of this world."

4:6. R. Yosé says, "Whoever honors the Torah himself is honored by people. And whoever disgraces the Torah himself is disgraced by people."

4:7. R. Ishmael, his son, says, "He who avoids serving as a judge avoids the power of enmity, robbery, and false swearing. And he who is arrogant about making decisions is a fool, evil, and prideful."

4:8. He would say, "Do not serve as a judge by yourself, for there is only One who serves as a judge all alone. And do not say, 'Accept my opinion,' for they have the choice in the matter, not you."

4:9. R. Jonathan says, "Whoever keeps the Torah when poor will in the end keep it in wealth. And whoever treats the Torah as nothing when he is wealthy in the end will treat it as nothing in poverty."

4:10. R. Meir says, "Keep your business to a minimum and make your business the Torah. And be humble before everybody. And if you treat the Torah as nothing, you will have many treating you as nothing. And if you have labored in the Torah, [the Torah] has a great reward to give you."

4:11A. R. Eleazar b. Jacob says, "He who does even a single religious duty gets himself a good advocate. He who does even a single transgression gets himself a powerful prosecutor. Penitence and good deeds are like a shield against punishment."

4:11B. R. Yohanan Hassandelar says, "Any gathering which is for the sake of Heaven is going to endure. And any which is not for the sake of Heaven is not going to endure."

4:12. R. Eleazar b. Shammua says, "The honor owing to your disciple should be as precious to you as yours. And the honor owing to your fellow should be like the reverence owing to your master. And the reverence owing to your master should be like the awe owing to Heaven."

4:13A. R. Judah says, "Be meticulous about learning, for error in learning leads to deliberate [violation of the Torah]."

4:13B. R. Simeon says, "There are three crowns: the crown of the Torah, the crown of priesthood, and the crown of sovereignty. But the crown of a good name is best of them all."

4:14. R. Nehorai says, "Go into exile to a place of the Torah, and do not suppose that it will come to you. For your fellow-disciples will make it solid in your hand. And on your own understanding do not rely."

4:15A. R. Yannai says, "We do not have in hand [an explanation] either for the prosperity of the wicked or for the suffering of the righteous."

4:15B. R. Matya b. Harash says, "Greet everybody first, and be a tail to lions. But do not be a head of foxes."

4:16. R. Jacobs says, "This world is like an antechamber before the world to come. Get ready in the antechamber, so you can go into the great hall."

4:17. He would say, "Better is a single moment spent in penitence and good deeds in this world than the whole of the world to come. And better is a single moment of inner peace in the world to come than the whole of a lifetime spent in this world."

4:18. R. Simeon b. Eleazar says, "(1) Do not try to make amends with your fellow when he is angry, or (2) comfort him when the corpse of his beloved is lying before him, or (3) seek to find absolution for him at the moment at which he takes vow, or (4) attempt to see him when he is humiliated."

4:19. Samuel the Small says, "Rejoice not when your enemy falls, and let not your heart be glad when he is overthrown, lest the Lord see it and it displease him, and he turn away his wrath from him" (Prov. 24:17).

4:20. Elisha b. Abuyah says, "He who learns when a child—what is he like? Ink put down on a clean piece of paper. And he who learns when an old man—what is he like? Ink put down on a paper full of erasures."

4:21A. R. Yosé b. R. Judah of Kefar Habbabli says, "He who learns from children— what is he like? One who eats sour grapes and drinks fresh wine. And he who learns from old men—what is he like? He who eats ripe grapes and drinks vintage wine."

4:21B. Rabbi says, "Do not look at the bottle but at what is in it. You can have a new bottle of old wine, and an old bottle which has not got even new wine."

4:22A. R. Eleazar Haqqappar says, "Jealousy, lust, and ambition drive a person out of this world."

4:22B. He would say, "Those who are born are [destined] to die, and those who die are [destined] for resurrection. And the living are [destined] to be judged—so as to know, to make known, and to confirm that (1) he is God, (2) he is the one who forms, (3) he is the one who creates, (4) he is the one who understands, (5) he is the one who judges, (6) he is the one who gives evidence, (7) he is the one who brings suit, (8) and he is the one who is going to make the ultimate judgment.

4:22C. "Blessed be he, for before him are no (1) guile, (2) forgetfulness, (3) respect for persons, or (4) bribe-taking, for everything is his. And know that everything is subject to reckoning. And do not let your evil impulse persuade you that Sheol is a place of refuge for you. For (1) despite your wishes were you formed, (2) despite your wishes were you born, (3) despite your wishes do you live, (4) despite your wishes do you die, and (5) despite your wishes are you going to give a full accounting before the King of kings of kings, the Holy One, blessed be he."

Chapter Five

5:1. By ten acts of speech was the world made. And what does Scripture mean [by having God say *say* ten times]? It is to exact punishment from the wicked, who destroy a world which was created through ten acts of speech, and to secure a good reward for the righteous, who sustain a world which was created through ten acts of speech.

5:2. There are ten generations from Adam to Noah, to show you how long-suffering is [God]. For all those generations went along spiting him until he brought the water of the flood upon them. There are ten generations from Noah to Abraham, to show you how long-suffering is [God]. For all those generations went along spiting him, until Abraham came along and took the reward which had been meant for all of them.

5:3. Ten trials were inflicted upon Abraham, our father, may he rest in peace, and he withstood all of them, to show you how great is his love for Abraham, our father, may he rest in peace.

5:4. Ten wonders were done for our fathers in Egypt, and ten at the Sea. Ten blows did the Holy One, blessed be he, bring upon the Egyptians in Egypt, and ten at the Sea. Ten trials did our fathers inflict upon the Omnipresent, blessed be he, in the wilderness, as it is said, 'Yet they have tempted me these ten times and have not listened to my voice' (Num. 14:22).

5:5. Ten wonders were done for our fathers in the Temple: (1) A woman never miscarried on account of the stench of the meat of Holy Things. (2) And the meat of the Holy Things never turned rotten. (3) A fly never made an appearance in the slaughter house. (4) A high priest never suffered a nocturnal emission on the eve of the Day of Atonement. (5) The rain never quenched the fire on the altar. (6) No wind ever blew away the pillar of smoke. (7) An invalidating factor never affected the 'omer, the Two Loaves, or the show bread. (8) When the people are standing, they are jammed together. When they go down and prostrate themselves, they have plenty of room. (9) A snake and a scorpion never bit anybody in Jerusalem. (10) And no one ever said to his fellow, "The place is too crowded for me" (Is. 49:20) to stay in Jerusalem.

5:6A. Ten things were created on the eve of the Sabbath [Friday] at twilight, and these are they: (1) the mouth of the earth [Num. 16:32]; (2) the mouth of the well [Num. 21:16–18]; (3) the mouth of the ass [Num. 22:38]; (4) the rainbow [Gen. 9:13]; (5) the manna [Ex. 16:15]; (6) the rod [Ex. 4:17]; (7) the Shamir; (8) letters, (9) writing, (10) and the tables of stone [of the Ten Commandments, Ex. 32:15f].

5:6B. And some say, "Also the destroyers, the grave of Moses, and the tamarisk of Abraham, our father."

5:6C. And some say, "Also: the tongs made with tongs [with which the first tongs were made]."

5:7. There are seven traits to an unformed clod, and seven to a sage. (1) A sage does not speak before someone greater than he in wisdom. (2) And he does not interrupt his fellow. (3) And he is not at a loss for an answer. (4) He asks a relevant question and answers properly. (5) And he addresses each matter in its proper sequence, first, then second. (6) And concerning something he has not heard, he says, "I have not heard the answer." (7) And he concedes the truth [when the other party demonstrates it]. And the opposite of these traits apply to a clod.

5:8. There are seven forms of punishment which come upon the world for seven kinds of transgression. (1) [If] some people give tithes and some people do not give tithes, there is a famine from drought. So some people are hungry and some have enough. (2) [If] everyone decided not to tithe, there is famine of unrest and drought. (3) [If all decided] not to remove dough-offering, there is a famine of totality. (4) Pestilence comes to the world on account of the death penalties which are listed in the Torah but which are not in the hands of the court [to inflict]; and because of the produce of the Seventh Year [which people buy and sell]. (5) A sword comes into the world because of the delaying of justice and perversion of justice, and because of those who teach the Torah not in accord with the law.

5:9A. (6) A plague of wild animals comes into the world because of vain oaths and desecration of the Divine Name. (7) Exile comes into the world because of those who worship idols, because of fornication, and because of bloodshed, and because of the neglect of the release of the land [in the year of release].

5:9B. At four turnings in the year pestilence increases: in the fourth year, in the Seventh Year, in the year after the Seventh Year, and at the end of the Festival [of Tabernacles] every year: (1) in the fourth year, because of the poorman's tithe of the third year [which people have neglected to hand over to the poor]; (2) in the Seventh Year, because of the poorman's tithe of the sixth year; (3) in the year after the Seventh Year, because of the dealing in produce of the Seventh Year; and (4) at the end of the Festival every year, because of the thievery of the dues [gleanings and the like] owing to the poor [not left for them in the antecedent harvest].

5:10. There are four sorts of people. (1) He who says, "What's mine is mine and what's yours is yours"—this is the average sort. (And some say, "This is the sort of Sodom.") (2) "What's mine is yours and what's yours is mine"—this is a boor. (3) "What's mine is yours and what's yours is yours"—this is a truly pious man. (4) "What's mine is mine and what's yours is mine"—this is a truly wicked man.

5:11. There are four sorts of personality: (1) easily angered, easily calmed—he loses what he gains; (2) hard to anger, hard to calm—what he loses he gains; (3) hard to anger and easy to calm—a truly pious man; (4) easy to anger and hard to calm—a truly wicked man.

5:12. There are four types of disciples: (1) quick to grasp, quick to forget—he loses what he gains; (2) slow to grasp, slow to forget—what he loses he gains; (3) quick to grasp, slow to forget—a sage; (4) slow to grasp, quick to forget—a bad lot indeed.

5:13. There are four traits among people who give charity: (1) he who wants to give, but does not want others to give—he begrudges what belongs to others; (2) he who wants others to give, but does not want to give—he begrudges what belongs to himself; (3) he who will give and wants others to give—he is truly pious; (4) he who will not give and does not want others to give—he is truly wicked.

5:14. There are four sorts among those who go to the study-house: (1) he who goes but does not carry out [what he learns]—he has at least the reward for the going. (2) he who practices but does not go [to study]—he has at least the reward for the doing. (3) he who both goes and practices—he is truly pious; (4) he who neither goes nor practices—he is truly wicked.

5:15. There are four traits among those who sit before the sages: a sponge, a funnel, a strainer, and a sifter. (1) A sponge—because he sponges everything up; (2) a funnel—because he takes in on one side and lets out on the other; (3) a strainer—for he lets out the wine and keeps in the lees; (4) and a sifter—for he lets out the [coarse] flour and keeps in the finest flour.

5:16. [In] any loving relationship which depends upon something, [when] that thing is gone, the love is gone. But any which does not depend upon something will never come to an end. What is a loving relationship which depends upon something? That is the love of Amnon and Tamar [II Sam. 13:15]. And one which does not depend upon something? That is the love of David and Jonathan.

5:17. Any dispute which is for the sake of Heaven will in the end yield results, and any which is not for the sake of Heaven will in the end not yield results. What is a dispute for the sake of Heaven? This is the sort of dispute between Hillel and Shammai. And what is one which is not for the sake of Heaven? It is the dispute of Korach and all his party.

5:18. He who brings merit to the community never causes sin. And he who causes the community to sin—they never give him a sufficient chance to attain penitence. Moses attained merit and bestowed merit on the community. So the merit of the community is assigned to his [credit], as it is said, "He executed the justice of the Lord and his judgments with Israel" (Deut. 33:21). Jeroboam sinned and caused the community of the Israelites to sin. So the sin of the community is assigned to his [debit], as it is said, "For the sins of Jeroboam which he committed and wherewith he made Israel to sin" (1 Kings 15:30).

5:19. Anyone in whom are these three traits is one of the disciples of Abraham, our father; but [if he bears] three other traits, he is one of the disciples of Balaam, the wicked; (1) a generous spirit, (2) a modest mien, and (3) a humble soul—he is one of the disciples of Abraham, our father. He who exhibits (1) a grudging spirit, (2) an arrogant mien, and (3) a proud soul—he is one of the disciples of Balaam, the wicked. What is the difference between the disciples of Abraham our father and the disciples of Balaam the wicked? The disciples of Abraham our father enjoy the benefit [of their learning] in this world and yet inherit the world to come, as it is said, "That I may cause those who love me to inherit substance, and so that I may fill their treasures" (Prov. 8:21). The disciples of Balaam the wicked inherit Gehenna and go down to the Pit of Destruction, as it is said, "But you, O God, shall bring them down into the pit of destruction; bloodthirsty and deceitful men shall not live out half their days" (ps. 55:24).

5:20A. Judah b. Tema says, "Be strong as a leopard, fast as an eagle, fleet as a gazelle, and grave as a lion, to carry out the will of your Father who is in heaven."

5:20B. He would say, "The shameless go to Gehenna, and the diffident to the garden of Eden.

5:20C. "May it be found pleasing before you, O Lord our God, that you rebuild your city quickly in our day and set our portion in your Torah."

5:21. He would say, "(1) At five to Scripture, (2) ten to Mishnah, (3) thirteen to religious duties, (4) fifteen to Talmud, (5) eighteen to the wedding canopy, (6) twenty to responsibility for providing for a family, (7) thirty to fullness of strength, (8) forty to understanding, (9) fifty to counsel, (10) sixty to old age, (11) seventy to ripe old age, (12) eighty to remarkable strength, (13) ninety to a bowed back, and (14) at a hundred—he is like a corpse who has already passed and gone from this world."

5:22. Ben Bag Bag says [in Aramaic], "Turn it over and over because everything is in it. And reflect upon it now, grow old and worn in it and do not leave it, [in Hebrew] for you have no better lot than that."

5:23. Ben He He says, "In accord with the effort is the reward."

Appendix to Chapter One:
Comparing The Fathers to The Fathers
According to Rabbi Nathan

Our twofold task is accomplished in a single experiment. We wish to know the basic structure of The Fathers and The Fathers According to Rabbi Nathan, and we also want to compare one to the other. We shall therefore juxtapose the entirety of the former with an outline of the latter (any other procedure would require an enormous book, since The Fathers According to Rabbi Nathan is approximately 250 printed pages). Let me remind the reader of what I have said earlier about the use of different type faces. In order to make clear the way in which the later document takes up the earlier one, I use typefaces that allow immediate recognition of the various sorts of materials and how they are put together.

    1. **Boldface type:** At issue is the relationship of The Fathers According to Rabbi Nathan to The Fathers. The Fathers therefore serves as the base structure; The Fathers According to Rabbi Nathan is the variable. Sayings of The Fathers are given in **boldface type,** and the outline of the contents of The Fathers According to Rabbi Nathan in regular type.

    2. SMALL CAPS: Where a saying in the The Fathers undergoes no treatment in The Fathers According to Rabbi Nathan, it is given in its proper place and order, but printed in SMALL CAPS. (That clear identification of material in The Fathers that is ignored by The Fathers According to Rabbi Nathan lays the foundations for the discussion in chapter 3 of how the documents differ in contents.) Furthermore, where a saying in The Fathers is treated at some location in The Fathers According to Rabbi Nathan other than in the normal sequence of the exposition of The Fathers, I present that saying also in small caps. In this way we see precisely the points at which The Fathers has governed the expository structure of The Fathers According to Rabbi Nathan, and where the order and program of the sayings of The Fathers have been ignored. It follows that sayings in small caps do not serve the redactor for the ordering and exposition of the composition at hand.

    3. *Italics:* Italics serve a special purpose. Since The Fathers According to Rabbi Nathan contains a fair amount of supplementary material (appendices inserted because they intersect with a theme introduced by the exegetical discourse), I indicate what is supplementary by *italics.* The reader will thus readily distinguish what I deem primary from what I take to be a secondary enrichment.

The Fathers Chapter One

1:1. **Moses received the Torah at Sinai . . .**
   I:I. **Moses** was sanctified in a cloud and **received Torah at Sinai.**
   I:I.1–2. As above.
   I:I.3. Appendix joined because of a named authority.
  I:II. By means of Moses the Torah was given at Sinai.
   I:II.1. As above.
   I:II.2. *Moses is the one who prepared lambs for the consecration of the priesthood, etc.*

1:1B. **. . . and handed it on to Joshua, Joshua to elders, and elders to prophets. And prophets handed it on to the men of the great assembly. They said three things, "Be prudent in judgment."**

  I:III–IV. The chain of tradition.
   I:III.1–5. Citation of successive names plus proof text.
   I:IV.1. As above.
  I:V. **Be prudent in judgment.**
   I:V.1. Spelled out ("tarry in giving judgment") plus proof text.
   I:V.2. Spelled out ("be forbearing in opinions and not too exacting") plus illustration in the case of Moses.
   I:V.3. Continuation of the foregoing.
   I:V.4. Ben Azzai's explanation of the same statement.

1:1D. **"Make a fence for the Torah."**

  I:VI. **Make a fence for the Torah.**
   I:VI.1. List of eight who made a fence for their words. These eight are then spelled out, with the fence they made described.
  I:VII. What is the fence that the Holy One made around his words?
  I:VIII. What is the fence that the first man made around his words?
    I:IX–XVIII. *Large anthology on the first man.*
  II:I.1. What sort of fence did the Torah make around its words? It was a stricter requirement than the law really demands in connection with separation from a woman during her menstrual period.
  I:I.2. As above.
  I:I.3. As above.
  I:I.4. As above.
  II:I.5. The same theme, namely, sexual taboos, is focused on a different conception, namely, there are minor religious duties that produce a great reward.
  II:II.1. What sort of fence did Moses make around his words? Moses on his own volition added to the instructions God gave him.
  II:III.1–4. Other instances in which Moses on his own volition did something with which, after the fact, God concurred.

II:IV.1. Instances in which Hezekiah on his own volition did something with which, after the fact, God [elsewhere: sages] concurred.

II:V.1. What sort of fence did Job make around his words? He avoided not only transgression but even something that might appear to lead to transgression.

II:V.2. *Because the foregoing refers to Job 1:8, which says that Job was unblemished, and which sages understand to mean that Job was born circumcised, we have a catalogue of others born circumcised.*

II:V.3. Specific instance of Job's making a fence around the divine law by avoiding something that might appear to lead to transgression, specifically, gazing even upon an unmarried woman.

II:VI. What sort of fence did prophets make for their words? This question is not given a clear answer. They understated God's attributes, rather than exaggerating the law's requirements.

II:VII.1. What sort of fence did the Writings make around their words? The basic point is that one should not only avoid wicked people but also not go anywhere near them.

II:VII.1. Avoid heretics and do not feel overconfident of being able to resist them.

II:VII.2. Avoid whores as above.

II:VIII.1. What sort of fence did sages make around their words?

II:VIII.1. Recite the *Shema* before taking a nap in the evening.

II:VIII.2. The same basic point about hedges around proper recitation of the *Shema*.

1:1C. "Raise up many disciples."

III:I.1. **Raise up many disciples,** plus the Houses on whether one should teach only appropriate candidates or whoever comes.

III:II.1–4. *Aqiba-sayings: If one lies about a condition from which he does not suffer, he will end up suffering from that condition.*

III:III.1. *Aqiba's ruling in a case. Not related to foregoing.* I have no idea why these items appear here.

III:IV. A set of sayings illustrative in diverse ways of Qoh. 11:6. Keep up a good practice early and late in life. This tangentially illustrates the notion of raising up many disciples.

III:IV.1. R. Dosa b. R. Yannai: Persist in what you do, because you do not know the result of your earlier effort, so keep it up.

III:IV.2. Ishmael: Study Torah when young and old.

III:IV.3. Aqiba: Study Torah when you are young and old. [Goldin adds: teach disciples when young and old.]

III:IV.4. Meir: Study with different masters.

III:IV.5. Study with four masters, such as Eliezer, Joshua, Aqiba, Tarfon.

III:IV.6. Joshua: Marry and have children when young and when old.

III:IV.7. Give charity to a beggar in the morning and do the same at night.

    III:V.1. *Story about a man who gave to charity.*

    III:VI.1. *Story about a man who gave to charity.*

    III:VII.1. *Story about a man who gave to charity.*

1:2. Simeon the Righteous was one of the last survivors of the great assembly. He would say, "On three things does the world stand: On the Torah, and on the Temple service, and on deeds of loving-kindness."

    IV:I.1. Citation of Simeon's statement.

    IV:II.1. **On the Torah:** how so? Burnt offering is most desirable. But study of the Torah is superior.

    IV:III.1. Sages should interrupt their study to carry out deeds of loving-kindness, if there is no one else available to do so. Comparison of importance of Torah study to deeds of loving-kindness. The latter are deemed more important.

    IV:III.2. Judah b. Ilai interrupted his teaching to celebrate a bride. [Omitted: if there is no one else available to do so.]

    IV:III.3. Same.

    IV:IV.1. **On the Temple service:** how so? When the Temple service is carried on, nature gives its blessings.

    IV:IV.2. Same point, different proof text. Nothing is more beloved than the Temple service.

    IV:V.1. **Deeds of loving-kindness:** how so? World was created only for loving-kindness.

    IV:V.2. Yohanan ben Zakkai: Deeds of loving-kindness are a means of atonement as effective as sacrifice of animals.

    IV:V.3. Daniel did such deeds, and not sacrifices. They were acts of celebration of the bride, burial of the dead, charity, and prayer.

    IV:VI.1. Destruction of the Temple.

    IV:VI.2. *Same.*

    IV:VI.3–4. *Same.*

    IV:VII.1. *God diversified human beings in three aspects.*

1:3. Antigonus of Sokho received [the Torah] from Simeon the Righteous. He would say, "Do not be like servants who serve the master on condition of receiving a reward, but [be] like servants who serve the master not on condition of receiving a reward. And let the fear of Heaven be upon you."

    V:I.1. Citation and gloss of Antigonus's saying.

    V:II.1. Story about what is at stake in that saying, with reference to the disciples, who formed two sects.

1:4. Yosé ben Yoezer of Zeredah and Yosé ben Yohanan of Jerusalem received [the Torah] from them. Yosé ben Yoezer says: "Let your house be a gathering place for sages. And wallow in the dust of their feet, and drink in their words with gusto."

VI:I.1. Citation and gloss of Yosé b. Yoezer's saying.

VI:II.1–2. Same as above.

VI:III.1. Same as above.

VI:IV.1. Prologue to stories about Aqiba and Eliezer, in a general way illustrative of **wallowing in the dust of the feet of sages:**

VI:V.1. *Aqiba began studying at forty, knew nothing.*

VI:V.2. *Simeon b. Eleazar: Parable on basic theme of foregoing.*

VI:V.3. *Tarfon on Aqiba, in line with basic theme.*

VI:V.4. *New theme: Aqiba supported himself in poverty.*

VI:V.5. *Same as above.*

VI:V.6. *Got rich.*

VI:VI.1. *Eliezer's beginnings in ignorance in mature years.*

VI:VI.2. *Starved, bad-breath saying.*

VI:VI.3. *Same as above.*

VI:VI.4. *Got rich in the end: father gave him his whole estate.*

VI:VII.1. *The mention in VI:VI.4 of three famous dignitaries of Jerusalem before whom Eliezer spoke leads to exposition of materials on all three of them.*

VI:VIII.1. *As above.*

VI:IX.1. *As above.*

VI:X.1. *As above.*

1:5. **Yosé ben Yohanan of Jerusalem says, "Let your house be open wide. And seat the poor at your table ["make the poor members of your household"]. And don't talk too much with women. (He referred to a man's wife; all the more so is the rule to be applied to the wife of one's fellow. In this regard did sages say, "So long as a man talks too much with a woman, he brings trouble on himself, wastes time better spent on studying the Torah, and ends up an heir of Gehenna.")**

VII:I.1. **Let your house be wide open**—north, south, etc., like Job.

VII:II.1. **And seat the poor at your table,** like Job. But Abraham was a greater model for the perfect host than Job.

VII:III.1. Illustrating how to treat the poor: Teach the members of your household humility. [This is illustrated by reference to appropriate hospitality to the poor.]

VII:IV.1. Same as above. Now illustrated by importance of avoiding contention.

VII:V.1. **Don't talk too much with women:** cited.

VII:VI.1. Foregoing is illustrated in terms of the life of the study-house. Specifically, do not bring home the quarrels of the study-house. It is demeaning to all concerned.

1:6. **Joshua ben Perahyah and Nittai the Arbelite received [the Torah] from them. Joshua ben Perahyah says, "Set up a master for yourself. And get yourself a companion-disciple. And give everybody the benefit of the doubt."**

VIII:I.1. Amplification of **Set up a master for yourself.** Have a single teacher for all subjects.

VIII:I.2. Same as above, parable.

VIII:II.1. Amplification of **Get yourself a companion-disciple.**

VIII:III.1–3. Special cases, if three, two, or one study by themselves, they get credit in heaven. Appendix on the same theme as the foregoing.

VIII:IV.1. **And give everybody the benefit of the doubt** spelled out, example.

VIII:V.1. Same as above.

VIII:VI.1–2. *Appendix on what captives eat.*

1:7. **Nittai the Arbelite says, "Keep away from a bad neighbor. And don't get involved with a bad person. And don't give up hope of retribution."**

IX:I.1. **Keep away from a bad neighbor,** because a bad neighbor may be the cause of having to tear down one's house. A bad neighbor, for example, may be a gossip and may therefore cause leprosy to develop on a wall that is shared both by him and by his fellow.

IX:II.1. *The evils of gossip.*

IX:III.1–5. *The evils of gossip. Aaron and Miriam.*

IX:III.6. *Appendix: Moses was meek.*

IX:IV.1. *The evils of gossip and of arrogance. Gehazi and Hezekiah.*

IX:V.1. **And don't get involved with a bad person:** three probative examples.

IX:VI.1. **Don't get involved with a bad person:** minor clarification.

IX:VII.1. **Don't despair of retribution:** means to expect punishment at any time.

IX:VIII.1. Same statement clarified in a different way.

1:8A. **Judah ben Tabbai and Simeon ben Shetah received [the Torah] from them.**

1:8B. **Judah ben Tabbai says, "Don't make yourself like one of those who advocate before judges [while you yourself are judging a case]. And when the litigants stand before you, regard them as guilty. But when they leave you, regard them as acquitted (when they have accepted your judgment)."**

X:I.1. Listen to the reasoning of a ruling before replying to it.

X:I.2. Do not favor either the rich or the poor, plus Dt. 1:17.

X:I.3. *Further comment on Dt. 1:17. Meir plus Judah.*

X:II.1. *Further saying of Judah.*

1:9. **Simeon ben Shetah says, "Examine the witnesses with great care. And watch what you say, lest they learn from what you say how to lie."**

X:III.1. Simeon b. Shetah's saying is paraphrased.

1:10. **Shemaiah and Avtalyon received [the Torah] from them. Shemaiah says, "Love work. Hate authority. Don't get friendly with the government."**

XI:I.1. **Love work,** and do not hate work. Work involves a covenant.

XI:I.2. Work may save one's life.

XI:I.3. If one does not work six days, he may end up working seven days.

XI:I.4. The first man had to work to eat.

XI:I.5. Israel had to work before the Presence of God came to rest in it.

XI:I.6. Any sort of work is better than idleness.

XI:I.7. One dies of idleness.

XI:I.8. Complement to foregoing.

XI:II.1. **Hate authority:** Do not honor yourself; let others do so.

XI:II.2. Same point as above, now with special reference to teachings of Torah.

XI:II.3. As above.

XI:III.1. **Do not get friendly with the government** means do not become known to the government, because they will take away everything you have.

XI:IV.1. As above.

XI:V.1. As above.

XI:VI.1. As above.

1:11. **Avtalyon says, "Sages, watch what you say, lest you become liable to the punishment of exile, and go into exile to a place of bad water, and disciples who follow you drink bad water and die, and the name of Heaven be thereby profaned."**

XI:VII.1. Gloss of Avtalyon's statement.

1:12. **Hillel and Shammai received [the Torah] from them. Hillel says, "Be disciples of Aaron, loving peace and pursuing grace, loving people and drawing them near to the Torah."**

1:13A. **He would say [in Aramaic], "A name made great is a name destroyed, and one who does not add, subtracts.**

1:13B. **"And who does not learn is liable to death. And the one who uses the crown, passes away."**

1:14. **He would say, "If I am not for myself, who is for me? And when I am for myself, what am I? And if not now, when?"**

XII:I.1. **Loving peace:** how so?

XII:I.2. What does it mean to love peace as Aaron did? Amplification of proof text in foregoing.

XII:I.3. Mourning for Aaron exceeded that of Moses: why?

XII:I.4. Same as above.

XII:I.5. Same as above.

XII:II.1. Continues foregoing.

XII:II.2. Continues foregoing.

XII:II.3. Continues foregoing.

XII:II.4. Continues foregoing.

XII:II.5. Continues foregoing.

XII:III.1. **. . . and pursuing peace:** how so?

XII:III.2. What it means to pursue peace.

XII:III.3. God does the same.

XII:IV.1. **Loving people:** how so?

XII:V.1. **And drawing them near to the Torah:** how so?
XII:VII.1. **He would say, "If I am not for myself, who is for me?"**
[XII:VI.1–2. Illustrate the foregoing and are presently out of place.]
XII:VIII.1. He would say, "If you will come to my house, I shall come to your house. To the place which my heart loves, there my feet lead me."
XII:IX.1. If I am here all are here . . . in accord with the pain is the gain: illustrated.

[2:7. **He saw a skull floating on the water. He said to it, "Because you drowned others, they drowned you, and those who drowned you will be drowned."**]

XII:X.1. **Skull floating on the water.**
XII:XI.1. **Name made great.**
XII:XII. Amplification of foregoing.
XII:XIII.1. **And who does not serve as disciple to sages is liable to death:** how so?
XII:XIV.1. **One who does not add subtracts:** how so?
XIV:XV.1. **One who makes worldly use of the crown:** how so?

1:15. Shammai says, **"Make your learning of the Torah a fixed obligation. Say little and do much. Greet everybody cheerfully."**

XIII:I.1. Shammai cited: **Make your study of Torah a fixed obligation.**
XIII:II.1. **Say little and do much.** Example of Abraham.
XIII:II.2. Continuation of foregoing.
XIII:II.3. Continuation of foregoing.
XIII:II.4. Continuation of foregoing.
XIII:III.1. **Greet everybody cheerfully.**

1:16. RABBAN GAMALIEL SAYS, "SET UP A MASTER FOR YOURSELF. AVOID DOUBT. DON'T TITHE BY TOO MUCH GUESSWORK."
1:17. SIMEON HIS SON SAYS: "ALL MY LIFE I GREW UP AMONG THE SAGES, AND I FOUND NOTHING BETTER FOR A PERSON [THE BODY] THAN SILENCE. AND NOT THE LEARNING IS THE THING, BUT THE DOING. AND WHOEVER TALKS TOO MUCH CAUSES SIN."
1:18. RABBAN SIMEON BEN GAMALIEL SAYS, "ON THREE THINGS DOES THE WORLD STAND: ON JUSTICE, ON TRUTH, AND ON PEACE. AS IT IS SAID, 'EXECUTE THE JUDGMENT OF TRUTH AND PEACE IN YOUR GATES.'" (ZECH. 8:16). [These do occur elsewhere.]

The Fathers Chapter Two

2:1. RABBI SAYS, "WHAT IS THE STRAIGHT PATH WHICH A PERSON SHOULD CHOOSE FOR HIMSELF? WHATEVER IS AN ORNAMENT TO THE ONE WHO FOLLOWS IT, AND AN ORNAMENT IN THE VIEW OF OTHERS. BE METICULOUS IN A SMALL RELIGIOUS DUTY AS IN A LARGE ONE, FOR YOU DO NOT KNOW WHAT SORT OF REWARD IS COMING FOR ANY OF THE VARIOUS RELIGIOUS DUTIES. AND RECKON WITH THE LOSS [REQUIRED]

IN CARRYING OUT A RELIGIOUS DUTY AGAINST THE REWARD FOR DOING IT; AND THE REWARD FOR COMMITTING A TRANSGRESSION AGAINST THE LOSS FOR DOING IT. AND KEEP YOUR EYE ON THREE THINGS, SO YOU WILL NOT COME INTO THE CLUTCHES OF TRANSGRESSION. KNOW WHAT IS ABOVE YOU. AN EYE WHICH SEES, AND AN EAR WHICH HEARS, AND ALL YOUR ACTIONS ARE WRITTEN DOWN IN A BOOK."

2:2. RABBAN GAMALIEL, A SON OF RABBI JUDAH THE PATRIARCH, SAYS, "FITTING IS LEARNING IN THE TORAH ALONG WITH A CRAFT, FOR THE LABOR PUT INTO THE TWO OF THEM MAKES ONE FORGET SIN. AND ALL LEARNING OF THE TORAH WHICH IS NOT JOINED WITH LABOR IS DESTINED TO BE NULL AND CAUSES SIN. AND ALL WHO WORK WITH THE COMMUNITY—LET THEM WORK WITH THEM [THE COMMUNITY] FOR THE SAKE OF HEAVEN. FOR THE MERIT OF THE FATHERS STRENGTHENS THEM, AND THE RIGHTEOUSNESS WHICH THEY DO STANDS FOREVER. AND, AS FOR YOU, I CREDIT YOU WITH A GREAT REWARD, AS IF YOU HAD DONE [ALL THE WORK RE-QUIRED BY THE COMMUNITY].

2:3. "BE WARY OF THE GOVERNMENT, FOR THEY GET FRIENDLY WITH A PERSON ONLY FOR THEIR OWN CONVENIENCE. THEY LOOK LIKE FRIENDS WHEN IT IS TO THEIR BENEFIT, BUT THEY DO NOT STAND BY A PERSON WHEN HE IS IN NEED."

2:4. HE WOULD SAY, "MAKE HIS WISHES INTO YOUR OWN WISHES, SO THAT HE WILL MAKE YOUR WISHES INTO HIS WISHES. PUT ASIDE YOUR WISHES ON ACCOUNT OF HIS WISHES, SO THAT HE WILL PUT ASIDE THE WISHES OF OTHER PEOPLE IN FAVOR OF YOUR WISHES." HILLEL SAYS: "DO NOT WALK OUT ON THE COMMUNITY. AND DO NOT HAVE CONFIDENCE IN YOURSELF UNTIL THE DAY YOU DIE. AND DO NOT JUDGE YOUR COMPANION UNTIL YOU ARE IN HIS PLACE. AND DO NOT SAY ANYTHING WHICH CANNOT BE HEARD, FOR IN THE END IT WILL BE HEARD. AND DO NOT SAY: 'WHEN I HAVE TIME, I SHALL STUDY,' FOR YOU MAY NEVER HAVE TIME."

2:5. HE WOULD SAY, "A COARSE PERSON WILL NEVER FEAR SIN, NOR WILL AN *AM HA-ARETZ* EVER BE PIOUS, NOR WILL A SHY PERSON LEARN, NOR WILL AN IGNO-RANT PERSON TEACH, NOR WILL ANYONE TOO OCCUPIED IN BUSINESS GET WISE. IN A PLACE WHERE THERE ARE NO INDIVIDUALS, TRY TO BE AN INDIVIDUAL."

2:7. HE WOULD SAY, "LOTS OF MEAT, LOTS OF WORMS; LOTS OF PROPERTY, LOTS OF WORRIES; LOTS OF WOMEN, LOTS OF WITCHCRAFT; LOTS OF SLAVE GIRLS, LOTS OF LUST; LOTS OF SLAVE BOYS, LOTS OF ROBBERY. LOTS OF THE TORAH, LOTS OF LIFE; LOTS OF DISCIPLESHIP, LOTS OF WISDOM; LOTS OF COUNSEL, LOTS OF UNDERSTAND-ING; LOTS OF RIGHTEOUSNESS, LOTS OF PEACE. [IF] ONE HAS GOTTEN A GOOD NAME, HE HAS GOTTEN IT FOR HIMSELF. [IF] HE HAS GOTTEN TEACHINGS OF THE TORAH, HE HAS GOTTEN HIMSELF LIFE ETERNAL."

2:8A. **Rabban Yohanan ben Zakkai received [the Torah] from Hillel and Shammai. He would say, "If you have learned much Torah, do not puff your-self up on that account, for it was for that purpose that you were created." He had five disciples, and these are they: Rabbi Eliezer ben Hyrcanus, Rabbi Joshua ben Hananiah, Rabbi Yosé the Priest, Rabbi Simeon ben Nethanel, and Rabbi Eleazar ben Arakh.**

2:8B. **He would list their good qualities, "Rabbi Eliezer ben Hyracanus—a plastered well, which does not lose a drop of water. Rabbi Joshua—happy is the one who gave birth to him. Rabbi Yosé—a pious man. Rabbi Simeon ben Nethanel—a man who fears sin, and Rabbi Eleazar ben Arakh—a surging spring."**

2:8C. He would say, "If all the sages of Israel were on one side of the scale, and Rabbi Eliezer ben Hyrcanus were on the other, he would outweigh all of them."

2:8D. Abba Saul says in his name, "If all of the sages of Israel were on one side of the scale, and Rabbi Eliezer ben Hyrcanus was also with them, and Rabbi Eleazar [ben Arakh] were on the other side, he would outweigh all of them."

2:9A. He said to them, "Go and see what is the straight path to which someone should stick."

2:9B. Rabbi Eliezer says, "A generous spirit." Rabbi Joshua says: "A good friend." Rabbi Yosé says: "A good neighbor." Rabbi Simeon says: "Foresight." Rabbi Eleazar says: "Good will."

2:9C. He said to them, "I prefer the opinion of Rabbi Eleazar ben Arakh, because in what he says is included everything you say."

2:9D. He said to them, "Go out and see what is the bad road, which someone should avoid." Rabbi Eliezer says, "Envy." Rabbi Joshua says: "A bad friend." "Rabbi Yosé says: "A bad neighbor." Rabbi Simeon says, "A loan. (All the same is a loan owed to a human being and a loan owed to the Omnipresent, the blessed, as it is said, 'The wicked borrows and does not pay back, but the righteous person deals graciously and hands over [what is owed]')" (Ps. 37:21).

2:9E. Rabbi Eleazar says, "Ill will."

2:9F. He said to them, "I prefer the opinion of Rabbi Eleazar ben Arakh, because in what he says is included everything you say."

XIV:I.1. **Yohanan ben Zakkai received the Torah from Hillel and Shammai.**

XIV:I.2. Identification of Yohanan ben Zakkai.

XIV:II.1. Gloss of Yohanan's saying.

XIV:III.1. As above.

XIV:IV.1. Story about death of Yohanan's son. Eleazar's departure.

2:10A. **They [each] said three things.**

2:10B. Rabbi Eliezer says, "Let the respect owing to your companion be as precious to you as the respect owing to yourself. And don't be easy to anger. And repent one day before you die. And warm yourself by the fire of the sages, but be careful of their coals, so you don't get burned—for their bite is the bite of a fox, and their sting is the sting of a scorpion, and their hiss is like the hiss of a snake, and everything they say is like fiery coals."

XV:I.1. Amplification of **respect owing to companion.**

XV:II.1. Same as above.

XV:III.1. **Don't be easy to anger,** plus prologue to Hillel-Shammai stories.

XV:IV.1. Patience of Hillel the Elder.

XV:V.1. Impatience of Shammai the Elder.

XV:V.2. As above.

XV:VI.1. Amplification of **Repent . . .**

XV:VII.1. Chain of tradition tied to Eliezer's sayings.

2:11. **Rabbi Joshua says, "Envy, desire of bad things, and hatred for people push a person out of the world."**

    XVI:I.1. **Envy:** how so?
    XVI:II.1. Same as above.
    XVI:III.1. **Evil impulse:** how so?
    XVI:III. Same as above.
    XVI:IV.1–4. Examples of those who have resisted the evil impulse.
    XVI:V.1–4. More on the evil impulse.
    XVI:VI.1–2. **Hatred for people,** how so?

2:12. **Rabbi Yosé says, "Let your companion's money be as precious to you as your own. And get yourself ready to learn the Torah, for it does not come as an inheritance to you. And may everything you do be for the sake of Heaven."**

    XVII:I.1. **Let your companion's property be as precious to you as your own:** how so?
    XVII:I.1. Another comment on the same.
    XVII:II.1. **And get yourself ready to learn Torah:** Moses' sons did not inherit, Joshua did. Proof text: Song 1:8.
    XVII:III.1. *Story of impoverished girl, connected to Song 1:8.*
    XVII:IV.1. *Story on girl taken captive.*
    XVII:V.1. *As above. All thus added because of Song 1:8 and its extenuation.*
    XVII:VI.1. **And may everything you do be for the sake of Heaven:** how so?

2:13. **Rabbi Simeon says, "Be meticulous about the recitation of the Shema and the Prayer. And when you pray, don't treat your praying as a matter of routine; but let it be a [plea for] mercy and supplication before the Omnipresent, the blessed, as it is said, 'For he is gracious and full of compassion, slow to anger and full of mercy, and repents of the evil' (Joel 2:13). And never be evil in your own eyes."**

2:14. **Rabbi Eleazar says, "Be constant in learning of the Torah; And know what to reply to an Epicurean; And know before whom you work, for your employer can be depended upon to pay your wages for what you do."**

    XVII:VII.1. **Sayings of Simeon and Eleazar cited without comment.**

    XVIII:I.1. Nicknames of Judah the Prince for Tarfon, Aqiba, Eleazar b. Azariah, Yohanan b. Nuri, and Yose the Galilean.
    XVIII:I.2. Tarfon.
    XVIII:I.3. Aqiba.
    XVIII:I.4. Eleazar b. Azariah.
        XVIII:II.1. Appendix on Eleazar b. Azariah.
    XVIII:II.1–2. Yohanan b. Nuri and Yose the Galilean.
    XVIII:III.1–2. Isi b. Judah would assign nicknames to sages. [I assume this

entire composition complements Yohanan's description of his disciples and is
inserted as a further illustration of the same basic principle.]

2:15. RABBI TARFON SAYS, "THE DAY IS SHORT, THE WORK FORMIDABLE, THE
WORKERS LAZY, THE WAGES HIGH, THE EMPLOYER IMPATIENT."
2:16. HE WOULD SAY, "IT'S NOT YOUR JOB TO FINISH THE WORK, BUT YOU ARE
NOT FREE TO WALK AWAY FROM IT. IF YOU HAVE LEARNED MUCH TORAH, THEY
WILL GIVE YOU A GOOD REWARD. AND YOUR EMPLOYER CAN BE DEPENDED UPON TO
PAY YOUR WAGES FOR WHAT YOU DO. AND KNOW WHAT SORT OF REWARD IS GOING
TO BE GIVEN TO THE RIGHTEOUS IN THE COMING TIME." [This occurs later.]

The Fathers Chapter Three

3:1A. **Aqabiah b. Mehallalel says, "Reflect upon three things and you will not
fall into the clutches of transgression: "Know (1) from whence you come, (2)
whither you are going, and (3) before whom you are going to have to give a full
account of yourself.**
3:1B. **"From whence do you come? From a putrid drop. Whither are you
going? To a place of dust, worms, and maggots.**
3:1C. **"And before whom are you going to hive a full account of yourself? Before the King of kings of kings, the Holy One, blessed be he."**

> XIX:I.1–2. **Aqabya b. Mehallel cited. Clause-by-clause gloss.**
> XIX:I.3. Same, now with proof text.
> XIX:I.4. Same, now with parable.
> XIX:II.1. *Eliezer's death scene. Intersects with who is his judge.*
> XIX:III.1. *More on Eliezer's death scene.*

3:2A. R. HANANIAH, PREFECT OF THE PRIESTS, SAYS, "PRAY FOR THE WELFARE
OF THE GOVERNMENT. FOR IF IT WERE NOT FOR FEAR OF IT, ONE MAN WOULD SWAL-
LOW HIS FELLOW ALIVE."
3:2B. R. HANANIAH B. TERADION SAYS, "[IF] TWO SIT TOGETHER AND BETWEEN
THEM DO NOT PASS TEACHINGS OF THE TORAH, LO, THIS IS A SEAT OF THE SCORN-
FUL, AS IT IS SAID, 'NOR SITS IN THE SEAT OF THE SCORNFUL' (PS. 1:1). BUT TWO
WHO ARE SITTING, AND WORDS OF THE TORAH DO PASS BETWEEN THEM—THE PRES-
ENCE IS WITH THEM, AS IT IS SAID, 'THEN THEY THAT FEARED THE LORD SPOKE
WITH ONE ANOTHER, AND THE LORD HEARKENED AND HEARD, AND A BOOK OF RE-
MEMBRANCE WAS WRITTEN BEFORE HIM, FOR THEM THAT FEARED THE LORD AND
GAVE THOUGHT TO HIS NAME' (MAL 3:16). I KNOW THAT THIS APPLIES TO TWO.
HOW DO I KNOW THAT EVEN IF A SINGLE PERSON SITS AND WORKS ON THE TORAH,
THE HOLY ONE, BLESSED BE HE, SET ASIDE A REWARD FOR HIM? AS IT IS SAID, 'LET
HIM SIT ALONE AND KEEP SILENT, BECAUSE HE HAS LAID IT UPON HIM'" (LAM.
3:28).
3.3. R. SIMEON SAYS, "THREE WHO ATE AT A SINGLE TABLE AND DID NOT TALK
ABOUT TEACHINGS OF THE TORAH WHILE AT THAT TABLE ARE AS THOUGH THEY ATE
FROM DEAD SACRIFICES (PS. 106:28), AS IT IS SAID, 'FOR ALL TABLES ARE FULL OF
VOMIT AND FILTHINESS [IF THEY ARE] WITHOUT GOD' (PS. 106:28). BUT THREE

WHO ATE AT A SINGLE TABLE AND DID TALK ABOUT TEACHINGS OF THE TORAH WHILE AT THAT TABLE ARE AS IF THEY ATE AT THE TABLE OF THE OMNIPRESENT, BLESSED IS HE, AS IT IS SAID, 'AND HE SAID TO ME, "THIS IS THE TABLE THAT IS BEFORE THE LORD"'" (EZ. 41:22).

3:4. R. HANANIAH B. HAKHINAI SAYS, "(1) HE WHO GETS UP AT NIGHT, AND (2) HE WHO WALKS AROUND BY HIMSELF, AND (3) HE WHO TURNS HIS DESIRE TO EMPTINESS—LO, THIS PERSON IS LIABLE FOR HIS LIFE."

3:5. R. NEHUNIA B. HAQQANEH SAYS, "FROM WHOEVER ACCEPTS UPON HIMSELF THE YOKE OF THE TORAH DO THEY REMOVE THE YOKE OF THE STATE AND THE YOKE OF HARD LABOR. AND UPON WHOEVER REMOVES FROM HIMSELF THE YOKE OF THE TORAH DO THEY LAY THE YOKE OF THE STATE AND THE YOKE OF HARD LABOR."

3:6. R. HALAFTA OF KEFAR HANANIAH SAYS, "AMONG TEN WHO SIT AND WORK HARD ON THE TORAH THE PRESENCE COMES TO REST, AS IT IS SAID, 'GOD STANDS IN THE CONGREGATION OF GOD' (PS. 82:1). AND HOW DO WE KNOW THAT THE SAME IS SO EVEN OF FIVE? FOR IT IS SAID, 'AND HE HAS FOUNDED HIS GROUP UPON THE EARTH' (AM. 9:6). AND HOW DO WE KNOW THAT THIS IS SO EVEN OF THREE? SINCE IT IS SAID, 'AND HE JUDGES AMONG THE JUDGES' (PS. 82:1). AND HOW DO WE KNOW THAT THIS IS SO EVEN OF TWO? BECAUSE IT IS SAID, 'THEN THEY THAT FEARED THE LORD SPOKE WITH ONE ANOTHER, AND THE LORD HEARKENED AND HEARD' (MAL. 3:16). AND HOW DO WE KNOW THAT THIS IS SO EVEN OF ONE? SINCE IT IS SAID, 'IN EVERY PLACE WHERE I RECORD MY NAME I WILL COME TO YOU AND I WILL BLESS YOU'" (EX. 20:24).

3:7A. R. ELEAZAR OF BARTOTA SAYS, "GIVE HIM WHAT IS HIS, FOR YOU AND YOURS ARE HIS. FOR SO DOES IT SAY ABOUT DAVID, 'FOR ALL THINGS COME OF YOU, AND OF YOUR OWN HAVE WE GIVEN YOU'" (I CHRON. 29:14).

3:7B. R. SIMEON SAYS, "HE WHO IS GOING ALONG THE WAY AND REPEATING [HIS TORAH TRADITION] BUT INTERRUPTS HIS REPETITION AND SAYS, 'HOW BEAUTIFUL IS THAT TREE! HOW BEAUTIFUL IS THAT PLOUGHED FIELD.!'—SCRIPTURE RECKONS IT TO HIM AS IF HE HAS BECOME LIABLE FOR HIS LIFE."

3:8. R. DOSETAI B. R. YANNAI IN THE NAME OF R. MEIR SAYS, "WHOEVER FORGETS A SINGLE THING FROM WHAT HE HAS LEARNED—SCRIPTURE RECKONS IT TO HIM AS IF HE HAS BECOME LIABLE FOR HIS LIFE, AS IT IS SAID, 'ONLY TAKE HEED TO YOURSELF AND KEEP YOUR SOUL DILIGENTLY, LEST YOU FORGET THE WORDS WHICH YOUR EYES SAW' (DEUT. 4:9). IS IT POSSIBLE THAT THIS IS SO EVEN IF HIS LEARNING BECAME TOO MUCH FOR HIM? SCRIPTURE SAYS, 'LEST THEY DEPART FROM YOUR HEART ALL THE DAYS OF YOUR LIFE.' THUS HE BECOMES LIABLE FOR HIS LIFE ONLY WHEN HE WILL SIT DOWN AND ACTUALLY REMOVE [HIS LEARNING] FROM HIS OWN HEART."

3.9A. **R. Haninah b. Dosa says, "For anyone whose fear of sin takes precedence over his wisdom, his wisdom will endure. And for anyone whose wisdom takes precedence over his fear of sin, wisdom will not endure."**

3.9B. **He would say, "Anyone whose deeds are more than his wisdom—his wisdom will endure. And anyone whose wisdom is more than his deeds—his wisdom will not endure."**

XXII:I.1 **Hanina cited,** lightly glossed with scriptural proof texts.

XXII:II.1. Story about Yohanan ben Zakkai that contains the same ideal as in Hanina's saying: that is, the importance of deeds as well as learning.

XXII:III.1–XXII:V.1. **Sayings in The Fathers that make the same point.**

3.10A. He [R. Haninah b. Dosa] would say, "Anyone from whom people take pleasure—the Omnipresent takes pleasure from him. And anyone from whom people do not take pleasure, the Omnipresent does not take pleasure from him."

XX:I.1. Hananiah's saying, plus Deut. 28:46–8.
XX:I.2. *Exposition of Deut. 28:46–8 in its own terms.*
XX:II.1. *He would interpret Song 1:6.*
XX:III.1. *Further interpretation of Song 1:6.*
XX:IV.1–2. *Continuation of above.*
XX:V.1. *Further interpretation of Song 1:6.*
XX:VI.1–2. *As above.*
XX:VII.1 Reversion to the theme of Deut. 28:46–8

3.10B. **R. Dosa b. Harkinas says, "(1) Sleeping late in the morning, (2) drinking wine at noon, (3) chatting with children, and (4) attending the synagogues of the ignorant drive a man out of the world."**

XXI:I.1. **Citation of Dosa plus sleeping late in the morning:** how so? It teaches, etc.
XXI:II.1. **Drinking wine at noon:** how so?
XXI:II.2. Secondary explanation of proof text.
XXI:III.1. **Chatting with children:** how so?
XXI:IV.1. **Attending the synagogues of the ignorant:** how so?
XXI:IV.2. Meir clarifies language of proof text cited above.
XXI:V.1. Pertinent case of Aqiba.

3:11. R. Eleazar the Modite says, "(1) He who treats Holy Things as secular, and (2) he who despises the appointed times, (3) he who humiliates his fellow in public, (4) he who removes the signs of the covenant of Abraham, our father, (may he rest in peace), and (5) he who exposes aspects of the Torah not in accord with the law, even though he has in hand learning in the Torah and good deeds, will have no share in the world to come."

3:12. R. Ishmael says, "(1) Be quick [in service] to a superior, (2) efficient in service [to the state], and (3) receive everybody with joy."

3:13. R. Aqiba says, "(1) Laughter and lightheadedness turn lewdness into a habit. (2) Tradition is a fence for the Torah. (3) Tithes are a fence for wealth. (4) Vows are a fence for abstinence. (5) A fence for wisdom is silence."

3.14A. He would say, "Precious is the human being, who was created in the image [of God]. It was an act of still greater love that it was made known to him that he was created in the image [of God]. As it is said, 'For in the image of God he made man' (Gen. 9:6).

3:14B. "Precious are Israelites, who are called children to the Om-

NIPRESENT. IT WAS AN ACT OF STILL GREATER LOVE THAT IT WAS MADE KNOWN TO THEM THAT THEY WERE CALLED CHILDREN TO THE OMNIPRESENT, AS IT IS SAID, 'YOU ARE THE CHILDREN OF THE LORD YOUR GOD' (DEUT. 14:1).

3:14C. "PRECIOUS ARE ISRAELITES, TO WHOM WAS GIVEN THE PRECIOUS THING. IT WAS AN ACT OF STILL GREATER LOVE THAT IT WAS MADE KNOWN TO THEM THAT TO THEM WAS GIVEN THAT PRECIOUS THING WITH WHICH THE WORLD WAS MADE, AS IT IS SAID, 'FOR I GIVE YOU A GOOD DOCTRINE. DO NOT FORSAKE MY TORAH' (PROV. 4:2).

3:15. "EVERYTHING IS FORESEEN, AND FREE CHOICE IS GIVEN. IN GOODNESS THE WORLD IS JUDGED. AND ALL IS IN ACCORD WITH THE ABUNDANCE OF DEED[S]."

3:16A. HE WOULD SAY, "(1) ALL IS HANDED OVER AS A PLEDGE, (2) AND A NET IS CAST OVER ALL THE LIVING. (3) THE STORE IS OPEN, (4) THE STOREKEEPER GIVES CREDIT, (5) THE ACCOUNT-BOOK IS OPEN, AND (6) THE HAND IS WRITING.

3:16B. "(1) WHOEVER WANTS TO BORROW MAY COME AND BORROW. (2) THE CHARITY-COLLECTORS GO AROUND EVERY DAY AND COLLECT FROM MAN WHETHER HE KNOWS IT OR NOT. (3) AND THEY HAVE GROUNDS FOR WHAT THEY DO. (4) AND THE JUDGMENT IS A TRUE JUDGMENT. (5) AND EVERYTHING IS READY FOR THE MEAL."

3:17A. R. ELEAZAR B. AZARIAH SAYS, "IF THERE IS NO LEARNING OF THE TORAH, THERE IS NO PROPER CONDUCT. IF THERE IS NO PROPER CONDUCT, THERE IS NO LEARNING IN THE TORAH. IF THERE IS NO WISDOM, THERE IS NO REVERENCE. IF THERE IS NO REVERENCE, THERE IS NO WISDOM. IF THERE IS NO UNDERSTANDING, THERE IS NO KNOWLEDGE. IF THERE IS NO KNOWLEDGE, THERE IS NO UNDERSTANDING. IF THERE IS NO SUSTENANCE, THERE IS NO TORAH-LEARNING. IF THERE IS NO TORAH-LEARNING, THERE IS NO SUSTENANCE."

3:17B. HE WOULD SAY, "ANYONE WHOSE WISDOM IS GREATER THAN HIS DEEDS— TO WHAT IS HE TO BE LIKENED? TO A TREE WITH ABUNDANT FOLIAGE, BUT FEW ROOTS. WHEN THE WINDS COME, THEY WILL UPROOT IT AND BLOW IT DOWN, AS IT IS SAID, 'HE SHALL BE LIKE A TAMARISK IN THE DESERT AND SHALL NOT SEE WHEN GOOD COMES, BUT SHALL INHABIT THE PARCHED PLACES IN THE WILDERNESS' (JER. 17:6). BUT ANYONE WHOSE DEEDS ARE GREATER THAN HIS WISDOM—TO WHAT IS HE TO BE LIKENED? TO A TREE WITH LITTLE FOLIAGE BUT ABUNDANT ROOTS. FOR EVEN IF ALL THE WINDS IN THE WORLD WERE TO COME AND BLAST AT IT, THEY WILL NOT MOVE IT FROM ITS PLACE, AS IT IS SAID, 'HE SHALL BE AS A TREE PLANTED BY THE WATERS, AND THAT SPREADS OUT ITS ROOTS BY THE RIVER, AND SHALL NOT FEAR WHEN HEAT COMES, AND HIS LEAF SHALL BE GREEN, AND SHALL NOT BE CARE-FUL IN THE YEAR OF DROUGHT, NEITHER SHALL CEASE FROM YIELDING FRUIT'" (JER. 17:8).

3:18. R. ELEAZAR HISMA SAYS, "THE LAWS OF BIRD-OFFERINGS AND OF THE BE-GINNING OF THE MENSTRUAL PERIOD—THEY ARE INDEED THE ESSENTIALS OF THE TORAH. CALCULATION OF THE EQUINOXES AND RECKONING THE NUMERICAL VALUE OF LETTERS ARE THE SAVORIES OF WISDOM."

The Fathers Chapter Four

4:1. Ben Zoma says, "Who is a sage? He who learns from everybody, as it is said, 'From all my teachers I have gotten understanding' (Ps. 119:99). Who

is strong? He who overcomes his desire, as it is said, 'He who is slow to anger is better than the mighty, and he who rules his spirit than he who takes a city' (Prov. 16:32). Who is rich? He who is happy in what he has, as it is said, 'When you eat the labor of your hands, happy will you be, and it will go well with you' (Ps. 128:2). [*"Happy will you be—in this world, and it will go well with you*—in the world to come."] Who is honored? He who honors everybody, as it is said, *'For those who honor me I shall honor, and they who despise me will be treated as of no account'"* (I Sam. 2:30).

XXIII:I.1. **Ben Zoma cited** and glossed with verses of Scripture.

4:2. BEN AZZAI SAYS, "RUN AFTER THE MOST MINOR RELIGIOUS DUTY AS AFTER THE MOST IMPORTANT, AND FLEE FROM TRANSGRESSION. FOR DOING ONE RELIGIOUS DUTY DRAWS IN ITS WAKE DOING YET ANOTHER, AND DOING ONE TRANSGRESSION DRAWS IN ITS WAKE DOING YET ANOTHER. FOR THE REWARD OF DOING A RELIGIOUS DUTY IS A RELIGIOUS DUTY, AND THE REWARD OF DOING A TRANSGRESSION IS A TRANSGRESSION."

4:3. HE WOULD SAY, "DO NOT DESPISE ANYBODY AND DO NOT TREAT ANYTHING AS UNLIKELY. FOR YOU HAVE NO ONE WHO DOES NOT HAVE HIS TIME, AND YOU HAVE NOTHING WHICH DOES NOT HAVE ITS PLACE."

4:4A. R. LEVITAS OF YAVNEH SAYS, "BE EXCEEDINGLY HUMBLE, FOR THE FUTURE OF HUMANITY IS THE WORM."

4:4B. R. YOHANAN B. BEROQA SAYS, "WHOEVER SECRETLY TREATS THE NAME OF HEAVEN AS PROFANE PUBLICLY PAYS THE PRICE. ALL THE SAME ARE THE ONE WHO DOES SO INADVERTENTLY AND THE ONE WHO DOES SO DELIBERATELY, WHEN IT COMES TO TREATING THE NAME OF HEAVEN AS PROFANE."

4:5A. R. ISHMAEL, HIS SON, SAYS, "HE WHO LEARNS SO AS TO TEACH—THEY GIVE HIM A CHANCE TO LEARN AND TO TEACH. HE WHO LEARNS SO AS TO CARRY OUT HIS TEACHINGS—THEY GIVE HIM A CHANCE TO LEARN, TO TEACH, TO KEEP, AND TO DO."

4:5B. R. SADOQ SAYS, "DO NOT MAKE [TORAH TEACHINGS] A CROWN IN WHICH TO GLORIFY YOURSELF OR A SPADE WITH WHICH TO DIG. SO DID HILLEL SAY, 'HE WHO USES THE CROWN PERISHES.' THUS HAVE YOU LEARNED: WHOEVER DERIVES WORLDLY BENEFIT FROM TEACHINGS OF THE TORAH TAKES HIS LIFE OUT OF THIS WORLD."

4:6. R. YOSÉ SAYS, "WHOEVER HONORS THE TORAH HIMSELF IS HONORED BY PEOPLE. AND WHOEVER DISGRACES THE TORAH HIMSELF IS DISGRACED BY PEOPLE."

4:7. R. ISHMAEL, HIS SON, SAYS, "HE WHO AVOIDS SERVING AS A JUDGE AVOIDS THE POWER OF ENMITY, ROBBERY, AND FALSE SWEARING. AND HE WHO IS AR-ROGANT ABOUT MAKING DECISIONS IS A FOOL, EVIL, AND PRIDEFUL.'

4:8. HE WOULD SAY, "DO NOT SERVE AS A JUDGE BY YOURSELF, FOR THERE IS ONLY ONE WHO SERVES AS A JUDGE ALL ALONE. AND DO NOT SAY, 'ACCEPT MY OPINION,' FOR THEY HAVE THE CHOICE IN THE MATTER, NOT YOU."

4:9. R. JONATHAN SAYS, "WHOEVER KEEPS THE TORAH WHEN POOR WILL IN THE END KEEP IT IN WEALTH. AND WHOEVER TREATS THE TORAH AS NOTHING WHEN HE IS WEALTHY IN THE END WILL TREAT IT AS NOTHING IN POVERTY."

4:10. R. MEIR SAYS, "KEEP YOUR BUSINESS TO A MINIMUM AND MAKE YOUR BUSI-NESS THE TORAH. AND BE HUMBLE BEFORE EVERYBODY. AND IF YOU TREAT THE

TORAH AS NOTHING, YOU WILL HAVE MANY TREATING YOU AS NOTHING. AND IF YOU HAVE LABORED IN THE TORAH, [THE TORAH] HAS A GREAT REWARD TO GIVE YOU."

4:11A. R. ELEAZAR B. JACOB SAYS, "HE WHO DOES EVEN A SINGLE RELIGIOUS DUTY GETS HIMSELF A GOOD ADVOCATE. HE WHO DOES EVEN A SINGLE TRANSGRESSION GETS HIMSELF A POWERFUL PROSECUTOR. PENITENCE AND GOOD DEEDS ARE LIKE A SHIELD AGAINST PUNISHMENT."

4:11B. R. YOHANAN HASSANDELAR SAYS, "ANY GATHERING WHICH IS FOR THE SAKE OF HEAVEN IS GOING TO ENDURE. AND ANY WHICH IS NOT FOR THE SAKE OF HEAVEN IS NOT GOING TO ENDURE."

4:12. R. ELEAZAR B. SHAMMUA SAYS, "THE HONOR OWING TO YOUR DISCIPLE SHOULD BE AS PRECIOUS TO YOU AS YOURS. AND THE HONOR OWING TO YOUR FELLOW SHOULD BE LIKE THE REVERENCE OWING TO YOUR MASTER. AND THE REVERENCE OWING TO YOUR MASTER SHOULD BE LIKE THE AWE OWING TO HEAVEN."

4:13A. R. JUDAH SAYS, "BE METICULOUS ABOUT LEARNING, FOR ERROR IN LEARNING LEADS TO DELIBERATE [VIOLATION OF THE TORAH]."

4:13B. R. SIMEON SAYS, "THERE ARE THREE CROWNS: THE CROWN OF THE TORAH, THE CROWN OF PRIESTHOOD, AND THE CROWN OF SOVEREIGNTY. BUT THE CROWN OF A GOOD NAME IS BEST OF THEM ALL."

4:14. **R. Nehorai says, "Go into exile to a place of the Torah, and do not suppose that it will come to you. For your fellow-disciples will make it solid in your hand. And on your own understanding do not rely."**

    XXIII:II.1. **Nehorai cited.**

    XXIII:III.1. **Nehorai cited** and glossed.

4:15A. R. YANNAI SAYS, "WE DO NOT HAVE IN HAND [AN EXPLANATION] EITHER FOR THE PROSPERITY OF THE WICKED OR FOR THE SUFFERING OF THE RIGHTEOUS."

4:15B. R. MATYA B. HARASH SAYS, "GREET EVERYBODY FIRST, AND BE A TAIL TO LIONS. BUT DO NOT BE A HEAD OF FOXES."

4:16. R. JACOB SAYS, "THIS WORLD IS LIKE AN ANTECHAMBER BEFORE THE WORLD TO COME. GET READY IN THE ANTECHAMBER, SO YOU CAN GO INTO THE GREAT HALL."

4:17. HE WOULD SAY, "BETTER IS A SINGLE MOMENT SPENT IN PENITENCE AND GOOD DEEDS IN THIS WORLD THAN THE WHOLE OF THE WORLD TO COME. AND BETTER IS A SINGLE MOMENT OF INNER PEACE IN THE WORLD TO COME THAN THE WHOLE OF A LIFETIME SPENT IN THIS WORLD."

4:18. R. SIMEON B. ELEAZAR SAYS, "(1) DO NOT TRY TO MAKE AMENDS WITH YOUR FELLOW WHEN HE IS ANGRY, OR (2) COMFORT HIM WHEN THE CORPSE OF HIS BELOVED IS LYING BEFORE HIM, OR (3) SEEK TO FIND ABSOLUTION FOR HIM AT THE MOMENT AT WHICH HE TAKES VOW, OR (4) ATTEMPT TO SEE HIM WHEN HE IS HUMILIATED."

4:19. SAMUEL THE SMALL SAYS, "REJOICE NOT WHEN YOUR ENEMY FALLS, AND LET NOT YOUR HEART BE GLAD WHEN HE IS OVERTHROWN, LEST THE LORD SEE IT AND IT DISPLEASE HIM, AND HE TURN AWAY HIS WRATH FROM HIM" (PROV. 24:17).

4:20. ELISHA B. ABUYAH SAYS, "HE WHO LEARNS WHEN A CHILD—WHAT IS HE LIKE? INK PUT DOWN ON A CLEAN PIECE OF PAPER. AND HE WHO LEARNS WHEN AN OLD MAN—WHAT IS HE LIKE? INK PUT DOWN ON A PAPER FULL OF ERASURES."

4:21A. R. Yosé b. R. Judah of Kefar Habbabli says, "He who learns from children—what is he like? One who eats sour grapes and drinks fresh wine. And he who learns from old men—what is he like? He who eats ripe grapes and drinks vintage wine."

4:21B. Rabbi says, "Do not look at the bottle but at what is in it. You can have a new bottle of old wine, and an old bottle which has not got even new wine."

4:22A. R. Eleazar Haqqappar says, "Jealousy, lust, and ambition drive a person out of this world."

4:22B. He would say, "Those who are born are [destined] to die, and those who die are [destined] for resurrection. And the living are [destined] to be judged—so as to know, to make known, and to confirm that (1) he is God, (2) he is the one who forms, (3) he is the one who creates, (4) he is the one who understands, (5) he is the one who judges, (6) he is the one who gives evidence, (7) he is the one who brings suit, (8) and he is the one who is going to make the ultimate judgment.

4:22C. "Blessed be he, for before him are no (1) guile, (2) forgetfulness, (3) respect for persons, or (4) bribe-taking, for everything is his. And know that everything is subject to reckoning. And do not let your evil impulse persuade you that Sheol is a place of refuge for you. For (1) despite your wishes were you formed, (2) despite your wishes were you born, (3) despite your wishes do you live, (4) despite your wishes do you die, and (5) despite your wishes are you going to give a full accounting before the King of kings of kings, the Holy One, blessed be he."

XXIII:IV.1–2. **Sayings regarding study the Torah in your youth.**
XXIII:IV.3–5. Appendix: *Sayings regarding study the Torah in your youth* by other authorities.

XXIV:I.1–XXIV:IV.1. **Both good deeds and Torah learning are necessary.** Four parables that make the same point.
XXIV:V.1. Studying Torah in one's youth is better than doing so in one's old age, because in the former case the teachings are absorbed in one's blood.
XXIV:VI.1. Hard to learn Torah teachings and easy to lose them.
XXIV:VII.1. Same as above.
XXIV:VIII.1. One should get his fellow to carry out religious duties, and if he does, he gets the credit too.

XXV:I.1. Ben Azzai: Omens on the death bed. What follows are death-bed scenes, which do not illustrate the omens. Hence they are inserted as thematic appendices, not as integral parts of the exegesis of Ben Azzai's saying.
XXV:II.1. *Death scene of Yohanan ben Zakkai.*
XXV:II.2–3. *Secondary expansions of No. 1.*
XXV:II.4. *Conclusion of No. 1.*
XXV:III.1. *More omens on the death bed.*
XXV:IV.1–5. *Eliezer b. Hyrcanus' death scene.*
XXV:V–IX.1. Further sayings of Ben Azzai.

XXVI:I.1. Sayings of Aqiba cited.
XXVI:II.1. More sayings of Aqiba. Proof text tacked on.
XXVI:III–V. Further sayings of Aqiba.
XXVI:VI.1. Simeon b. Eliezer provides a restatement of Aqiba's view.
XXVI:VII.1. Eliezer the Modite's sayings.
XXVI:VIII–IX. Further sayings of Aqiba.
XXVI:X–XI. Sayings of Judah b. Ilai, Eliezer Haqqappar.

XXVII:I.1. Yose cited and glossed with 1 Sam. 2:30.
XXVII:II.1. *Further interpretation of 1 Sam. 2:30. Proof text: Song 1:9.*
XXVII:II.2. *Further interpretation of Song 1:9.*
XXVII:II.3. Reversion to XXVII:II.1.
XXVII:II.4. As above.
XXVII:III.1. Ishmael cited.
XXVII:IV.1. Tarfon cited.
XXVII:V.1. Eleazar Hisma cited.
XXVII:VI.1. Foregoing complemented by Yohanan b. Nuri.
XXVII:VII.1. More in name of Yohanan b. Nuri.
XXVII:VIII.1. Saying of Yohanan b. Danabai.
XXVII:IX.1. Tarfon cited.
XXVII:X.1. Tarfon further cited, with parable.
XXVII:XI.1. Eleazar b. Shammua cited and glossed.
XXVII:XII.1. Saying included for no clear reason.

XXVIII:I.1. Saying of Nathan on the outstanding traits of various parties, e.g., the Torah, Land of Israel, Jerusalem, Rome, Persia, the Arabs, etc.
XXVIII:II.1. Further sayings on the superiority of the Torah study of Land of Israel.
XXVIII:III.1. Sayings attributed to Simeon b. Gamaliel.
XXVIII:IV–V. Sayings attributed to Gamaliel.
XXVIII:VI–VIII. Sayings attributed to Judah the Patriarch.
XVIII:IX–X. Sayings attributed to Hillel.
XXVIII:XI.1. Eleazar b. Shammua's sayings.
XXVIII:XII.1. Judah b. Ilai's sayings.

XXIX:I–IV. Simeon b. Eleazar cited.
XXIX:V.1. Abba Saul b. Nannos: Four traits in a disciple.
XXIX:VI.1. Hanania b. Jacob's sayings.
XXIX:VII.1–3. Eliezer Haqqappar's sayings.
XXIX:VIII.1. Mattia consults Eleazar [sic] Haqqappar on a teaching of Ishmael.
XXIX:IX.1. Issi b. Judah's sayings.
XXIX:X–XII. Isaac b. Phineas's sayings.

XXX:I.1–XXX:II.1. Citation of Nathan b. Joseph's sayings.
XXX:III–IV. Further sayings that make the same point: that merely thinking is tantamount to doing.

XXX:VI.1. *Secondary amplification of a minor detail of* XXX: IV.2.

XXX:VI.1–XXX:VII.1. Sayings of Ahai b. Josiah on a separate point entirely.

XXXI:I.1. Whoever carries out one religious duty is as if he sustained the whole world. This point leads to the one of importance: a human being is equivalent to the whole of creation.

XXXI:I.2. The point repeated, now for Cain.

XXXI:I.3. The point repeated in general terms.

XXXI:I.4. *Secondary appendix added because of thematic association.*

Chapter Five

5:1. By ten acts of speech was the world made. And what does Scripture mean [by having God say *say* ten times]? But it is to exact punishment from the wicked, who destroy a world which was created through ten acts of speech, and to secure a good reward for the righteous, who sustain a world which was created through ten acts of speech.

XXXI:II.1. **Ten acts of speech** linked to the Torah, thus reversion to original assertion.

XXXI:III.1. *Man is equivalent to created world.*

5:2. There are ten generations from Adam to Noah, to show you how long-suffering is [God]. For all those generations went along spiting him until he brought the water of the flood upon them. There are ten generations from Noah to Abraham, to show you how long-suffering is [God]. For all those generations went along spiting him, until Abraham came along and took the reward which had been meant for all of them.

XXXII:I.1. Why is it necessary to count the generations? To show how long-suffering God is. He waited for Methuselah to die.

XXXII:I.2. God waited for them to repent but they did not.

XXXII:I.3. God gave them signals that something was wrong, but they did not listen.

XXXII:I.4. God showed them what they would lose.

XXXII:II.1. Exegesis of Gen. 6:3: God gave them their reward in this world.

XXXII:II.2. Good impulse/evil impulse.

XXXII:II.3. Same as above.

XXXII:II.4. Exegesis of Gen. 6:3: God paid reward coming to the righteous.

XXX:II.5. They were arrogant.

XXXII:II.6. They did not believe there was judgment.

XXXII:II.7. They did not set up courts.

5:3. Ten trials were inflicted upon Abraham, our father, may he rest in peace, and he withstood all of them, to show you how great is his love for Abraham, our father, may he rest in peace.

5:4. Ten wonders were done for our fathers in Egypt, and ten at the Sea. Ten blows did the Holy One, blessed be he, bring upon the Egyptians in Egypt, and ten at the Sea. Ten trials did our fathers inflict upon the Omnipresent, blessed be he, in the wilderness, as it is said, "Yet they have tempted me these ten times and have not listened to my voice" (Num. 14:22).

XXXIII:I.1. Base statement cited and glossed.
XXXIII:I.2–3. *Appendix on Abraham.*
XXXIII:II.1. Base statement cited and glossed.
XXXIII:III.1. In response to the ten trials, the Holy One performed ten miracles in Egypt, ten plagues on the Egyptians in Egypt, ten miracles for Israelites at the Sea, ten plagues on Egyptians at the Sea.
XXXIII:IV.1. *Foregoing statement given a thematic appendix, in which what the Egyptians did to Israel has as its counterpart what the Holy One did to the Egyptians.*
XXXIII:V.1. *Miracles done at the sea for the Israelites. No reference to foregoing.*

XXXIV:I.1. **Ten trials** plus systematic amplification and proof texts.
XXXIV:II.1. *Ten terms of praise apply to God.*
XXXIV:III.1. *Ten terms of denigration apply to idolatry.*
XXXIV:IV.1. *Two signifying markers occur in a single passage.*
XXXIV:V.1. *More of same.*
XXXIV:VI.1. *Ten passages in the Torah are dotted.*
XXXIV:VII.1. *Eleven passages in which the word for* she *is written with a* Y.
XXXIV:VIII.1. *Ten descents of God's presence into the world.*
XXXIV:IX.1. *Ten ascents out of the world.*
XXXIV:X.I. *Prophet called by ten names.*
XXXIV:XI.1. *Holy Spirit called by ten names.*
XXXIV:XII. *Joy called by ten names.*
XXXIV:XIII.1. *Ten are called living.*

5:5. Ten wonders were done for our fathers in the Temple: (1) A woman never miscarried on account of the stench of the meat of Holy Things. (2) And the meat of the Holy Things never turned rotten. (3) A fly never made an appearance in the slaughter house. (4) A high priest never suffered a nocturnal emission on the eve of the Day of Atonement. (5) The rain never quenched the fire on the altar. (6) No wind ever blew away the pillar of smoke. (7) An invalidating factor never affected the 'omer, the Two Loaves, or the show bread. (8) When the people are standing, they are jammed together. When they go down and prostrate themselves, they have plenty of room. (9) A snake and a scorpion never bit anybody in Jerusalem. (10) And no one ever said to his fellow, "The place is too crowded for me" (Is. 49:20) to stay in Jerusalem.

XXXV:I.1. **Ten wonders** saying amplified.
XXXV:II.1. *Ten rulings in connection with Jerusalem.*
XXXV:III.1–3. *Appendix on Jerusalem.*
XXXV:IV.1. **Ten wonders done for our fathers in the Temple.**
XXXV:IV.2–3. *Appendix on wonders in Temple.*

XXXVI:I.1. *Men of Sodom and world to come (Eliezer vs. Joshua).*
XXXVI:II.1. *Minor children of wicked and world to come, last judgment (Eliezer vs. Joshua).*
XXXVI:III.1. *Korach and his party (Eliezer vs. Joshua).*
XXXVI:IV.1. *Generation of wilderness (Eliezer vs. Joshua).*
XXXVI:V.1. *Ten tribes.*
XXXVI:VI.1. *Seven who have no share in the world to come.*
XXXVI:VII.1. *Continuation of foregoing.*
XXXVI:VII.2. *Others who have no share in the world to come.*
My best guess is that this entire chapter serves as a supplement to materials in chapter 37.

XXXVII:I.1. *Seven categories of created beings.*
XXXVII:II.1. *Continuation of foregoing: Six traits have been stated with respect to humanity, three like traits of a beast, three like traits of ministering angels.*
XXXVII:III.1. *Continuation of foregoing: Six traits have been stated with respect to demons.*
XXXVII:IV.1. *Seven types of Pharisee.*
XXXVII:V.1. *Seven things which in large volume are bad and in small volume are good.*
XXXVII:VI.1. *With seven things did the Holy One, blessed be he, create his world.*
XXXVII:VII.1. *Seven attributes serve before the throne of glory.*
XXXVII:VIII.1. *Seven stages [to the universe].*
XXXVII:IX.1. *Seven points of distinction between one righteous person and another.*
XXXVII:X.1. *There are seven exegetical principles by which Hillel the Elder interpreted [Scripture] before the sons of Batera.*

5:6A. TEN THINGS WERE CREATED ON THE EVE OF THE SABBATH [FRIDAY] AT TWILIGHT, AND THESE ARE THEY: (1) THE MOUTH OF THE EARTH [NUM. 16:32]; (2) THE MOUTH OF THE WELL [NUM. 21:16–18]; (3) THE MOUTH OF THE ASS [NUM. 22:38]; (4) THE RAINBOW [GEN. 9:13]; (5) THE MANNA [EX. 16:15]; (6) THE ROD [EX. 4:17]; (7) THE *SHAMIR*; (8) LETTERS, (9) WRITING, (10) AND THE TABLES OF STONE [OF THE TEN COMMANDMENTS, EX. 32:15F.].
5:6B. AND SOME SAY, "ALSO THE DESTROYERS, THE GRAVE OF MOSES, AND THE TAMARISK OF ABRAHAM, OUR FATHER."
5:6C. AND SOME SAY, "ALSO: THE TONGS MADE WITH TONGS [WITH WHICH THE FIRST TONGS WERE MADE]."
5:7. **There are seven traits to an unformed clod, and seven to a sage. (1) A sages does not speak before someone greater than he in wisdom. (2) And he**

does not interrupt his fellow. (3) And he is not at a loss for an answer. (4) He asks a relevant question and answers properly. (5) And he addresses each matter in its proper sequence, first, then, second. (6) And concerning something he has not heard, he says, "I have not heard the answer." (7) And he concedes the truth [when the other party demonstrates it]. And the opposite of these traits apply to a clod.

> XXXVII:XI.1. There are seven traits that characterize an unformed clod, and seven a sage.
>> XXXVII:XII.1. Clarification of foregoing.
>> XXXVII:XIII.1. As above.
>> XXXVII:XIV.1. As above.
>> XXXVII:XV.1. As above.
>> XXXVII:XVI.1. As above.
>> XXXVII:XVII.1. As above.

5:8. There are seven forms of punishment which come upon the world for seven kinds of transgression. (1) [If] some people give tithes and some people do not give tithes, there is a famine from drought. So some people are hungry and some have enough. (2) [If] everyone decided not to tithe, there is famine of unrest and drought. (3) [If all decided] not to remove dough-offering, there is a famine of totality. (4) Pestilence comes to the world on account of the death penalties which are listed in the Torah but which are not in the hands of the court [to inflict]; and because of the produce of the Seventh Year [which people buy and sell]; (5) A sword comes into the world because of the delaying of justice and perversion of justice, and because of those who teach the Torah not in accord with the law.

5:9A. (6) A plague of wild animals comes into the world because of vain oaths and desecration of the Divine Name. (7) Exile comes into the world because of those who worship idols, because of fornication, and because of bloodshed, and because of the neglect of the release of the land [in the year of release].

> XXXVIII:I.1. Amplification of causes of famine.
>> XXXVIII:II.1. Josiah on causes of famine.
>> XXXVIII:III.1. Neglect of the gifts to the poor.
>> XXXVIII:IV.1. Case illustrative of the foregoing.
> XXXVIII:V.1. Base saying cited.
>> XXXVIII:V.2. Base saying illustrated.
>> XXXVIII:V.3. Secondary expansion of foregoing.
> XXXVIII:VI.1. Base sayings supplied with proof texts.

5:9B. AT FOUR TURNINGS IN THE YEAR PESTILENCE INCREASES: IN THE FOURTH YEAR, IN THE SEVENTH YEAR, IN THE YEAR AFTER THE SEVENTH YEAR, AND AT THE END OF THE FESTIVAL [OF TABERNACLES] EVERY YEAR: (1) IN THE FOURTH YEAR, BECAUSE OF THE POORMAN'S TITHE OF THE THIRD YEAR [WHICH PEOPLE HAVE NEGLECTED TO HAND OVER TO THE POOR]; (2) IN THE SEVENTH YEAR, BECAUSE OF THE POORMAN'S TITHE OF THE SIXTH YEAR; (3) IN THE YEAR AFTER THE SEVENTH YEAR, BECAUSE OF THE DEALING IN PRODUCE OF THE SEVENTH YEAR;

AND (4) AT THE END OF THE FESTIVAL EVERY YEAR, BECAUSE OF THE THIEVERY OF
THE DUES [GLEANINGS AND THE LIKE] OWING TO THE POOR [NOR LEFT FOR THEM IN
THE ANTECEDENT HARVEST].

XXXIX:I.1. Further sayings.
XXXIX:II.1. Further sayings.
XXXIX:III.1. Aqiba cited, with some glosses.
XXXIX:IV.1. As above.
XXXIX:V.1. Further sayings.
XXXIX:VI.1. Further sayings.
XXXIX:VII.1. Further sayings.
XXXIX:VIII.1. Further sayings.
XXXIX:IX.1. Further sayings.
XXXIX:X.1. Parable *possibly* illustrative of XXIX:VII.1.
XXXIX:XI.1. Further sayings: list of six items.
XXXIX:XII.1. As above.
XXXIX:XIII.1. As above.
   As earlier, many of these sayings simply follow the pattern of The Fathers:
attributive plus connective plus wise saying.

XL:I.1. List of four items.
XL:II.1. List of four items.
XL:III.1. *Secondary expansion of foregoing.*
XL:IV.1. Matched sayings on the penalties of causing public sin and the re-
wards of bringing about public merit.
   XL:V.1. Continuation of foregoing.

5:10. THERE ARE FOUR SORTS OF PEOPLE. (1) HE WHO SAYS, "WHAT'S MINE IS
MINE AND WHAT'S YOURS IS YOURS"—THIS IS THE AVERAGE SORT. (AND SOME SAY,
"THIS IS THE SORT OF SODOM.") (2) "WHAT'S MINE IS YOURS AND WHAT'S YOURS IS
MINE"—THIS IS A BOOR. (3) "WHAT'S MINE IS YOURS AND WHAT'S YOURS IS
YOURS"—THIS IS A TRULY PIOUS MAN. (4) "WHAT'S MINE IS MINE AND WHAT'S
YOURS IS MINE"—THIS IS A TRULY WICKED MAN.
5:11. THERE ARE FOUR SORTS OF PERSONALITY: (1) EASILY ANGERED, EASILY
CALMED—HE LOSES WHAT HE GAINS; (2) HARD TO ANGER, HARD TO CALM—WHAT
HE LOSES HE GAINS; (3) HARD TO ANGER AND EASY TO CALM—A TRULY PIOUS MAN;
(4) EASY TO ANGER AND HARD TO CALM—A TRULY WICKED MAN.
5:12. THERE ARE FOUR TYPES OF DISCIPLES: (1) QUICK TO GRASP, QUICK TO FOR-
GET—HE LOSES WHAT HE GAINS; (2) SLOW TO GRASP, SLOW TO FORGET—WHAT HE
LOSES HE GAINS; (3) QUICK TO GRASP, SLOW TO FORGET—A SAGE; (4) SLOW TO
GRASP, QUICK TO FORGET—A BAD LOT INDEED.
5:13. THERE ARE FOUR TRAITS AMONG PEOPLE WHO GIVE CHARITY: (1) HE WHO
WANTS TO GIVE, BUT DOES NOT WANT OTHERS TO GIVE—HE BEGRUDGES WHAT BE-
LONGS TO OTHERS; (2) HE WHO WANTS OTHERS TO GIVE, BUT DOES NOT WANT TO
GIVE—HE BEGRUDGES WHAT BELONGS TO HIMSELF; (3) HE WHO WILL GIVE AND
WANTS OTHERS TO GIVE—HE IS TRULY PIOUS; (4) HE WHO WILL NOT GIVE AND DOES
NOT WANT OTHERS TO GIVE—HE IS TRULY WICKED.
5:14. THERE ARE FOUR SORTS AMONG THOSE WHO GO TO THE STUDY-HOUSE: (1) HE

WHO GOES BUT DOES NOT CARRY OUT [WHAT HE LEARNS]—HE HAS AT LEAST THE
REWARD FOR THE GOING. (2) HE WHO PRACTICES BUT DOES NOT GO [TO STUDY]—HE
HAS AT LEAST THE REWARD FOR THE DOING. (3) HE WHO BOTH GOES AND PRAC-
TICES—HE IS TRULY PIOUS; (4) HE WHO NEITHER GOES NOR PRACTICES—HE IS
TRULY WICKED.

    XL:VI.1. Four types of persons.
    XL:VII.1. More of the same, in the model of the foregoing.

5:15. **There are four traits among those who sit before the sages: a sponge, a
funnel, a strainer, and a sifter. (1)A sponge—because he sponges everything
up; (2) a funnel—because he takes in on one side and lets out on the other; (3) a
strainer—for he lets out the wine and keeps in the lees; (4) and a sifter—for he
lets out the [coarse] flour and keeps in the finest flour.**

    XL:VIII.1. Four types of disciples.
    XL:IX.1. Four types of disciples.
    XL:X.1. Four types of disciples.
    XL:XI.1. *Four sorts [of sources] of bad things.*
    XL:XII.1. *Four sorts of sages whom one might see in a dream.*
    XL:XIII.1. *Three sorts of sages whom one might see in a dream.*
    XL:XIV.1. *Three sorts of prophets whom one might see in a dream.*
    XL:XV.1. *Three sorts of writings one might see in a dream.*
    XL:XVI.1. *Death, sleep, quiet.*
    XL:XVII.1. *Four rules for the privy.*

5:16. **[In] any loving relationship which depends upon something, [when] that
thing is gone, the love is gone. But any which does not depend upon something
will never come to an end. What is a loving relationship which depends upon
something? That is the love of Amnon and Tamar [II Sam. 13:15]. And one
which does not depend upon something? That is the love of David and
Jonathan.**
5:17. **Any dispute which is for the sake of Heaven will in the end yield results,
and any which is not for the sake of Heaven will in the end not yield results.
What is a dispute for the sake of Heaven? This is the sort of dispute between
Hillel and Shammai. And what is one which is not for the sake of Heaven? It is
the dispute of Korach and all his party.**

    XL:XVIII.1. Verbatim transcription of above saying in The Fathers.
        XL:XIX.1. As above.
        XL:XX.1. As above.
        XL:XX.1. Further example of the same.

    XLI:I.1. **Exposition of three-crowns saying of The Fathers.**
        XLI:II.1. Amplification of Torah theme, with story about a rabbi and
blasphemy.
        XLI:III.1. Story about a rabbi, relevant to blasphemy.
    XLI:IV.1. *Further lists of threes.*

XLI: V.1. *As above.*
XLI: VI.1. *As above.*
XLI: VII.1. *A set of six, complementing the foregoing.*
XLI: VIII.1. *Set of three.*
XLI: IX.1. *Set of three.*
XLI: X.1. *Set of four.*
XLI: XI.1. *Another set of four.*
XLI: XII.1. *Set of three.*

5:18. HE WHO BRINGS MERIT TO THE COMMUNITY NEVER CAUSES SIN. AND HE WHO CAUSES THE COMMUNITY TO SIN—THEY NEVER GIVE HIM A SUFFICIENT CHANCE TO ATTAIN PENITENCE. MOSES ATTAINED MERIT AND BESTOWED MERIT ON THE COMMUNITY. SO THE MERIT OF THE COMMUNITY IS ASSIGNED TO HIS [CREDIT], AS IT IS SAID, "HE EXECUTED THE JUSTICE OF THE LORD AND HIS JUDGMENTS WITH ISRAEL" (DEUT. 33:21). JEROBOAM SINNED AND CAUSED THE COMMUNITY OF THE ISRAELITES TO SIN. SO THE SIN OF THE COMMUNITY IS ASSIGNED TO HIS [DEBIT], AS IT IS SAID, "FOR THE SINS OF JEROBOAM WHICH HE COMMITTED AND WHEREWITH HE MADE ISRAEL TO SIN" (I KINGS 15:30).

5:19. ANYONE IN WHOM ARE THESE THREE TRAITS IS ONE OF THE DISCIPLES OF ABRAHAM, OUR FATHER; BUT [IF HE BEARS] THREE OTHER TRAITS, HE IS ONE OF THE DISCIPLES OF BALAAM, THE WICKED; (1) A GENEROUS SPIRIT, (2) A MODEST MIEN, AND (3) A HUMBLE SOUL—HE IS ONE OF THE DISCIPLES OF ABRAHAM, OUR FATHER. HE WHO EXHIBITS (1) A GRUDGING SPIRIT, (2) AN ARROGANT MIEN, AND (3) A PROUD SOUL—HE IS ONE OF THE DISCIPLES OF BALAAM, THE WICKED. WHAT IS THE DIFFERENCE BETWEEN THE DISCIPLES OF ABRAHAM OUR FATHER AND THE DISCIPLES OF BALAAM THE WICKED? THE DISCIPLES OF ABRAHAM OUR FATHER ENJOY THE BENEFIT [OF THEIR LEARNING] IN THIS WORLD AND YET INHERIT THE WORLD TO COME, AS IT IS SAID, "THAT I MAY CAUSE THOSE WHO LOVE ME TO INHERIT SUB-STANCE, AND SO THAT I MAY FILL THEIR TREASURES" (PROV. 8:21). THE DISCIPLES OF BALAAM THE WICKED INHERIT GEHENNA AND GO DOWN TO THE PIT OF DE-STRUCTION, AS IT IS SAID, "BUT YOU, O GOD, SHALL BRING THEM DOWN INTO THE PIT OF DESTRUCTION; BLOODTHIRSTY AND DECEITFUL MEN SHALL NOT LIVE OUT HALF THEIR DAYS" (PS. 55:24).

5:20A. **Judah b. Tema says, "Be strong as a leopard, fast as an eagle, fleet as a gazelle, and grave as a lion, to carry out the will of your Father who is in heaven."**

5:20B. HE WOULD SAY, "THE SHAMELESS GO TO GEHENNA, AND THE DIFFIDENT TO THE GARDEN OF EDEN.

5:20C. "MAY IT BE FOUND PLEASING BEFORE YOU, O LORD OUR GOD, THAT YOU REBUILD YOUR CITY QUICKLY IN OUR DAY AND SET OUR PORTION IN YOUR TORAH."

5:21. HE WOULD SAY, "(1) AT FIVE TO SCRIPTURE, (2) TEN TO MISHNAH, (3) THIRTEEN TO RELIGIOUS DUTIES, (4) FIFTEEN TO TALMUD, (5) EIGHTEEN TO THE WEDDING CANOPY, (6) TWENTY TO RESPONSIBILITY FOR PROVIDING FOR A FAMILY, (7) THIRTY TO FULLNESS OF STRENGTH, (8) FORTY TO UNDERSTANDING, (9) FIFTY TO COUNSEL, (10) SIXTY TO OLD AGE, (11) SEVENTY TO RIPE OLD AGE, (12) EIGHTY TO REMARKABLE STRENGTH, (13) NINETY TO A BOWED BACK, AND (14) AT A HUN-

DRED—HE IS LIKE A CORPSE WHO HAS ALREADY PASSED AND GONE FROM THIS WORLD."

5:22. BEN BAG BAG SAYS [IN ARAMAIC], "TURN IT OVER AND OVER BECAUSE EVERYTHING IS IN IT. AND REFLECT UPON IT NOW, GROW OLD AND WORN IN IT AND DO NOT LEAVE IT, [IN HEBREW] FOR YOU HAVE NO BETTER LOT THAN THAT."

5:23. BEN HE HE SAYS, "IN ACCORD WITH THE EFFORT IS THE REWARD."

XLI:XIII.1. **Judah b. Tema's saying.**

XLI:XIV.1. Further sayings of Judah b. Tema.

XLI:XV.1. As above.

XLI:XVI.1. As above.

XLI:XVII.1. *Five things that were made and hidden away.*

XLI:XVIII.1. *[Conjectural: Five things done for a bride.]*

XLI:XIX.1. *Five who have no portion in the world to come.*

XLI:XX.1. *Appendix regarding the world to come.*

XLI:XXI.1–XLLI:XXII.1. *Liturgical conclusion.*

The Fathers According to Rabbi Nathan Chapters XXIV–XXX Compared to The Fathers

The Fathers According to Rabbi Nathan Chapter XXV and The Fathers 4:2

4:2. **Ben Azzai says, "Run after the most minor religious duty as after the most important, and flee from transgression. For doing one religious duty draws in its wake doing yet another, and doing one transgression draws in its wake doing yet another. For the reward of doing a religious duty is a religious duty, and the reward of doing a transgression is a transgression."**

XXV:I.1.   A. Ben Azzai says, "Whoever has a serene mind on account of his learning has a good omen for himself, and who does not have a serene mind on account of his learning has a bad omen for himself."

XXV:II.1.   A. *At the time that Rabban Yohanan ben Zakkai was departing from this life, he raised up his voice and wept. His disciples said to him, "Lord, tall pillar, eternal light, mighty hammer, why are you weeping?"* [The appendix does not illustrate the saying, but complements its theme.]

XXV:II.2.   A. In regard to Moses, Scripture says, "And I will take away my hand and you shall see my back, but my face shall not be seen" (Ex. 33:23).

XXV:II.3.   A. "And there was written therein lamentations and jubilant sound and woe" (Ez. 2:10):

XXV:II.4.   A. *[Yohanan ben Zakkai] would say, "Clear the house on account of uncleanness and prepare a throne for King Hezekiah of Judah."*

XXV:III.1.   A. [Ben Azzai] would say, "If one dies in a serene mind, it is a good omen for him; in derangement, it is a bad omen. We now have a long appendix, in which the theme of one's mind at depth is complemented by the repertoire of stories about Eliezer's death scene.

XXV:IV.1.   A. *When R. Eliezer was dying—they say it was the eve of the Sabbath [toward dusk]—R. Aqiba and his colleague came in to see him, and he was dozing in the room, sitting back [Goldin:] on a canopied couch. . . .*

XXV:IV.2.   A. *R. Aqiba entered and took a seat before him and said to him, "My lord, now repeat traditions for me. . . .*

XXV:IV.3.   A. *"But no one ever asked me anything about it, except for Aqiba b. Joseph. . . ."*

XXV:IV.4.   A. *Said R. Eleazar b. Azariah to him, "My lord, as to a shoe that is on the shoemaker's last, what is the law? [Is it susceptible to uncleanness, as a useful object, or insusceptible, since it is not fully manufactured and so finished as a useful object?] . . ."*

XXV:IV.5.   A. *After the Sabbath R. Aqiba came and found [Eliezer's corpse being conveyed for burial] on the road from Caesarea to Lud. Then he tore his clothes and ripped his hair, and his blood flowed, and he fell to the earth, crying out and weeping, saying, "Woe is me for you, my Lord, woe is me, my master, for you have left the entire generation orphaned. . . ."*

XXV:V.1.   A. **Ben Azzai says, "Run after the most minor religious duty** and flee from a transgression."

XXV:VI.1.   A. He would say, "If you have fulfilled one religious duty and do not regret it, in the end it will bring about the doing of many more religious duties, and if you have done one transgression and do not worry about that transgression, in the end it will cause the doing of many more transgressions,

B. **"for doing one religious duty draws in its wake doing yet another, and doing one transgression draws in its wake doing yet another. For the reward of doing a religious duty is a religious duty, and the reward of doing a transgression is a transgression."**

XXV:VII.1.   A. He would say, "On your own refrain [from sinning] [following Goldin:], and there will be a reward for your restraint."

XXV:VIII.1.   A. He would say, "Go two or three steps below the place suitable for you and take your seat there."

XXV:IX.1.   A. There are three whose lives are no life, and these are they: one who depends on the table of his fellow, one who lives in a cramped attic, and one whose wife runs his life.

XXV:X.1.   A. He would say, "It is easier to rule the whole world than to sit and repeat Mishnah traditions before people clothed in linen."

There is no formal difference between this chapter and the ones that are geared to The Fathers. We have sayings in the normal form and appendices that are joined for clear and defensible reasons. But the substance is quite fresh, as we shall see later on.

The Fathers According to Rabbi Nathan Chapter XXVI
and The Fathers 3:13, 2:5, 3:11

3:13.   R. Aqiba says, "(1) Laughter and lightheadedness turn lewdness into a habit. (2) Tradition is a fence for the Torah. (3) Tithes are a fence for wealth. (4) Vows are a fence for abstinence. (5) A fence for wisdom is silence."

2:5.   He [Hillel, son of R. Judah the Patriarch] would say, "A coarse person will never fear sin, nor will an *am ha-Aretz* ever be pious, nor will a shy person learn, nor will an ignorant person teach, nor will anyone too occupied in business get wise. In a place where there are no individuals, try to be an individual."

3:11.   R. Eleazar the Modite says, "(1) He who treats Holy Things as secular, and (2) he who despises the appointed times, (3) he who humiliates his fellow in public, (4) he who removes the signs of the covenant of Abraham, our father, (may he rest in peace), and (5) he who exposes aspects of the Torah not in accord with the law, even though he has in hand learning in the Torah and good deeds, will have no share in the world to come."

XXVI:I.1.   A. R. Aqiba says, "A fence for honor is not acting in a silly way, **a fence for wisdom is silence, a fence for vows is abstaining [from vowing]**, a fence for sanctity is cleanness, a fence for humility is fear of sin."

XXVI:II.1.   A. He would say, "Do not come among gentiles, lest you learn from what they do. Do not eat bread with a priest who does not observe the rules of cultic cleanness properly, lest you commit sacrilege against Holy Things [given to the priest to eat, which the priest may not consume in accord with the law].

B. "Do not break out in vows, lest you commit sacrilege against oaths. Do not become accustomed to eating at banquets, lest you end up eating what is [Goldin:] forbidden to you. Do not get involved in what is doubt[fully forbidden], lest you end up involved in what is certainly forbidden. And do not go outside of the Land [of Israel], lest you worship idols.

C. "For lo, David is the one who says, 'For they have driven me out this day that I should not cleave to the inheritance of the Lord, saying, "Go serve other gods"'" (1 Sam. 26:19).

D. "Now can you imagine that King David would ever have served idols? But this is what David said, 'Whoever abandons the Land of Israel and goes outside of the Land is regarded by Scripture as though he were an idolater.'"

XXVI:III.1.   A. He would say, "Whoever is buried in other lands is as though he were buried in Babylonia. Whoever is buried in Babylonia is as if he were buried in the Land of Israel. Whoever is buried in the Land of Israel is as if he were buried under the altar.

XXVI:IV.1.   A. **He would say, "A common person cannot be pious, nor can a shy person learn, nor can an impatient person teach."**

XXVI:V.1.   A. He would say, "Why do disciples of sages die young? Not because they commit adultery nor because they steal, but because they leave off the study of words of the Torah and take up idle conversation, and, furthermore, because they do not take up at the place at which they left off."

XXVI:VI.1.   A. R. Simeon b. Eliezer says, "Israelites who live outside of the Land worship idols [Goldin:] in all innocence."

XXVI:VII.1.   A. R. Eliezer the Modite says, "He who violates the Sabbath and treats the appointed times with contempt, **he who removes the signs of the covenant of circumcision, and he who exposes aspects of the Torah, even though he has in hand learning in the Torah and good deeds, will have no share in the world to come.**"

XXVI:VIII.1.   A. R. Aqiba says, "Whoever marries a woman inappropriate to his station in life violates no fewer than five negative commandments: "not taking vengeance" (Lev. 19:19), "not bearing a grudge" (Lev. 19:19), "not hating your brother in your heart" (Lev. 19:17), "loving your neighbor as yourself" (Lev. 19:18), "that your brother may live with you" (Lev. 25:36).

XXVI:IX.1.   A. He would say, "He who eats food which [Goldin:] does not agree with him violates three negative commandments, for he has treated himself with contempt, treated food with disrespect, and said a blessing [for the food] which is inappropriate [since the food has brought no blessing]."

XXVI:X.1.   A. R. Judah b. Ilai says, "He who dies and leaves a son who has not learned the Torah from his father, and [after his father's death] goes and studies the Torah from other people—lo, this one seeks compliments."

XXVI:XI.1.   A. R. Eliezer Haqqappar says, "Do not be like the highest lintel, which people cannot reach up and touch, nor like the lintel on high, which . . . [what follows makes no sense], nor like the middle lintel, which bruises peoples' feet, but be like the lowest one, on which everyone tramples, for in the end, even though the entire building is demolished, that lintel still remains in its place.

The conclusion announced in connection with The Fathers According to Rabbi Nathan chapter XXV applies here as well.

The Fathers According to Rabbi Nathan Chapter XXVII
and The Fathers 4:6, 4:5, 2:15–16, 3:18, 4:12

4:6.   **R. Yosé says, "Whoever honors the Torah himself is honored by people. And whoever disgraces the Torah himself is disgraced by people."**

4:5.   **R. Ishmael, his [R. Yohanan b. Beroqa's] son, says, "He who learns so as to teach—they give him a chance to learn and to teach. He who learns so as to carry out his teachings—they give him a chance to learn, to teach, to keep, and to do.**

2:15.   **Rabbi Tarfon says: "The day is short, the work formidable, the workers lazy, the wages high, the employer impatient."**

2:16.   **He [Rabbi Tarfon] would say: "It's not your job to finish the work, but you are not free to walk away from it. If you have learned much Torah, they will give you a good reward. And your employer can be depended upon to pay your wages for what you do. And know what sort of reward is going to be given to the righteous in the coming time."**

3:18.   **R. Eleazar Hisma says, "The laws of bird-offerings and of the beginning of the menstrual period—they are indeed the essentials of the Torah. Calculation of the equinoxes and reckoning the numerical value of letters are the savories of wisdom."**

4:12.   **R. Eleazar b. Shammua says, "The honor owing to your disciple should be as precious to you as yours. And the honor owing to your fellow should be like the reverence owing to your master. And the reverence owing to your master should be like the awe owing to Heaven."**

XXVII:I.1.   A. R. Yosé says, "Whoever honors the Torah himself is honored by people. And whoever disgraces the Torah himself is disgraced by people.

B. "For it is said, 'For those that honor me shall I honor, and those that abuse me will be treated as null' " (1 Sam. 2:30).

XXVII:II.1.   A. *Another interpretation of "For those that honor me shall I honor, and those that abuse me will be treated as null" (1 Sam. 2:30).*

B. *This refers to Pharaoh, king of Egypt, who treated with respect him who spoke and by his word brought the world into being. For he came forth at the head of his retinue. His staff said to him, "The custom of the world is that all kings go forth only after their retinue, but you have gone forth at the head of your retinue. . . ."*

E. *As it is said, "I have compared you, O my love, to my own horse, which charged against Pharaoh's chariots" (Song 1:9).*

XXVII:II.2. A. R. *Pappias says, [In the cited verse of Song of Songs,] "The congregation of Israel was praising [Goldin: what God did against] the cavalry and chariotry of Pharaoh."*

XXVII:II.3. A. R. *Joshua b. Qorha says, "When Pharaoh came to the sea, he rode a stallion, and the Holy One, blessed be he, appeared to him on a mare,*

B. *"as it is said, 'To my mare among Pharaoh's chariots' (Song 1:9).*

XXVII:II.4. A. *" '[For those that honor me shall I honor,] and those that abuse me will be treated as null' (1 Sam. 2:30):*

C. *"Accordingly, the Holy One, blessed be he, treated him with utter contempt, and exacted a penalty from him only through an angel . . ."*

XXVII:III.1. A. **R. Ishmael says, "He who learns so as to teach—they give him a chance to learn and to teach. He who learns so as to carry out his teachings—they give him a chance to learn, to teach, to keep, and to do."**

XXVII:IV.1. A. **He [The Fathers: Tarfon] would say: "It's not your job to finish the study of the entire Torah, but you are not free to walk away from it. But to whoever puts in great effort and masters more [of the Torah] do they add a great reward."**

XXVII:V.1. A. **R. Eleazar b. Hisma says, "The laws of bird-offerings and of the beginning of the menstrual period—they are indeed the essentials of the laws. Calculation of the equinoxes and reckoning the numerical value of letters are the savories of wisdom."**

XXVII:VI.1. A. R. Yohanan b. Nuri says, "The laws, the rules of cultic cleanness, and the regulations on the menstrual period and on bird offerings—lo, they are the essentials of the Torah."

XXVII:VII.1. A. He would say, "Laying out a sizable spread, building courts of justice, and maintaining them bring good to the world."

XXVII:VIII.1. A. R. Yohanan b. Dahabai says, "He who says, 'This law does not make sense to me' has no share in the world to come."

XXVII:IX.1. A. **Rabbi Tarfon says: "The day is short, the work formidable, the workers lazy, the wages high, the employer impatient. And know that the reward that is coming to the righteous in the time to come is great."**

XXVII:X.1. A. He would say, "Do not keep your distance from a good trait without limit and from labor without end.

B. "There is a parable. To what may the matter be compared? To someone who was [hired for the purpose of] drawing water from the sea and pouring it out on the land. The one loses nothing, the other is not filled up."

XXVII:XI.1. A. **R. Eleazar b. Shammua says, "The honor owing to your disciple should be as precious to you as yours. And the honor owing to your fellow should be like the reverence owing to your master. And the reverence owing to your master should be like the awe owing to Heaven."**

B. How do we know that **the honor owing to one's disciple should be as precious to one as his own?**

C. Let everyone learn from the case of our lord, Moses, who said to Joshua, "Choose men for us" (Ex. 17:9).

E. How do we know that **the honor owing to one's fellow should be like the reverence owing to his master?**

F. As it is said, "And Aaron said to Moses, 'Please, my lord'" (Num. 12:11).

H. And how do we know that **the reverence owing to one's master should be like the awe owing to Heaven?**

I. As it is said, "And Joshua b. Nun, servant of Moses from his youth, answered and said, 'My lord, Moses, destroy them'" Num. 11:28), so treating Moses as though he were equal [in power] to the Presence of God.

XXVII:XII.1. A. Since to begin with people said, "There is grain in Judea, straw in Galilee, and chaff in Transjordan," they reverted and said, "There is no grain in Judah but straw, no straw in Galilee but chaff, and in Transjordan, neither this nor that." [I have no idea why this item is included.]

Other than the final item, we have no difficulty in following the formal program of chapter XXVII. We have a sequence of sayings given in the manner of The Fathers, to which we find either secondary exegesis of a proposition or supplementary amplification of a thematic character.

The Fathers According to Rabbi Nathan Chapter XXVIII and The Fathers 2:4, 7

2:4. **Hillel [son of Judah the Patriarch] says, "Do not walk out on the community. And do not have confidence in yourself until the day you die. And do not judge your companion until you are in his place. And do not say anything which cannot be heard, for in the end it will be heard. And do not say, 'When I have time, I shall study,' for you may never have time."**

2:7. **He would say, "Lots of meat, lots of worms."**

XXVIII:I.1. A. R. Nathan says, "You have no love like the love for the Torah, wisdom like the wisdom of the Land of Israel, beauty like the beauty of Jerusalem, wealth like the wealth of Rome, power like the power of Persia, lewdness like the lewdness of the Arabs, arrogance like the arrogance of Elam, hypocrisy like the hypocrisy of Babylonia."

XXVIII:II.1. A. R. Simeon b. Eleazar says, "A sage who has dwelled in the Land of Israel and then left for overseas becomes flawed. One who remains in the Land is more praiseworthy than he."

XXVIII:III.1. A. R. Simeon b. Gamaliel says, "Whoever brings peace to his own household is credited by Scripture as though he brought peace in Israel, for every individual."

XXVIII:IV.1. A. R. Gamaliel says, "In four ways the empire [of Rome] supports itself: tolls, baths, theaters, and crop-levies."

XXVIII:V.1. A. He would say, "The words of Torah are as hard to acquire as garments made of fine wool and easy to destroy as linen garments."

XXVIII:VI.1. A. R. Judah the Patriarch says, "From whoever is glad to get the pleasures of this world are held back the pleasures of the world to come."

XXVIII:VII.1.   A. He would say, "As to the righteous who have it bad in this world, to what are they compared? To a cook who fixes a meal for himself. Even though he has to trouble himself, he is preparing not for others but for himself."
XXVIII:VIII.1.   A. "He would say, Let your actions in secret in your own view be as though they were in public."
XXVIII:IX.1.   A. **Hillel says: "Do not walk out on the community. And do not have confidence in yourself until the day you die. And do not judge your companion until you are in his place. And do not say anything which cannot be heard, for in the end it will be heard. And do not say 'When I have time, I shall study,' for you may never have time."**
XXVIII:X.1.   A. **He would say,** "Lots of eating, lots of shitting. **Lots of meat, lots of worms** and maggots."
XXVIII:XI.1.   A. R. Eleazar b. Shammua says, "There are three traits that may characterize disciples of sages: they may be like either hewn stone, a corner stone, or a polished stone."
XXVIII:XII.1.   A. R. Judah b. Ilai says, "Whoever treats the words of the Torah as the main thing and earning a living as trivial is treated as the main thing in the world to come. . . .
    B. ". . . earning a living as the main thing and the words of the Torah as second is treated as trivial in the world to come."

The Fathers According to Rabbi Nathan Chapter XXIX and The Fathers 4:18, 15

4:18. **R. Simeon b. Eleazar says, "(1) Do not try to make amends with your fellow when he is angry, or (2) comfort him when the corpse of his beloved is lying before him, or (3) seek to find absolution for him at the moment at which he takes vow, or (4) attempt to see him when he is humiliated."**
4:15. **R. Matya b. Harash says, "Greet everybody first, and be a tail to lions. But do not be a head of foxes."**

XXIX:I.1.   A. **R. Simeon b. Eleazar says** in the name of R. Meir, **"Do not try to make amends with your fellow when he is angry, or comfort him when the corpse of his beloved is lying before him, or seek to find absolution for him at the moment at which he takes vow,** or come to his house on a day which he has suffered a reverse, **or attempt to see him when he is humiliated."**
XXIX:II.1.   A. He would say, "If you have friends, some of whom give you criticism and some of whom give you praise, love the ones who give you criticism and hate the ones who give you praise."
XXIX:III.1.   A. He would say, "Wherever a person goes, his heart follows. If he stops, his heart stops. If he sits, things settle down for him [Goldin: wheresoever he sits, things are clarified for him]."
XXIX:IV.1.   A. He would say, "To whoever pays careful attention to teachings of Torah they give those who will keep watch over him.
    B. "And to whoever pays slight attention to the words of the Torah they give [Goldin:] [forces] that will make him idle . . ."
XXIX:V.1.   A. Abba Saul b. Nannos says, "There are four traits in a disciple of a sage:

B. "There is one who studies for himself but does not teach others, there is one who teaches others but does not teach himself, there is one who teaches himself and others, and one who does not teach himself or others."
XXIX: VI.1.   A. R. Hanania b. Jacob says, "He who wakes up in the middle of the night on account of words of the Torah has a good omen for himself. If it is on account of the words of an idle conversation he may have had, it is a bad omen for him."
B. R. Jacob b. Hanania says, "He who wakes up in the middle of the night and does not open his mouth with words of the Torah, it would have been befitting for him and better for him had the afterbirth of his mother been turned over on his face [to suffocate him as an infant] so that he should not go forth into the air of the world or see the world."
XXIX: VII.1.   A. R. Eliezer Haqqappar says, "Whoever honors his fellow for the sake of money, in the end will take his leave from him in disgrace, but whoever treats his fellow lightly on account of [a prior obligation to perform] a religious duty in the end will take his leave from him in dignity."
B. And how do we know that whoever honors his fellow for the sake of money in the end will take his leave from him in disgrace?
XXIX: VII.2.   A. And was Pharaoh standing on the room and Moses standing down on the ground?
XXIX: VII.3.   A. And how do we know that in the end he took his leave from him in dignity?
XXIX: VIII.1.   A. In order to investigate four types of atonement R. Mattia b. Harash went to R. Eleazar Haqqappar in Laodicea to visit him. He said to him, "Have you heard about the four types of atonement that R. Ishmael expounded?"
XXIX: IX.1.   A. Issi b. Judah says, "On what account do disciples of sages die before their time?
B. "It is not because they commit adultery or steal but because they treat themselves lightly."
XXIX: X.1.   A. R. Isaac b. Phineas says, "Whoever has mastered exegesis but not laws has never tasted the flavor of wisdom."
XXIX: XI.1.   A. He would say, "Whoever has mastered exegesis but has not mastered laws is a mighty man who is not armed."
XXIX: XII.1.   A. He would say, "**Be careful to greet other people first,** and to not get involved in contention, and do not try to be [following Goldin:] seen in session with disciples of sages,
B. "and **be a tail to lions but do not be head of foxes.**"

The Fathers According to Rabbi Nathan Chapter XXX and The Fathers 4:9

4:9. R. Jonathan says, "Whoever keeps the Torah when poor will in the end keep it in wealth. And whoever treats the Torah as nothing when he is wealthy in the end will treat it as nothing in poverty."

XXX: I.1.   A. R. Nathan b. Joseph says, **"Whoever neglects the words of the Torah when he is wealthy in the end will neglect the Torah when he is poor,**

and whoever carries out the words of the Torah when he is poor in the end will carry out the Torah when he is wealthy."

XXX:II.1.   A. He would say, "Bringing words of consolation to mourners, visiting the sick, and carrying out acts of loving-kindness bring good to the world."

XXX:III.1.   A. R. Meir says, "Whoever as a matter of doubt thinks that he has committed a transgression [of sacrilege, e.g., unknowingly eating food that is in the status of Holy Things] is regarded by Scripture as though he had assuredly done it" (so that he pays the penalty that would accrue had he actually committed sacrilege, as we shall now see).

XXX:III.2.   A. R. Nathan b. Joseph says, "Whoever inadvertently commits a transgression is regarded by Scripture as though he had done it deliberately."

XXX:IV.1.   A. R. Aqiba says, "Whoever associates with transgressors, even though he does not do the things they do, lo, this one receives a punishment like theirs. And whoever associates with those who do religious deeds, even though he does not do the things they do, lo, this one receives a reward like theirs."

XXX:V.1.   A. R. Simeon says, "The punishment of a liar is that even when he is telling the truth, people do not believe him."

XXX:VI.1.   A. R. Ahai b. Josiah says, "One who has to buy grain in the marketplace—to what is he compared? To an infant whose mother died, and whom people pass from door to door among wetnurses, but who is not satisfied."

XXX:VII.1.   A. He would say, "When someone eats of his own [produce], his mind is serene."

The Repertoire of Formal Rhetoric
of The Fathers According to Rabbi Nathan

What follows is a catalogue of the components of The Fathers According to Rabbi Nathan laid out in the formal classifications that seem to me required.

1. Name plus Attributive (*says*) plus Wise Saying [formally comparable to sayings in The Fathers]. This category includes secondary amplification of a wise saying, for example: *How so? This teaches that . . .* (exclusive of sayings in The Fathers, which are not catalogued when amplified in The Fathers According to Rabbi Nathan).

I: V.4
I: II.2   (Not a good example)
III: II.1–IV.1
III: IV.1–7   (Saying plus proof texts)
IV: III.1   (Lacks name)
IV: VII.1   (Lacks name)
VI: II.2
VII: III.1–2
VIII: I.2
IX: IV.1
X: 1.3–4
XI: I.2–8
XII: III.2–3
XII: VI.1–2
XII: VII.1
XII: VIII.1
XII: IX.1
XVI: V.1–4
XVI: VI.2
XVIII: I.1–XVIII: I.4
XVIII: II.1–XVIII: III.2
XX: I.1–II.1
XXI: V.1

XXIII: IV.1–2
XXIII: IV.4–55
XXIV I.1–XXIV: VIII.1
XXV: I.1
XXV: III.1
XXV: VIII.1–X.1
XXVI: II.1–III.1
XXVI: V.1
XXVI: VIII.1–XI.1
XXVII: XII.1
XXVIII: I.1–XXVIII: VIII.1
XXVIII: XI.1–XXVIII: XII.1
XXIX: II.1–VIII: 1 [2–3]
XXIX: VII.1–XI.1
XXX: II.1–VII.1
XXXI: III.1
XXXV: IV.3
XXXVI: I.1–VII.2   (Series of propositions in Mishnaic dispute form)
XXXIX: V.1–VII.1
XXXIX: X.1
XLI: XIV.1–XLI.1
XLI: XX.1

2. Scriptural proof text introduced and expounded.

I:I.1   (Dispute)   XIII:II.1−4
I:I.2   XVI:III.2
I:II.1   XX:III.1−XX:VII.1
I:V.1.C−J   XXI:IV.2
I:V.2.C−G   XXV:II.2−3
I:V.3   XXVII:II.1−4
I:VII.1−I:VIII.2   XXXI:I.2−XXXI:II.1
II:I.3−5   XXXII:1.2−XXXII:II.7
II:VII.2   XXXIV:V.1−2
III.IV.1−7   XXXV:III.1−2
IV:IV.2   XXXVII:XIII.2−4
XII:1.2−5

3. Story illustrative of wise saying or providing a narrative setting for a wise saying.

I:I.3−4   XII:IX.1
III:III.1   XVI:IV.1−4
III:V.1−III:VII.1   XXXIII:I.3
IV:III.2−3   XXXVIII:IV.1
V:II.1   XLI:II.1
VIII:V.1

4. The appendix.

II:III.1−II:IV.1   (Proposition plus   II:V.2   (As above)
scriptural proof texts)   IX:II.1−IX:III.5 plus 6

5. The genre of story, including the subgenre of biographical tale. These stories do not illustrate a point made by a saying, either of The Fathers or of The Fathers According to Rabbi Nathan, but they stand on their own.

I:VIII:1.D−I:XVIII.3 (An extended narrative about the First Man and Woman.)

II:I.2   (Why did a disciple of sages   XVII:III.1
die young?)   XVII:IV.1
IV:V.2−IV:VI.4   (Treated as   XVII:V.1
continuous)   XVIII:II.1−2
VI:V.1−VI:X.3   XIX:II.1−XIX:III.1
VIII:VI.1−2   XXV:II.1−4
XII:II.1−5   XXV:IV.1−5
XII:XIII.1.C−J   XXXVIII:V.2 (plus 3)
XIV:IV.1   XLI:III.1
XV:IV.1−XV:V.2

6. List of items of a single classification.

XXXIII:III.1−V.1   XXXIV:VI.1−XIII.1
XXXIV:II.1   XXXV:II.1

XXXVII:I.1–X:1

XXXIX:I.1–2

XXXIX:XI.1–XIII.1

XL:I.1–III.1

XL:VII.1–VIII.1

XL:X.1–XVII.I

XLI:IV.1–XII.1

XLI:XVII.1–XIX.1

Topics Treated in The Fathers and Not in The Fathers According to Rabbi Nathan

We first review the items that receive no treatment at all in The Fathers According to Rabbi Nathan (items printed in small capital letters), excluding items that appear in The Fathers According to Rabbi Nathan but not in the location dictated by the arrangement of The Fathers. The topical plan of The Fathers According to Rabbi Nathan, as distinct from the redactor's arrangement of materials in correspondence with The Fathers, now takes center stage. Thus where those redactors merely cite, but do not discuss, a passage in The Fathers, we treat that passage as distinctive to the earlier document and neglected by the later one. I specify my reasons for claiming that a passage not treated explicitly in The Fathers According to Rabbi Nathan nonetheless falls into the frame of reference of the later authorship. It goes without saying that neglect of a passage cannot testify to rejection of the sentiments it contains. In a traditional system such as the one at hand, we must assume that everything people received and handed on they implicitly affirmed. Points of stress and special interest are the focus here.

2:1. RABBI SAYS: "WHAT IS THE STRAIGHT PATH WHICH A PERSON SHOULD CHOOSE FOR HIMSELF? WHATEVER IS AN ORNAMENT TO THE ONE WHO FOLLOWS IT, AND AN ORNAMENT IN THE VIEW OF OTHERS. BE METICULOUS IN A SMALL RELIGIOUS DUTY AS IN A LARGE ONE, FOR YOU DO NOT KNOW WHAT SORT OF REWARD IS COMING FOR ANY OF THE VARIOUS RELIGIOUS DUTIES. AND RECKON WITH THE LOSS [REQUIRED] IN CARRYING OUT A RELIGIOUS DUTY AGAINST THE REWARD FOR DOING IT; AND THE REWARD FOR COMMITTING A TRANSGRESSION AGAINST THE LOSS FOR DOING IT. AND KEEP YOUR EYE ON THREE THINGS, SO YOU WILL NOT COME INTO THE CLUTCHES OF TRANSGRESSION. KNOW WHAT IS ABOVE YOU. AN EYE WHICH SEES, AND AN EAR WHICH HEARS, AND ALL YOUR ACTIONS ARE WRITTEN DOWN IN A BOOK."

While there is no exegesis of Rabbi's statement, The Fathers According to Rabbi Nathan XVIII is devoted to his nicknames for earlier masters. So there is surely no bias against discussing Rabbi's materials. As to the substance, Ben Azzai, The Fathers 4:2, says pretty much the same thing, though, to be sure, that also is not discussed in The Fathers According to Rabbi Nathan XXV.

2:2. RABBAN GAMALIEL, A SON OF RABBI JUDAH THE PATRIARCH, SAYS: "FIT-
TING IS LEARNING IN THE TORAH ALONG WITH A CRAFT, FOR THE LABOR PUT
INTO THE TWO OF THEM MAKES ONE FORGET SIN. AND ALL LEARNING OF THE
TORAH WHICH IS NOT JOINED WITH LABOR IS DESTINED TO BE NULL AND CAUSES
SIN. AND ALL WHO WORK WITH THE COMMUNITY—LET THEM WORK WITH THEM
[THE COMMUNITY] FOR THE SAKE OF HEAVEN. FOR THE MERIT OF THE FATHERS
STRENGTHENS THEM, AND THE RIGHTEOUSNESS WHICH THEY DO STANDS FOR-
EVER. AND, AS FOR YOU, I CREDIT YOU WITH A GREAT REWARD, AS IF YOU HAD
DONE [ALL THE WORK REQUIRED BY THE COMMUNITY]."

Praise of working for a living along with study of Torah does not occur in The
Fathers According to Rabbi Nathan, so far as I can see. Study of Torah sayings emphasizes the importance of perpetual learning. Repeating Torah traditions, for instance,
helps keep the angel of death at bay. The importance of working for the community for
the sake of Heaven finds its counterpart at The Fathers 5:18, which is discussed at The
Fathers According to Rabbi Nathan XL:IV.1.

2:3. "BE WARY OF THE GOVERNMENT, FOR THEY GET FRIENDLY WITH A PERSON
ONLY FOR THEIR OWN CONVENIENCE. THEY LOOK LIKE FRIENDS WHEN IT IS TO
THEIR BENEFIT, BUT THEY DO NOT STAND BY A PERSON WHEN HE IS IN NEED."

This saying does not differ from Shemaiah's, "Don't get friendly with the govern-
ment," The Fathers 1:10, which is fully discussed at The Fathers According to Rabbi
Nathan XI:III.1–XI:V.1. The same position is at The Fathers According to Rabbi
Nathan XII:XII.1.

2:4. HE WOULD SAY: "MAKE HIS WISHES INTO YOUR OWN WISHES, SO THAT HE
WILL MAKE YOUR WISHES INTO HIS WISHES. PUT ASIDE YOUR WISHES ON AC-
COUNT OF HIS WISHES, SO THAT HE WILL PUT ASIDE THE WISHES OF OTHER
PEOPLE IN FAVOR OF YOUR WISHES."

I can find no counterpart in The Fathers According to Rabbi Nathan.

[HILLEL SAYS]: "DO NOT HAVE CONFIDENCE IN YOURSELF UNTIL THE DAY YOU
DIE. AND DO NOT JUDGE YOUR COMPANION UNTIL YOU ARE IN HIS PLACE. AND
DO NOT SAY ANYTHING WHICH CANNOT BE HEARD, FOR IN THE END IT WILL BE
HEARD. AND DO NOT SAY: 'WHEN I HAVE TIME, I SHALL STUDY,' FOR YOU MAY
NEVER HAVE TIME."

Eliezer's sayings at The Fathers 2:10 go over the same ground and are fully discussed at The Fathers According to Rabbi Nathan XV:II and VI.1 ["repent one day
before your death"]. The latter saying is explicit: one does not know when he is going
to die, and that covers the same ground as, "You may never have time."

2:5. HE WOULD SAY: "A COARSE PERSON WILL NEVER FEAR SIN, . . . NOR WILL
ANYONE TOO OCCUPIED IN BUSINESS GET WISE. IN A PLACE WHERE THERE ARE
NO INDIVIDUALS, TRY TO BE AN INDIVIDUAL."

The correspondence between Torah study and fear of sin, also wisdom, is not taken for granted in The Fathers According to Rabbi Nathan. Quite to the contrary, extensive discourse emphasizes the importance of joining Torah study with fear of sin. But the discussion also takes for granted materials in The Fathers that make the same point. So this sentiment does not seem to me alien to the later exegetes' interests.

2:7. HE WOULD SAY: "LOTS OF PROPERTY, LOTS OF WORRIES; LOTS OF WOMEN, LOTS OF WITCHCRAFT; LOTS OF SLAVE GIRLS, LOTS OF LUST; LOTS OF SLAVE BOYS, LOTS OF ROBBERY. LOTS OF THE TORAH, LOTS OF LIFE; LOTS OF DISCIPLESHIP, LOTS OF WISDOM; LOTS OF COUNSEL, LOTS OF UNDERSTANDING; LOTS OF RIGHTEOUSNESS, LOTS OF PEACE. [IF] ONE HAS GOTTEN A GOOD NAME, HE HAS GOTTEN IT FOR HIMSELF. [IF] HE HAS GOTTEN TEACHINGS OF THE TORAH, HE HAS GOTTEN HIMSELF LIFE ETERNAL."

The formal pattern—correlations and opposites—does attract interest, and some of the elements of this saying are discussed. The mode of thought is commonplace, and so are the sentiments.

3:2A. HANANIAH, PREFECT OF THE PRIESTS, SAYS, "PRAY FOR THE WELFARE OF THE GOVERNMENT. FOR IF IT WERE NOT FOR FEAR OF IT, ONE MAN WOULD SWALLOW HIS FELLOW ALIVE."

This saying has no counterpart in The Fathers According to Rabbi Nathan.

3:2B. R. HANANIAH B. TERADION SAYS, "[IF] TWO SIT TOGETHER AND BETWEEN THEM DO NOT PASS TEACHINGS OF THE TORAH, LO, THIS IS A 'SEAT OF THE SCORNFUL,' AS IT IS SAID, 'NOR SITS IN THE SEAT OF THE SCORNFUL' (PS. 1:1). BUT TWO WHO ARE SITTING, AND WORDS OF THE TORAH DO PASS BETWEEN THEM—THE PRESENCE IS WITH THEM, AS IT IS SAID, 'THEN THEY THAT FEARED THE LORD SPOKE WITH ONE ANOTHER, AND THE LORD HEARKENED AND HEARD, AND A BOOK OF REMEMBRANCE WAS WRITTEN BEFORE HIM, FOR THEM THAT FEARED THE LORD AND GAVE THOUGHT TO HIS NAME' (MAL. 3:16). I KNOW THAT THIS APPLIES TO TWO. HOW DO I KNOW THAT EVEN IF A SINGLE PERSON SITS AND WORKS ON THE TORAH, THE HOLY ONE, BLESSED BE HE, SETS ASIDE A REWARD FOR HIM? AS IT IS SAID, 'LET HIM SIT ALONE AND KEEP SILENT, BECAUSE HE HAS LAID IT UPON HIM'" (LAM. 3:28).

3:3. R. SIMEON SAYS, "THREE WHO ATE AT A SINGLE TABLE AND DID NOT TALK ABOUT TEACHINGS OF THE TORAH WHILE AT THAT TABLE ARE AS THOUGH THEY ATE FROM 'DEAD SACRIFICES' (PS. 106:28), AS IT IS SAID, 'FOR ALL TABLES ARE FULL OF VOMIT AND FILTHINESS [IF THEY ARE] WITHOUT GOD' (PS. 106:28). BUT THREE WHO ATE AT A SINGLE TABLE AND DID TALK ABOUT TEACHINGS OF THE TORAH WHILE AT THAT TABLE ARE AS IF THEY ATE AT THE TABLE OF THE OMNIPRESENT, BLESSED IS HE, AS IT IS SAID, 'AND HE SAID TO ME, "THIS IS THE TABLE THAT IS BEFORE THE LORD"'" (EZ. 41:22).

The importance of studying Torah in groups is well established (e.g., by the treatment of the destiny of Eleazar b. Arakh). While the notion that study of Torah in groups or alone yields a reward is not taken up, so far as I can see, at any point, it seems to me a premise of both documents.

3:4. R. HANANIAH B. HAKHINAI SAYS, "(1) HE WHO GETS UP AT NIGHT, AND (2) HE WHO WALKS AROUND BY HIMSELF, AND (3) HE WHO TURNS HIS DESIRE TO EMPTINESS—LO, THIS PERSON IS LIABLE FOR HIS LIFE."

This has no counterpart in The Fathers According to Rabbi Nathan.

3:5. R. NEHUNIA B. HAQQANEH SAYS, "FROM WHOEVER ACCEPTS UPON HIMSELF THE YOKE OF THE TORAH DO THEY REMOVE THE YOKE OF THE STATE AND THE YOKE OF HARD LABOR. AND UPON WHOEVER REMOVES FROM HIMSELF THE YOKE OF THE TORAH DO THEY LAY THE YOKE OF THE STATE AND THE YOKE OF HARD LABOR."

The contrast of the authority of the Torah as against the authority of the state is not drawn in The Fathers According to Rabbi Nathan.

3:6. R. HALAFTA OF KEFAR HANANIAH SAYS, "AMONG TEN WHO SIT AND WORK HARD ON THE TORAH THE PRESENCE COMES TO REST, AS IT IS SAID, 'GOD STANDS IN THE CONGREGATION OF GOD' (PS. 82:1). AND HOW DO WE KNOW THAT THE SAME IS SO EVEN OF FIVE? FOR IT IS SAID, 'AND HE HAS FOUNDED HIS GROUP UPON THE EARTH' (AM. 9:6). AND HOW DO WE KNOW THAT THIS IS SO EVEN OF THREE? SINCE IT IS SAID, 'AND HE JUDGES AMONG THE JUDGES' (PS. 82:1). AND HOW DO WE KNOW THAT THIS IS SO EVEN OF TWO? BECAUSE IT IS SAID, 'THEN THEY THAT FEARED THE LORD SPOKE WITH ONE ANOTHER, AND THE LORD HEARKENED AND HEARD' (MAL. 3:16). AND HOW DO WE KNOW THAT THIS IS SO EVEN OF ONE? SINCE IT IS SAID, 'IN EVERY PLACE WHERE I RECORD MY NAME I WILL COME TO YOU AND I WILL BLESS YOU'" (EX. 20:24).

As noted above, the premise of this saying seems to me the foundation of both documents.

3:7A. ELEAZAR OF BARTOTA SAYS, "GIVE HIM WHAT IS HIS, FOR YOU AND YOURS ARE HIS. FOR SO DOES IT SAY ABOUT DAVID, 'FOR ALL THINGS COME OF YOU, AND OF YOUR OWN HAVE WE GIVEN YOU'" (I CHRON. 29:14).

This seems to me a commonplace sentiment, no different in status from the foregoing.

3:7B. R. SIMEON SAYS, "HE WHO IS GOING ALONG THE WAY AND REPEATING [HIS TORAH TRADITION] BUT INTERRUPTS HIS REPETITION AND SAYS, 'HOW BEAUTIFUL IS THAT TREE! HOW BEAUTIFUL IS THAT PLOUGHED FIELD!'—SCRIPTURE RECKONS IT TO HIM AS IF HE HAS BECOME LIABLE FOR HIS LIFE."

This saying is to be read along with the following.

3:8. R. DOSETAI B. R. YANNAI IN THE NAME OF R. MEIR SAYS, "WHOEVER FORGETS A SINGLE THING FROM WHAT HE HAS LEARNED—SCRIPTURE RECKONS IT TO HIM AS IF HE HAS BECOME LIABLE FOR HIS LIFE, AS IT IS SAID, 'ONLY TAKE HEED TO YOURSELF AND KEEP YOUR SOUL DILIGENTLY, LEST YOU FORGET THE WORDS WHICH YOUR EYES SAW' (DEUT. 4:9). IS IT POSSIBLE THAT THIS IS SO EVEN IF HIS LEARNING BECAME TOO MUCH FOR HIM? SCRIPTURE SAYS, 'LEST THEY DEPART FROM YOUR HEART ALL THE DAYS OF YOUR LIFE.' THUS HE BECOMES LIABLE FOR HIS LIFE ONLY WHEN HE WILL SIT DOWN AND ACTUALLY REMOVE [HIS LEARNING] FROM HIS OWN HEART."

The uncompromising stress on the centrality of Torah study, to the exclusion of all other considerations, however extreme the present expression of that view, seems to me at the foundation of The Fathers According to Rabbi Nathan.

3:10A. HE [R. HANANIAH B. DOSA] WOULD SAY, "ANYONE FROM WHOM PEOPLE TAKE PLEASURE—THE OMNIPRESENT TAKES PLEASURE FROM HIM. AND ANYONE FROM WHOM PEOPLE DO NOT TAKE PLEASURE, THE OMNIPRESENT DOES NOT TAKE PLEASURE FROM HIM."

The notion that a principal task of a person is to please other people and to exercise self-restraint in favor of the will of others has no counterpart in The Fathers According to Rabbi Nathan. But stress on being accommodating and swaying with popular opinion is a commonplace (e.g., be as malleable as a reed and not as strong as a cedar).

3:12. R. ISHMAEL SAYS, "(1) BE QUICK [IN SERVICE] TO A SUPERIOR, (2) EFFICIENT IN SERVICE [TO THE STATE], AND (3) RECEIVE EVERYBODY WITH JOY."

4:3. HE [BEN AZZAI] WOULD SAY, "DO NOT DESPISE ANYBODY AND DO NOT TREAT ANYTHING AS UNLIKELY. FOR YOU HAVE NO ONE WHO DOES NOT HAVE HIS TIME, AND YOU HAVE NOTHING WHICH DOES NOT HAVE ITS PLACE."

4:4A. R. LEVITAS OF YAVNEH SAYS, "BE EXCEEDINGLY HUMBLE, FOR THE FUTURE OF HUMANITY IS THE WORM."

These sayings fall into the same classification as The Fathers 3:10A. Advice to be humble and therefore patient is given in diverse ways, for example, in the contrast of Shammai's impatience and Hillel's patience.

4:4B. R. YOHANAN B. BEROQA SAYS, "WHOEVER SECRETLY TREATS THE NAME OF HEAVEN AS PROFANE PUBLICLY PAYS THE PRICE. ALL THE SAME ARE THE ONE WHO DOES SO INADVERTENTLY AND THE ONE WHO DOES SO DELIBERATELY, WHEN IT COMES TO TREATING THE NAME OF HEAVEN AS PROFANE."

The conception that secret sin yields public punishment is routine in The Fathers According to Rabbi Nathan (e.g., in discussion of gossip).

4:5B. R. SADOQ SAYS, "DO NOT MAKE [TORAH TEACHINGS] A CROWN IN WHICH TO GLORIFY YOURSELF OR A SPADE WITH WHICH TO DIG. SO DID HILLEL

SAY, 'HE WHO USES THE CROWN PERISHES.' THUS HAVE YOU LEARNED: WHO-
EVER DERIVES WORLDLY BENEFIT FROM TEACHINGS OF THE TORAH TAKES HIS
LIFE OUT OF THIS WORLD."

One should not make a living from Torah study, but should both study the Torah
and work for a living. As noted earlier, I find no counterpart in The Fathers According
to Rabbi Nathan. But the notion of exploiting the Torah one has mastered for private
ends is familiar to the later document's authorship.

4:7. R. ISHMAEL, HIS SON, SAYS, "HE WHO AVOIDS SERVING AS A JUDGE
AVOIDS THE POWER OF ENMITY, ROBBERY, AND FALSE SWEARING. AND HE WHO
IS ARROGANT ABOUT MAKING DECISIONS IS A FOOL, EVIL, AND PRIDEFUL."
4:8. HE WOULD SAY, "DO NOT SERVE AS A JUDGE BY YOURSELF, FOR THERE IS
ONLY ONE WHO SERVES AS A JUDGE ALL ALONE. AND DO NOT SAY, 'ACCEPT MY
OPINION,' FOR THEY HAVE THE CHOICE IN THE MATTER, NOT YOU."

These sayings form a counterpart to those of Judah b. Tabbai and Simeon b.
Shetah, The Fathers 1:8–9, which are discussed.

4:10. R. MEIR SAYS, "KEEP YOUR BUSINESS TO A MINIMUM AND MAKE YOUR
BUSINESS THE TORAH. AND BE HUMBLE BEFORE EVERYBODY. AND IF YOU TREAT
THE TORAH AS NOTHING, YOU WILL HAVE MANY TREATING YOU AS NOTHING.
AND IF YOU HAVE LABORED IN THE TORAH, [THE TORAH] HAS A GREAT REWARD
TO GIVE YOU."
4:11B. R. YOHANAN HASSANDELAR SAYS, "ANY GATHERING WHICH IS FOR THE
SAKE OF HEAVEN IS GOING TO ENDURE. AND ANY WHICH IS NOT FOR THE SAKE
OF HEAVEN IS NOT GOING TO ENDURE."

It seems to me that The Fathers According to Rabbi Nathan XL:XIX.1–XX.1 goes
over this same matter; disputes for the sake of Heaven yield results; those not for the
sake of Heaven do not.

4:13A. R. JUDAH SAYS, "BE METICULOUS ABOUT LEARNING, FOR ERROR IN
LEARNING LEADS TO DELIBERATE [VIOLATION OF THE TORAH]."
4:15A. R. YANNAI SAYS, "WE DO NOT HAVE IN HAND [AN EXPLANATION]
EITHER FOR THE PROSPERITY OF THE WICKED OR FOR THE SUFFERING OF THE
RIGHTEOUS."
4:16. R. JACOB SAYS, "THIS WORLD IS LIKE AN ANTECHAMBER BEFORE THE
WORLD TO COME. GET READY IN THE ANTECHAMBER, SO YOU CAN GO INTO THE
GREAT HALL."
4:17. HE WOULD SAY, "BETTER IS A SINGLE MOMENT SPENT IN PENITENCE AND
GOOD DEEDS IN THIS WORLD THAN THE WHOLE OF THE WORLD TO COME. AND
BETTER IS A SINGLE MOMENT OF INNER PEACE IN THE WORLD TO COME THAN
THE WHOLE OF A LIFETIME SPENT IN THIS WORLD."

The stress in these sayings is on the individual, this life, and the life of the resurrection. It is not on this age and the age to come, and the life of Israel restored to its land
and government. These sayings are ignored in The Fathers According to Rabbi Nathan.

Here I do discern a shift in focus, and a striking one. The move from a teleology defined by individual conduct in this life tied to life eternal to one defined by national and social suffering in this age compensated by national and social prosperity in the age to come is marked by a persistent tendency to add an eschatological and salvific motif to passages which, in The Fathers, rest on an essentially ahistorical and noneschatological teleology. The latter persists, but is joined by the former.

4:19. SAMUEL THE SMALL SAYS, "REJOICE NOT WHEN YOUR ENEMY FALLS, AND LET NOT YOUR HEART BE GLAD WHEN HE IS OVERTHROWN, LEST THE LORD SEE IT AND IT DISPLEASE HIM, AND HE TURN AWAY HIS WRATH FROM HIM" (PROV. 24:17).

4:20. ELISHA B. ABUYAH SAYS, "HE WHO LEARNS WHEN A CHILD—WHAT IS HE LIKE? INK PUT DOWN ON A CLEAN PIECE OF PAPER. AND HE WHO LEARNS WHEN AN OLD MAN—WHAT IS HE LIKE? INK PUT DOWN ON A PAPER FULL OF ERASURES."

4:21A. R. YOSÉ B. R. JUDAH OF KEFAR HABBABLI SAYS, "HE WHO LEARNS FROM CHILDREN—WHAT IS HE LIKE? ONE WHO EATS SOUR GRAPES AND DRINKS FRESH WINE. AND HE WHO LEARNS FROM OLD MEN—WHAT IS HE LIKE? HE WHO EATS RIPE GRAPES AND DRINKS VINTAGE WINE."

The exact sentiment about studying in youth and not waiting for old age is at The Fathers According to Rabbi Nathan XXIII:IV.1–2 (Nehorai) and XXIII:IV.3 (Eliezer b. Jacob and Gamaliel).

4:21B. RABBI SAYS, "DO NOT LOOK AT THE BOTTLE BUT AT WHAT IS IN IT. YOU CAN HAVE A NEW BOTTLE OF OLD WINE, AND AN OLD BOTTLE WHICH HAS NOT GOT EVEN NEW WINE."

4:22A. R. ELEAZAR HAQQAPPAR SAYS, "JEALOUSY, LUST, AND AMBITION DRIVE A PERSON OUT OF THIS WORLD."

This forms the counterpart of the sayings on the importance of self-abnegation.

4:22B. HE WOULD SAY, "THOSE WHO ARE BORN ARE [DESTINED] TO DIE, AND THOSE WHO DIE ARE [DESTINED] FOR RESURRECTION. AND THE LIVING ARE [DESTINED] TO BE JUDGED—SO AS TO KNOW, TO MAKE KNOWN, AND TO CONFIRM THAT (1) HE IS GOD, (2) HE IS THE ONE WHO FORMS, (3) HE IS THE ONE WHO CREATES, (4) HE IS THE ONE WHO UNDERSTANDS, (5) HE IS THE ONE WHO JUDGES, (6) HE IS THE ONE WHO GIVES EVIDENCE, (7) HE IS THE ONE WHO BRINGS SUIT, (8) AND HE IS THE ONE WHO IS GOING TO MAKE THE ULTIMATE JUDGMENT.

4:22C. "BLESSED BE HE, FOR BEFORE HIM ARE NO (1) GUILE, (2) FORGETFULNESS, (3) RESPECT FOR PERSONS, OR (4) BRIBE-TAKING, FOR EVERYTHING IS HIS. AND KNOW THAT EVERYTHING IS SUBJECT TO RECKONING. AND DO NOT LET YOUR EVIL IMPULSE PERSUADE YOU THAT SHEOL IS A PLACE OF REFUGE FOR YOU. FOR (1) DESPITE YOUR WISHES WERE YOU FORMED, (2) DESPITE YOUR WISHES WERE YOU BORN, (3) DESPITE YOUR WISHES DO YOU LIVE, (4) DESPITE YOUR WISHES DO YOU DIE, AND (5) DESPITE YOUR WISHES ARE YOU GOING TO GIVE A FULL ACCOUNTING BEFORE THE KING OF KINGS OF KINGS, THE HOLY ONE, BLESSED BE HE."

The stress of these sayings on the individual and personal judgment has no counterpart in The Fathers According to Rabbi Nathan, and they are not discussed there. But the story about the death of Yohanan b. Zakkai goes over precisely the ground of this story: God does not take bribes, and one cannot take for granted his fate after death. So, as I said, the received teleology of individual reward and punishment persists, but is augmented by a second (complementary) one.

5:6A. TEN THINGS WERE CREATED ON THE EVE OF THE SABBATH [FRIDAY] AT TWILIGHT, AND THESE ARE THEY: (1) THE MOUTH OF THE EARTH [NUM. 16:32]; (2) THE MOUTH OF THE WELL [NUM. 21:16–18]; (3) THE MOUTH OF THE ASS [NUM. 22:38]; (4) THE RAINBOW [GEN. 9:13]; (5) THE MANNA [EX. 16:15]; (6) THE ROD [EX. 4:17]; (7) THE *SHAMIR;* (8) LETTERS, (9) WRITING, (10) AND THE TABLES OF STONE [OF THE TEN COMMANDMENTS, EX. 32:15F.]. AND SOME SAY, "ALSO THE DESTROYERS, THE GRAVE OF MOSES, AND THE TAMARISK OF ABRAHAM, OUR FATHER." AND SOME SAY, "ALSO: THE TONGS MADE WITH TONGS [WITH WHICH THE FIRST TONGS WERE MADE]."

I do not know why this list was made, and I also do not know why it was ignored in The Fathers According to Rabbi Nathan, since I cannot specify the proposition that the list proposes to make.

5:9B. AT FOUR TURNINGS IN THE YEAR PESTILENCE INCREASES: IN THE FOURTH YEAR, IN THE SEVENTH YEAR, IN THE YEAR AFTER THE SEVENTH YEAR, AND AT THE END OF THE FESTIVAL [OF TABERNACLES] EVERY YEAR: (1) IN THE FOURTH YEAR, BECAUSE OF THE POORMAN'S TITHE OF THE THIRD YEAR [WHICH PEOPLE HAVE NEGLECTED TO HAND OVER TO THE POOR]: (2) IN THE SEVENTH YEAR, BECAUSE OF THE POORMAN'S TITHE OF THE SIXTH YEAR; (3) IN THE YEAR AFTER THE SEVENTH YEAR, BECAUSE OF THE DEALING IN PRODUCE OF THE SEVENTH YEAR; AND (4) AT THE END OF THE FESTIVAL EVERY YEAR, BECAUSE OF THE THIEVERY OF THE DUES [GLEANINGS AND THE LIKE] OWING TO THE POOR [NOT LEFT FOR THEM IN THE ANTECEDENT HARVEST].

While this passage is not discussed, The Fathers According to Rabbi Nathan XXXVIII goes over the related sayings.

5:11. THERE ARE FOUR SORTS OF PERSONALITY: (1) EASILY ANGERED, EASILY CALMED—HE LOSES WHAT HE GAINS; (2) HARD TO ANGER, HARD TO CALM—WHAT HE LOSES HE GAINS; (3) HARD TO ANGER AND EASY TO CALM—A TRULY PIOUS MAN; (4) EASY TO ANGER AND HARD TO CALM—A TRULY WICKED MAN.
5:12. THERE ARE FOUR TYPES OF DISCIPLES: (1) QUICK TO GRASP, QUICK TO FORGET—HE LOSES WHAT HE GAINS; (2) SLOW TO GRASP, SLOW TO FORGET—WHAT HE LOSES HE GAINS; (3) QUICK TO GRASP, SLOW TO FORGET—A SAGE; (4) SLOW TO GRASP, QUICK TO FORGET—A BAD LOT INDEED.
5:13. THERE ARE FOUR TRAITS AMONG PEOPLE WHO GIVE CHARITY: (1) HE WHO WANTS TO GIVE, BUT DOES NOT WANT OTHERS TO GIVE—HE BEGRUDGES WHAT BELONGS TO OTHERS; (2) HE WHO WANTS OTHERS TO GIVE, BUT DOES NOT WANT TO GIVE—HE BEGRUDGES WHAT BELONGS TO HIMSELF; (3) HE WHO WILL GIVE AND WANTS OTHERS TO GIVE—HE IS TRULY PIOUS; (4) HE WHO WILL NOT

GIVE AND DOES NOT WANT OTHERS TO GIVE—HE IS TRULY WICKED.

5:14. THERE ARE FOUR SORTS AMONG THOSE WHO GO TO THE STUDY-HOUSE: (1) HE WHO GOES BUT DOES NOT CARRY OUT [WHAT HE LEARNS]—HE HAS AT LEAST THE REWARD FOR THE GOING. (2) HE WHO PRACTICES BUT DOES NOT GO [TO STUDY]—HE HAS AT LEAST THE REWARD FOR THE DOING. (3) HE WHO BOTH GOES AND PRACTICES—HE IS TRULY PIOUS; (4) HE WHO NEITHER GOES NOR PRACTICES—HE IS TRULY WICKED.

It seems to me that The Fathers According to Rabbi Nathan XL amply treats the counterpart sayings. The basic mode of thought revealed here is fully revealed in the later document.

5:19. ANYONE IN WHOM ARE THESE THREE TRAITS IS ONE OF THE DISCIPLES OF ABRAHAM, OUR FATHER; BUT [IF HE BEARS] THREE OTHER TRAITS, HE IS ONE OF THE DISCIPLES OF BALAAM, THE WICKED; (1) A GENEROUS SPIRIT, (2) A MODEST MIEN, AND (3) A HUMBLE SOUL—HE IS ONE OF THE DISCIPLES OF ABRAHAM, OUR FATHER. HE WHO EXHIBITS (1) A GRUDGING SPIRIT, (2) AN ARROGANT MIEN, AND (3) A PROUD SOUL—HE IS ONE OF THE DISCIPLES OF BALAAM, THE WICKED. WHAT IS THE DIFFERENCE BETWEEN THE DISCIPLES OF ABRAHAM OUR FATHER AND THE DISCIPLES OF BALAAM THE WICKED? THE DISCIPLES OF ABRAHAM OUR FATHER ENJOY THE BENEFIT [OF THEIR LEARNING] IN THIS WORLD AND YET INHERIT THE WORLD TO COME, AS IT IS SAID, "'*THAT I MAY CAUSE THOSE WHO LOVE ME TO INHERIT SUBSTANCE, AND SO THAT I MAY FILL THEIR TREASURES*' (PROV. 8:21). THE DISCIPLES OF BALAAM THE WICKED INHERIT GEHENNA AND GO DOWN TO THE PIT OF DESTRUCTION, AS IT IS SAID, '*BUT YOU, O GOD, SHALL BRING THEM DOWN INTO THE PIT OF DESTRUCTION; BLOODTHIRSTY AND DECEITFUL MEN SHALL NOT LIVE OUT HALF THEIR DAYS*'" (PS. 55:24).

5:20B. HE WOULD SAY, "THE SHAMELESS GO TO GEHENNA, AND THE DIFFIDENT TO THE GARDEN OF EDEN.

5:20C. "MAY IT BE FOUND PLEASING BEFORE YOU, O LORD OUR GOD, THAT YOU REBUILD YOUR CITY QUICKLY IN OUR DAY AND SET OUR PORTION IN YOUR TORAH."

5:21. HE WOULD SAY, "(1) AT FIVE TO SCRIPTURE, (2) TEN TO MISHNAH, (3) THIRTEEN TO RELIGIOUS DUTIES, (4) FIFTEEN TO TALMUD, (5) EIGHTEEN TO THE WEDDING CANOPY, (6) TWENTY TO RESPONSIBILITY FOR PROVIDING FOR A FAMILY, (7) THIRTY TO FULLNESS OF STRENGTH, (8) FORTY TO UNDERSTANDING, (9) FIFTY TO COUNSEL, (10) SIXTY TO OLD AGE, (11) SEVENTY TO RIPE OLD AGE, (12) EIGHTY TO REMARKABLE STRENGTH, (13) NINETY TO A BOWED BACK, AND (14) AT A HUNDRED—HE IS LIKE A CORPSE WHO HAS ALREADY PASSED AND GONE FROM THIS WORLD."

5:22. BEN BAG BAG SAYS [IN ARAMAIC], "TURN IT OVER AND OVER BECAUSE EVERYTHING IS IN IT. AND REFLECT UPON IT NOW, GROW OLD AND WORN IN IT AND DO NOT LEAVE IT, [IN HEBREW] FOR YOU HAVE NO BETTER LOT THAN THAT."

5:23. BEN HE HE SAYS, "IN ACCORD WITH THE EFFORT IS THE REWARD."

APPENDIX SIX

Topics Treated in The Fathers According to Rabbi Nathan and Not in The Fathers

We follow the outline given in chapter 1 (with its appendix), now omitting reference to those entries that serve directly to clarify statements in The Fathers or to provide secondary expansion of materials that do so. The remaining items then occur in The Fathers According to Rabbi Nathan and not in The Fathers, serving neither directly nor indirectly to amplify The Fathers. Discussion of these entries is postponed to sections 4 and 5 of chapter 3, where I classify and then generalize on the items catalogued here.

I:IX–XVIII.	Large anthology on the first man.
IV:VII.1.	God diversified human beings in three aspects.
VI:V.1.	Aqiba began studying at forty, knew nothing.
VI:V.2.	Simeon b. Eleazar: Parable on basic theme of foregoing.
VI:V.3.	Tarfon on Aqiba, in line with basic theme.
VI:V.4.	New theme: Aqiba supported himself in poverty.
VI:V.5.	Same as above.
VI:V.6.	Got rich.
VI:VI.1.	Eliezer's beginnings in ignorance in mature year.
VI:VI.2.	Starved, bad-breath saying.
VI:V.3.	Same as above.
VI:VI.4.	Got rich in the end; father gave him his whole estate.
VI:VII.1.	The mention in VI:VI.4 of three famous dignitaries of Jerusalem before whom Eliezer spoke leads to exposition of materials on all three of them.
VI:VII.1. As above.	
VI:IX.1. As above.	
VI:X.1. As above.	
XV:IV.1.	Patience of Hillel the Elder.
XV:V.1.	Impatience of Shammai the Elder.
XV:V.2.	As above.
XVII:III.1.	Story of impoverished girl, connected to Song 1:8.
XVII:IV.1.	Story on girl taken captive.
XVII:V.1.	As above. Added because of Song 1:8 and its extenuation.

XXVII:X.1	Tarfon further cited, with parable.
XXVII:XI.1.	Eleazar b. Shammua cited from The Fathers and glossed.
XXVII:XII.1.	Saying included for no clear reason.
XXVIII:I.1.	Saying of Nathan on the outstanding traits of various parties (e.g., the Torah, Land of Israel, Jerusalem, Rome, Persia, the Arabs, etc.).
XXVIII:II.1.	Further saying on the superiority of the Torah study of Land of Israel.
XXVIII:III.1.	Sayings attributed to Simeon b. Gamaliel.
XXVIII:IV–V.	Gamaliel-sayings.
XXVIII:VI–VIII.	Sayings attributed to Judah the Patriarch.
XVIII:IX–X.	Sayings attributed to Hillel from the Fathers.
XXVIII:XI.1.	Eleazar b. Shammua's sayings.
XXVIII:XII.1.	Judah b. Ilai's sayings.
XXIX:I–IV.	Simeon b. Eleazar cited.
XXIX:V.1.	Abba Saul b. Nannos: four traits in a disciple.
XXIX:VI.1.	Hanania b. Jacob's sayings.
XXIX:VII.1–3.	Eliezer Haqqappar's sayings.
XXIX:VIII.1.	Mattia consults Eleazar [*sic*] Haqqappar on a teaching of Ishmael.
XXIX:IX.1.	Issi b. Judah's saying.
XXIX:X–XII.	Isaac b. Phineas's sayings.
XXX:I.1–II.1.	Citation of Nathan b. Joseph's sayings.
XXX:III–IV.	Further sayings that make the same point: that merely thinking is tantamount to doing.
XXX:V.1.	Secondary amplification of a minor detail of XXX:IV.2.
XXX:VI.1–XXX:VII.1.	Sayings of Ahai b. Josiah on a separate point entirely.
XXXI:I.1.	Whoever carries out one religious duty is as if he sustained the whole world. This point leads to the one of importance: a human being is equivalent to the whole of creation.
XXXI:I.2	The point repeated, now for Cain.
XXXI:I.3	The point repeated in general terms.
XXXI:I.4	Secondary appendix added because of thematic association.
XXXIV:II.1.	Ten terms of praise apply to God.
XXXIV:III.1.	Ten terms of denigration apply to idolatry.
XXXIV:IV.1.	Two signifying markers occur in a single passage.
XXXIV:V.1.	More of same.
XXXIV:VI.1.	Ten passages in the Torah are dotted.
XXXIV:VII.1.	Eleven passages in which the word for *she* is written with a Y.
XXXIV:VIII.1.	Ten descents of God's presence into the world.
XXXIV:IX.1.	Ten ascents out of the world.
XXXIV:X.1.	Prophet called by ten names.
XXXIV:XI.1.	Holy Spirit called by ten names.
XXXIV:XII.	Joy called by ten names.
XXXIV:XIII.1.	Ten are called living.

XXXVI:I.1.	Men of Sodom and world to come (Eliezer vs. Joshua).
XXXVI:II.1.	Minor children of wicked and world to come, last judgment (Eliezer vs. Joshua).
XXXVI:III.1.	Korach and his party (Eliezer vs. Joshua).
XXXVI:IV.1.	Generation of wilderness (Eliezer vs. Joshua).
XXXVI:V.1.	Ten tribes.
XXXVI:VI.1.	Seven who have no share in the world to come.

XXXVI:VII.1. Continuation of foregoing.

XXXVI:VII.2 Others who have no share in the world to come.

XXXVII:I.1.	Seven categories of created beings.

XXXVII:II.1. Continuation of foregoing: six traits have been stated with respect to humanity, three like traits of a beast, three like traits of ministering angels.

XXXVII:III.1. Continuation of foregoing: six traits have been stated with respect to demons.

XXXVII:IV.1.	Seven types of Pharisee.
XXXVII:V.1.	Seven things which in large volume are bad and in small volume are good.
XXXVII:VI.1.	With seven things did the Holy One, blessed be he, create his world.
XXXVII:VII.1.	Seven attributes serve before the throne of glory.
XXXVII:VIII.1.	Seven stages [to the universe].
XXXVII:IX.1.	Seven points of distinction between one righteous person and another.
XXXVII:X.1.	There are seven exegetical principles by which Hillel the Elder interpreted [Scripture] before the sons of Batera.
XXXIX:I.1.	Further sayings.
XXXIX:II.1.	Further sayings.
XXXIX:III.1.	Aqiba cited, with some glosses.

XXXIX:IV.1 As above.

XXXIX:V.1.	Further sayings.
XXXIX:VI.1.	Further sayings.
XXXIX:VII.1.	Further sayings.
XXXIX:VIII.1.	Further sayings.
XXXIX:IX.1.	Further sayings.
XXXIX:XI.1.	Further sayings: list of six items.

XXXIX:XII.1. As above.

XXXIX:XIII.1. As above.

XL:I.1.	List of four items.
XL:II.1.	List of four items.

XL:III.1. Secondary expansion of foregoing.

XL:XI.1.	Four sorts [of sources] of bad things.
XL:XII.1.	Four sorts of sages whom one might see in a dream.

Life, Death, and Torah Study

At stake in studying the Torah as a disciple of sages is life. That proposition emerges in the following story.

XII:XIII.1.   A. **And who does not serve as disciple to sages is liable to death:** how so?

B. How so?

C. There was the case of someone who lived in Beth Ramah, who applied to himself the rules of piety.

D. Rabban Yohanan ben Zakkai sent a disciple to him to investigate his character. The disciple came and found that he took oil and put it on the stove and took it from the stove and put it into the bean soup.

E. He said to him, "What are you doing?"

F. He said to him, "I am in the status of a high priest, and I am preparing in a condition of cultic purity to eat my food in the status of priestly rations."

G. He said to him, "Is this stove in a state of cultic cleanness or uncleanness? [Can the stove become cultically unclean, or is it neutral and perpetually in a state of insusceptibility?]."

H. He said to him, "And in the Torah do we have a rule covering the cultic uncleanness of a stove? [A stove, in the man's view, simply cannot become cultically unclean at all, the uncleanness pertaining solely to an oven, while the stove is a neutral object.] For it is said, 'Whatever is in [the oven] shall be unclean' (Lev. 11:33). [The stress on the oven means an oven can become cultically unclean but the stove remains perpetually insusceptible.]"

I. He said to him, "Just as the Torah has given the rule that an oven can become cultically unclean, so the Torah has given the rule that a stove can be cultically unclean, for it is said, 'Whether oven or stove for pots, it shall be broken in pieces, they are unclean' (Lev. 11:35) [hence as much as an oven falls into the classification of cultic uncleanness, if it is subjected to a source of uncleanness, so a stove falls into that same category].

J. "If, therefore, this is how you have been doing things, you have never in your life eaten your priestly rations in a state of cultic cleanness."

The *ma'aseh* before us does not present a case or precedent but teaches a lesson. The lesson is not made explicit—who does not serve as disciple to sages is liable to death—but is told solely through the tale itself. On that basis I classify the narrative as a story. The narrative plan, moreover, predominates, and the lesson that is illustrated, or the law embodied in a case, does not appear within the framework of the narrative at all. That again points toward the classification of the story. The tale unfolds with a beginning which tells of someone who lived outside the circles of master and disciples (C–D). We know that is the case because Yohanan had to send a discile to investigate the character of this person, who thought that he would on his own conform to the rules of cultic purity. So the tension is established in C–D. But the narrative then works itself out solely through the format of *he said to him*. There is no unfolding action. But the interchange preserves a narrative tone by presenting a conversation, rather than an exchange of formalized sayings. The climax and resolution at the end—you have never kept the law properly—draw the whole to a suitable and dramatic close.

XLI:II.1.   A. Labor in words of the Torah and do not occupy yourself with words of no worth.

B. There is the case of R. Simeon b. Yohai, who would visit the sick. He came across a person who was bloated and suffering with a belly ache, and [in pain] blaspheming before the Holy One, blessed be he.

C. He said to him, "Empty head! You should have sought mercy for yourself instead of blaspheming."

D. He said to him, "May the Holy One, blessed be he, arise from me and alight on you."

E. He said to him, "The Holy One, blessed be he, did to you what is coming to you, for you have neglected words of the Torah and occupied yourself with words of no worth."

Once more the narrative shelters a conversation, rather than unfolding through a sequence of actions. But there is implicit action: Simeon would visit the sick, came across a person who was suffering, who said . . . Still, the contrast between this brief story and the sizable ones involving Hillel and Shammai is striking. The narrative nonetheless falls into the classification of a story, not an illustration of a fixed saying, for the reasons stated with reference to the preceding passage.

Abbreviations

A.Z.	Abodah Zarah	Ker.	Keritot
Ar.	Arakhin	Ket.	Ketubot
B.	Bavli, Talmud of Babylonia	Kil.	Kilayim
B.B.	Baba Batra	Lam.	Lamentations
B.M.	Baba Mesia	Lev.	Leviticus
B.Q.	Baba Qamma	M.	Mishnah
Bek.	Bekhorot	M.Q.	Moed Qatan
Ber.	Berakhot	M.S.	Maaser Sheni
Bes.	Besah	Ma.	Maaserot
Bikkur.,		Mak.	Makkot
Bik.	Bikkurim	Makh.	Makhshirin
Chron.	Chronicles	Mal.	Malachi
Dan.	Daniel	Me.	Meilah
Dem.	Demai	Meg.	Megillah
Deut.	Deuteronomy	Men.	Menahot
Ed.	Eduyyot	Mic.	Micah
Er.	Erubin	Mid.	Middot
Est.	Esther	Miq.	Miqvaot
Ex.	Exodus	Nah.	Nahum
Ez.	Ezekiel	Naz.	Nazir
Gen.	Genesis	Ned.	Nedarim
Git.	Gittin	Neg.	Negaim
Hab.	Habakkuk	Neh.	Nehemiah
Hag.	Haggai	Nid.	Niddah
Hag.	Hagigah	Num.	Numbers
Hal.	Hallah	Ob.	Obadiah
Hor.	Horayot	Oh.	Oholot
Hos.	Hosea	Orl.	Orlah
Hul.	Hullin	Par.	Parah
Is.	Isaiah	Pe.	Peah
Jer.	Jeremiah	Pes.	Pesahim
Josh.	Joshua	Prov.	Proverbs
Jud.	Judges	Ps.	Psalms
Kel.	Kelim	Qid.	Qiddushin

229

Qin.	Qinnim	Ta.	Taanit
Qoh.	Qohelet [Ecclesiastes]	Tam.	Tamid
R.	Rabbi	Tem.	Temurah
R.H.	Rosh Hashshanah	Ter.	Terumot
Sam.	Samuel	Toh.	Tohorot
San.	·Sanhedrin	Uqs.	Uqsin
Shab.	Shabbat	Y.	Yerushalmi, Talmud of the
Sheb.	Shebiit		Land of Israel
Shebu.	Shebuot	Yad.	Yadayim
Sheq	Sheqalim	Yeb.	Yebamot
Song	Song of Songs	Zab.	Zabim
Sot.	Sotah	Zeb.	Zebahim
Suk.	Sukkah	Zech.	Zechariah
T.	Tosefta	Zeph.	Zephaniah
T.Y.	Tebul Yom		

Index of Biblical and Talmudic References

Arthur W. Woodman

General Index

Arthur W. Woodman

Abba Saul, 182
Abba Saul b. Nannos, 191, 206–7
Abba Sikra, Yohanan's escape from Jerusalem, 151
Ahai b. Josiah, 192, 208
Antigonus of Sokho, 161, 176; in logical discourse, 44
Aqabiah b. Mehalel, 164, 184; expanding wise sayings, 19–21
Aqiba, 166, 175, 177, 186, 191, 200; biographical accounts, 13, 79–86, 117–19, 134, 147–49; on death of sages, 102, 104; expanding wise sayings, 23, 35, 37, 202, 208; in logical narrative, 51–52, 55; scriptural heroes, 107
Aqiba b. Joseph, on death of sages, 103
Authorship of story, 3–13
Avtalyon, 162, 178

Ben Azzai, 167, 188, 190, 216; on death of sages, 100, 102, 104; religious duty and serene life, 200–201, 212
Ben Bag Bag, 172, 199, 220
Ben He He, 172, 199, 220
Ben Zoma, 167, 187–88
Bornkamm, Gunther, 157

Canonical writings of sages, 115–39, 144–46
Communal respect for others, 35–36
Creation, embellishment of story, 61–73

Death of Sages, 98–106, 109, 130–32, 135, 152–55, 219
Destruction of the Temple, narratives on, 149–52
Dosa b. Harkinas, 166; expanding wise sayings, 25

Dosa b. R. Yannai, 175
Dosetai b. R. Yannai, 165, 185, 216
Dungan, David L., 17

Eleazar, 164
Eleazar b. Arakh, 163–64, 181–83, 214; on death of sages, 99–100
Eleazar b. Azariah, 166–67, 187; on death of sages, 104–5; in logical narrative, 49
Eleazar of Bartota, 165, 185, 215
Eleazar Haqqappar, 169, 190–91, 207; expanding wise sayings, 32, 35, 203
Eleazar Hisma, 167, 187, 191, 203–4
Eleazar b. Jacob, 168, 189, 218
Eleazar the Modite, 166, 186, 191, 201–2
Eleazar b. Shammua, 168, 189, 191, 203–4, 206
Eliezer, 164, 175, 177; biographical accounts, 79–86, 117–21, 135, 147–48; on death of sages, 99–103, 105, 109, 135, 152; expanding wise sayings, 23–24, 37; in history of Israel, 92
Eliezer ben Hyrcanus, 163, 181–82; biographical accounts of sages, 83; on death of sages, 130–32; expanding wise sayings, 24
Elisha b. Abuyah, 169, 189, 218; Torah study and good deeds, 10–11, 35, 37

Fall of mankind, 63

Gamaliel, 162, 180–81, 205, 213, 218; untold stories, 110
Gentiles, 35
Good deeds and Torah study, 10–11

Halafta of Kefar Hananiah, 165, 185, 215
Hanania b. Jacob, 191, 207

239